Prison Reform And Criminal Law...

Eugene Smith, Russell Sage Foundation

CORRECTION AND PREVENTION

FOUR VOLUMES PREPARED FOR THE EIGHTH INTER-
NATIONAL PRISON CONGRESS

Edited by
CHARLES RICHMOND HENDERSON

I

PRISON REFORM, by CHARLES RICHMOND HENDER-
SON (Editor), F. B. SANBORN, F. H. WINES, and
Others

CRIMINAL LAW IN THE UNITED STATES, by
EUGENE SMITH

II

PENAL AND REFORMATORY INSTITUTIONS,
by SIXTEEN LEADING AUTHORITIES

III

PREVENTIVE AGENCIES AND METHODS, by
CHARLES RICHMOND HENDERSON

IV

PREVENTIVE TREATMENT OF NEGLECTED
CHILDREN, by HASTINGS H. HART
With Special Papers by Leading Authorities

E C Wines.

RUSSELL SAGE
FOUNDATION
—

CORRECTION AND PREVENTION

FOUR VOLUMES PREPARED FOR THE
EIGHTH INTERNATIONAL PRISON
CONGRESS

EDITED BY

CHARLES RICHMOND HENDERSON, PH.D. (LEIPSIC)

PROFESSOR OF SOCIOLOGY IN THE UNIVERSITY OF CHICAGO
COMMISSIONER FOR THE UNITED STATES ON THE INTER-
NATIONAL PRISON COMMISSION

NEW YORK
CHARITIES PUBLICATION
COMMITTEE . . . . . MCMX

PRESS OF WM. F. FELL CO.,
PHILADELPHIA

LIST OF COMMITTEES

EIGHTH INTERNATIONAL PRISON CONGRESS

INTERNATIONAL PRISON COMMISSION

PRESIDENT:
Charles R. Henderson — Chicago, Illinois

SECRETARY:
Dr. Guillaume — Berne, Switzerland

FINANCIAL DIRECTOR:
Frederick H. Mills — 97 Warren St., New York City

HONORARY PRESIDENTS

His Excellency M. Galkine-Wraskoy — President of the St. Petersburg Congress
M. Duflos — President of the Paris Congress
M. Rickl de Bellye — President of the Budapest Congress

TREASURER:
Fred Woxen — Christiania, Norway

UNITED STATES GENERAL COMMISSION

Amos W. Butler	Indianapolis, Indiana, *Chairman*
Joseph P. Byers	New York, New York, *Secretary*
Alva Adams	Pueblo, Colorado
Edwin A. Alderman	University, Virginia
Charles F. Amidon	Fargo, North Dakota
Joshua L. Baily	Philadelphia, Pennsylvania
Simeon E. Baldwin	New Haven, Connecticut
Levi L. Barbour	Detroit, Michigan
George A. Beecher	Omaha, Nebraska
Frank Billings, M.D.	Chicago, Illinois
Frank W. Blackmar	Lawrence, Kansas
Maud Ballington Booth	New York, New York
Desha Breckinridge	Lexington, Kentucky
Demarchus C. Brown	Indianapolis, Indiana
William Jennings Bryan	Lincoln, Nebraska
John Burke	Bismarck, North Dakota
Walter Clark	Raleigh, North Carolina
Allan D. Conover	Madison, Wisconsin
*John H. Converse	Philadelphia, Pennsylvania
Sarah Platt Decker	Denver, Colorado
H. E. Deemer	Red Oak, Iowa
Robert W. deForest	New York, New York
Charles S. Deneen	Springfield, Illinois
George H. Denny	Lexington, Virginia
Edward T. Devine	New York, New York

* Deceased

William F. Drewry, M.D.	Petersburg, Virginia
John Joy Edson	Washington, District of Columbia
Richard T. Ely	Madison, Wisconsin
Henry W. Farnam	New Haven, Connecticut
J. Sloat Fassett	Elmira, New York
W. H. P. Faunce	Providence, Rhode Island
Homer Folks	New York, New York
John Franklin Fort	Trenton, New Jersey
Hugh F. Fox	Plainfield, New Jersey
David R. Francis	St. Louis, Missouri
W. T. Gardner	Portland, Oregon
James, Cardinal Gibbons	Baltimore, Maryland
Albert W. Gilchrist	Tallahassee, Florida
Washington Gladden	Columbus, Ohio
William E. Gonzales	Columbia, South Carolina
George Gray	Wilmington, Delaware
Allan G. Hall	Nashville, Tennessee
G. Stanley Hall	Worcester, Massachusetts
Judson Harmon	Columbus, Ohio
M. E. Hay	Olympia, Washington
J. A. Herring	Huntsville, Texas
Julia Ward Howe	Boston, Massachusetts
Charles E. Hughes	Albany, New York
William DeWitt Hyde	Brunswick, Maine
Edmund J. James	Urbana, Illinois
David Starr Jordan	Stanford University, California
Hiram W. Kellogg	Wilmington, Delaware
Frederick Kohler	Cleveland, Ohio
Ira Landrith	Nashville, Tennessee
Ben. B. Lindsey	Denver, Colorado
C. Lombardi	Dallas, Texas
Julian W. Mack	Chicago, Illinois
James R. Mann	Chicago, Illinois
Robert H. Marr	New Orleans, Louisiana
Thomas R. Marshall	Indianapolis, Indiana
M. A. Matthews	Seattle, Washington
S. C. Mitchell	Columbia, South Carolina
Mrs. Philip N. Moore	St. Louis, Missouri
Thomas M. Mulry	New York, New York
Henry B. F. McFarland	Washington, District of Columbia
Fanny McKinney McKee	Indianapolis, Indiana
Timothy Nicholson	Richmond, Indiana
W. J. Northen	Atlanta, Georgia
Cyrus B. Northrop ·	Minneapolis, Minnesota
William H. O'Connell	Boston, Massachusetts
Thomas M. Osborn	Louisville, Kentucky
Robert L. Owen	Muskogee, Oklahoma

Rutherford H. Platt	Columbus, Ohio
Aram J. Pothier	Providence, Rhode Island
James P. Ramsay	Lowell, Massachusetts
Joseph Rauch	Sioux City, Iowa
Charles A. Rook	Pittsburgh, Pennsylvania
T. P. Shields	New Orleans, Louisiana
Hoke Smith	Atlanta, Georgia
Samuel G. Smith	St. Paul, Minnesota
William Spry	Salt Lake City, Utah
B. M. Spurr	Moundsville, West Virginia
Wendell P. Stafford	Washington, District of Columbia
Lillian M. N. Stevens	Portland, Maine
J. H. Stolper, M.D.	Krebs, Oklahoma
Thomas N. Strong	Portland, Oregon
Walter R. Stubbs	Topeka, Kansas
Richard Sylvester	Washington, District of Columbia
Charles H. Taylor	Massachusetts
Francis J. Torrance	Pittsburgh, Pennsylvania
F. S. Towle, M.D.	Portsmouth, New Hampshire
Victor C. Vaughan, M.D.	Ann Arbor, Michigan
George Vaux, Jr.	Philadelphia, Pennsylvania
R. S. Vessey	Pierre, South Dakota
Maurice M. Wall	Buffalo, New York
Booker T. Washington	Tuskegee, Alabama
William H. Welch, M.D.	Baltimore, Maryland
Benjamin Ide Wheeler	Berkeley, California
Albert Hall Whitfield	Jackson, Mississippi
Frederick Howard Wines	Springfield, Illinois

CO-OPERATING COMMITTEES

AMERICAN PRISON ASSOCIATION

Cornelius V. Collins	Albany, New York
*John L. Milligan	Allegheny, Pennsylvania
Frederick G. Pettigrove	Boston, Massachusetts
Albert Garvin	Wethersfield, Connecticut
Frederick H. Wines	Springfield, Illinois
Henry Wolfer	Stillwater, Minnesota
R. W. McClaughry	Leavenworth, Kansas
John M. Glenn	New York, New York
Frank B. Sanborn	Concord, Massachusetts
Robert V. LaDow	Washington, District of Columbia
John Joy Edson	Washington, District of Columbia
Ernest P. Bicknell	Washington, District of Columbia
F. H. Mills	New York, New York
Amos W. Butler	Indianapolis, Indiana
James A. Leonard	Mansfield, Ohio
John H. Wigmore	Evanston, Illinois

*Deceased

Decatur M. Sawyer	Montclair, New Jersey
*E. F. Morgan	Richmond, Virginia
Eugene Smith	New York, New York
Joseph P. Byers	New York, New York
Z. R. Brockway	Elmira, New York
Roeliff Brinkerhoff	Mansfield, Ohio
Edward S. Wright	Pittsburgh, Pennsylvania
Joseph F. Scott	Elmira, New York
E. J. Murphy	Joliet, Illinois

NATIONAL CONFERENCE OF CHARITIES AND CORRECTION

Jane Addams	Chicago, Illinois
Homer Folks	New York, New York
F. H. Nibecker	Glen Mills, Pennsylvania
Katharine B. Davis	Bedford, New York
Thomas M. Mulry	New York, New York
William Calhoun	Chicago, Illinois
Julian W. Mack	Chicago, Illinois
Julia C. Lathrop	Rockford, Illinois
Alexander Johnson	Fort Wayne, Indiana
Ernest P. Bicknell	Washington, District of Columbia

AMERICAN INSTITUTE OF CRIMINAL LAW AND CRIMINOLOGY

Joseph P. Byers	New York, New York
Homer Folks	New York, New York
J. W. Garner	Champaign, Illinois
Charles R. Henderson	Chicago, Illinois
Joseph Jastrow	Madison, Wisconsin
Adolph Meyer, M.D.	Baltimore, Maryland
Boris Sidis, M.D.	Brookline, Massachusetts
William W. Smithers	Philadelphia, Pennsylvania

NATIONAL CONFERENCE ON THE EDUCATION OF DEPENDENT, TRUANT, BACK-WARD AND DELINQUENT CHILDREN

Mornay Williams	New York, New York
J. C. Kalleen	Jamesburg, New Jersey
O. E. Darnall	Washington, District of Columbia
Elmer L. Coffeen	Westboro, Massachusetts
F. H. Nibecker	Glen Mills, Pennsylvania
C. D. Hillis	Washington, District of Columbia .
George S. Addams	Cleveland, Ohio
Ophelia L. Amigh	Geneva, Illinois
Margaret E. Fairbank	Middletown, Connecticut
John B. Montgomery	Coldwater, Michigan
E. P. Wentworth	Portland, Maine

AMERICAN BAR ASSOCIATION

William W. Smithers	Philadelphia, Pennsylvania
Julian W. Mack	Chicago, Illinois
John D. Lindsay	New York, New York
William H. DeLacy	Washington, District of Columbia
Albert H. Hall	Minneapolis, Minnesota

---

* Deceased

EDITORIAL INTRODUCTION

By CHARLES RICHMOND HENDERSON

IN the year 1905 at the meeting of the American (then "National") Prison Association at Lincoln, Nebraska, the late Dr. S. J. Barrows, then United States Commissioner on the International Prison Commission, and President of the International Prison Congress, requested the American Prison Association to appoint a committee "to co-operate with the government in making the necessary arrangements for the meeting." It was the duty of this committee to assist the Commissioner in making suitable arrangements for the entertainment of the delegates to the International Prison Congress in 1910. The following persons were appointed for this purpose: John L. Milligan, Cornelius V. Collins, Albert Garvin, Frederick Howard Wines, Robert W. McClaughry, Henry Wolfer, Frederick G. Pettigrove, John M. Glenn, with Charles R. Henderson as chairman.* This Committee was given power to enlarge its numbers and fill vacancies.

Dr. Barrows suggested to this general committee the formation of a special sub-committee to help him prepare several volumes to be called Souvenir Volumes and presented to the official delegates to the International Prison Congress; the purpose of these books being to exhibit as fully as possible the essential features and principles of American methods of dealing with crime and delinquents. It was proposed that the scope of this work should correspond to the four sections of the International Prison Congress,—criminal law, prison systems, preventive agencies and treatment of delinquent and neglected children. The following persons were appointed to constitute this sub-committee: Frank B. Sanborn, F. H. Wines, J. M. Glenn, with C. R. Henderson as chairman. Later, after giving very valuable and fruitful suggestions, Dr. F. H. Wines resigned from the committee and Mr. Eugene Smith was added. The following division of labor was finally accepted: Dr. Barrows was to have general editorial direction; several specialists were to be invited to prepare

* Proceedings of the National Prison Association, 1905, p. 304.

Volumes I and II; C. R. Henderson was requested to prepare Volume III, and Dr. H. H. Hart, Volume IV.

To the great satisfaction of the friends of the Congress, all anxiety about the expense of the undertaking was removed by the generous action of the Russell Sage Foundation, which offered to give $5,000 to pay the expenses of publication; the labor of the writers being given without pecuniary recompense, as a patriotic service.

The sad loss of our esteemed friend, Dr. Barrows, on April 21, 1909, made necessary several changes in the plans. He had already carefully worked out, in collaboration with the committee, the outlines of the work and had selected all of the writers; he had examined the first sketches to assure himself that conflicts and duplication would be avoided; then he passed away from us and we took up his task as well as we could.

The responsibility of the general editor then fell to the chairman of the sub-committee, who having been appointed by President Taft to succeed Dr. Barrows as United States Commissioner on the International Prison Commission on May 28, 1909, resigned as chairman of the general committee of the American Prison Association at its meeting in Seattle in August, 1909. Mr. C. V. Collins succeeded him.

It has been the purpose of all concerned to present in these volumes, with fidelity to truth, the most essential facts, without controversy and without boasting, and to interpret the historical movements treated so as to discover their genuine significance. Perhaps some important facts have been overlooked; perhaps being so near the events described the perspective has not always been duly regarded, or perhaps the personal convictions of the writers (all of them persons having strong convictions) may sometimes have over-emphasized particular arguments on disputed points; but at least an honest attempt has been made to put the reader in a position to form an independent judgment on the basis of all relevant facts and differing opinions. Many of the laws and activities and institutions described are in the stage of experiment; some of these will drop away and leave only negative results; but on the whole we believe that we have made a record of some permanent contributions to human welfare and progress in this series of volumes.

GENERAL ASPECTS OF OUR GOVERNMENT

All the papers of these four volumes are written by persons familiar with the relations of their topics to the working of federal, state and local governments in the United States; and there are certain facts that must be kept in mind in reading these papers.

The fundamental law of the land was originally derived from Great Britain, the Mother Country, and all our legal institutions to this day show traces of this origin, however much they have been modified to meet new and different conditions and problems. The Constitution of the Union was an instrument drawn up in the beginning of the Republic as an independent nation, to give a large framework for future development of legal and political institutions. Several important amendments were adopted at later dates. Such amendments are very difficult to secure and require long time to carry through the process of discussion and enactment. The method of amendment is too cumbrous for meeting emergencies and changed conditions, so that the more speedy and effective method of adaptation of old principles to new needs is judicial interpretation. Whatever the legal theory may be, the practical fact is that the Supreme Court finds in the Constitution no permanent obstacle to progressive measures, if these are persistently demanded, after thorough consideration, by the will of the nation. The fundamental law is thus far more flexible than might be supposed from the apparently rigid lines of the written Constitution. The preamble to the Constitution recites the origin, authority and purpose of government: "We, the people of the United States, in order to form a more perfect Union, establish justice, insure domestic tranquility, provide for the common defence, promote the general welfare, and secure the blessings of liberty to ourselves and our posterity, do ordain and establish this Constitution for the United States of America."

An analysis of this instrument reveals the outline of the federal organization:

(1) A national legislature composed of a Senate and House of Representatives. The qualifications, privileges and duties of the members are carefully defined. (2) The executive power is vested in the President. His cabinet is simply advisory and is not responsible to Congress. (3) The judicial power is vested in one Supreme Court. In the amendments are set down important principles relating to criminal law.

There are 46 states, besides the territories of Alaska, Arizona,

Hawaii, New Mexico, the District of Columbia, the colony of Guam, the Philippine Islands and Porto Rico. A government for Porto Rico was established by the Fifty-sixth Congress. The Philippines are under a permanent civil government; Guam and Tutuila under governors; and the Isthmian Canal Zone is under a commission, all appointed by the President. The District of Columbia is governed by Congress through a commission.

The territorial limits of the United States extend into the ocean the distance of a cannon shot and the boundaries between the United States and countries adjacent are determined by treaties. The territorial limits of the states are fixed by charters, compacts and by acts of Congress admitting to the Union. The limits of counties are fixed by the acts of the state legislature. The following principles are of general significance:

The courts of the country can punish a person only for acts committed within its territorial limits, with certain exceptions relating to crimes committed on ships or in foreign countries. The jurisdiction of federal courts is determined by Congress, although where Congress has declared certain crimes without defining them the courts may seek a definition in the common law. Powers conferred on federal courts by Congress must be such as are authorized by the Constitution.

Generally speaking all persons who are within the territorial limits of the nation or a state are subject to its laws; certain exceptions are made with regard to foreign citizens.

THE CRIMINAL LAW

The criminal law consists of statutes which have been enacted by Congress or the legislature, and of the common law. The principles of the common law are expressly stated in court decisions and at this point the English common law has great influence, though without final authority.

Congress is limited in its power to define crimes and fix penalties by the Federal Constitution. The Constitution has given Congress power to provide for the punishment of counterfeiting and piracy. The state legislatures have inherent power to prohibit and punish any act unless the statute violates the state or federal constitution.

PENAL ACTS

Some states have adopted penal codes which, in certain cases, are intended to cover the whole law, so that no act is a crime unless it is expressly declared to be so; in others the code abrogates the common law only in relation to acts prohibited, leaving in force the common law where it is not expressly set aside.

For the development of the essential principles of criminal law in this country we refer at once to the able discussion by Mr. Eugene Smith, in this volume, as to a competent authority.*

We thus see the possibility of great confusion, perplexity and contradiction in the criminal law and in the modes of punishment established within the United States. The Federal Legislature, and the legislatures of all the forty-six states are constantly putting forth new statutes, while the courts of all ranks are interpreting and applying these laws in every part of the vast region. The consequence may be anticipated. The penalties for the same crime are different for each state. There is no great country which has tried so many experiments with the retributive principle. When it is asserted that a legislature is competent to measure the degree of guilt in the length of the punishment, this absurd assertion is contradicted by the facts before us. Dr. F. H. Wines, Dr. S. J. Barrows, Mr. Eugene Smith and others have given abundant illustrations of these necessary contradictions, and have drawn from them a strong argument for abandoning the attempt to give any approximate measure for retribution. They have shown that we must seek in the character and conduct of the criminal rather than in abstract definitions and penalties the amount of punishment necessary for social protection. Illustrations of these unequal penalties are given in this volume.

The definitions and conceptions of "justice" are changing under the influence of a more scientific analysis and a deeper appreciation of the value of human life. We are coming to see that "justice" must mean the condition of social welfare at a given time, the spirit and the method of furthering human life in all its elements of good and in all the members of the nation. The notion that "justice" looks merely to the past and demands a fair equivalent for the wrong done, will not bear calm and rational inspection. The ideal is not some remote condition which is utterly impracticable here and now, but a principle which can be made to regulate action at once, in this world, and among all the members of the common-

*See also: L'Organisation judiciare aux États-Unis, par Alf. Nerincx, 1909.

wealth. It is possible, at least for all practical purposes, to discuss rules of conduct which can be tested by results before all eyes. Justice, as we now see it, asks not for destruction or retribution,—a purely negative and fruitless demand,—but it wills positively just and upright character and conduct. The malefactor is to be transformed into a benefactor, or at least placed under conditions most favorable to produce this result.

The tendency to promote general well-being is the test of measures of law as of all other modes of action among men. By careful observation, with records in statistical form as far as possible, the effects of various measures on the individual delinquents and on the persons tempted to crime may be measured. The laws of influence, made clear by psychologists, teachers and directors of reformatories are reliable guides and may be trusted.

This practical conception of justice is at the basis of the movements toward reform of laws and prison methods throughout the civilized world, and of those which are described in these pages. The moment "good time" laws or rules were admitted there was a breach in the Chinese wall of the retributive theory of punishment; from that moment the admission was made that the conduct of the convict after conviction ought to have some effect on the time of liberation, on the length of the sentence. From that moment the ancient assumption that legislator or judge should attempt to measure out punishment was dead and a new and more reasonable principle came into play.

The discretion of the judge and his authority to be "lenient" was another door of entrance for the modern conception; the fact that "leniency" without supervision by agents of the court was in reality cruelty to the individual and dangerous to public order, revealed the necessity of providing probation officers, just as the defective results of absolute release on "good time" demonstrated the necessity for having parole officers and a system of conditional release.

The governors of states, under the pressure of politicians, attorneys and friends, tempted and urged to abuse their pardon power, discovered the arbitrary nature of the pardon power itself; and what Blackstone had praised was found to be dangerous and capricious. The governors besought the legislators to give them pardon boards to divide and dilute their responsibility,—a mere unprincipled makeshift without foundation in reason, supported only by tradition. It is not surprising that several governors became enthusiastic advocates of the parole system, because it placed the responsibility on the shoulders of the convict himself, where it belongs, and introduced the principle that a man's freedom depends not on an act of grace but on his own disposition as shown in his habitual deeds.

Thus it will be seen that this movement toward a real "indeterminate sentence" has its sources in experience, and is the logical outcome of the obvious failures and contradictions of a theory of retribution.

All the improvements thus far brought about in the United States have their roots in the principle of social protection through educative agencies:—parental and industrial schools for reform; numerous preventive agencies and methods; probation of first offenders; parole for convicts who give reason for hope of reform; prolonged sentences for hardened criminals; colonies for the cure of habitual inebriates; reformatory methods for all; higher demands on prison officers made imperative by the higher requirements of an educative system as compared with those of a merely brutal repressive and retributive system.

Perhaps the so-called "indeterminate sentence" is popularly regarded as, in some sense, distinctive and central in the reforms of prisons and criminal law in the United States. It is sometimes said that the indeterminate sentence has been accepted universally in the United States and is maintained without opposition. This is far from the truth, and it is desirable that the truth should be known.

In the strict and legal sense of the word the indeterminate sentence—defined as a "sentence to reformation" and without limits in time,—has not been made legal by a single legislature.* In all states where a beginning has been made with the reformatory principle the maximum term of imprisonment is fixed by law for each kind of crime, and often the minimum period also. This is in no proper or exact sense an indeterminate sentence, and it is seriously confusing, as practice shows, to employ it, even though most of us qualify it by the term "so-called" indeterminate sentence. It might be well to reserve this expression to use accurately and truthfully when we finally secure what we on principle are striving hard to attain. But habit and custom are tyrannous; the term indeterminate sentence at least designates a hope, an ideal and a tendency; and, with the usual explanations we shall probably continue to use it, with all its defects. We shall not waste time quibbling over a

* This is shown by Judge Simeon Baldwin in his " rapport " to the International Prison Congress, 1910.

phrase. The substantial fact is that the American public has entered upon a new era of criminal law and the phrase indeterminate sentence is the watchword of the movement. From the beginning the members of the legal profession, and properly, as conservators of the rights of men against executive arbitrariness, have looked with suspicion on the undue extension of the powers of an administrative board in restraining convicts, even when on conditional parole. This antagonism has broken out in violent speech of heated controversy, and the parole law has been arraigned before the public as giving free and unjust control to the executive branch of government.

In the very first experiment, in the establishment of the Elmira Reformatory, New York, this antagonism of the legal profession was felt. The first draft of the law contained a provision for a really indeterminate sentence, and would have given power to the board of managers to keep a prisoner for life. This clause was stricken out, because it might have defeated the entire reformatory plan. Even the modified and limited power entrusted to the board of managers was not given without question. Mr. Scott cites the language of the report of the commissioners who selected the site of Elmira in 1869:

"Should it be thought that too much power is given to the board of managers and warden to determine whether reformation has taken place, the answer is that their decision is not to be arbitrary but based on some report of facts showing regular and satisfactory improvement."

But this answer has not hushed controversy among many lawyers who insist that giving such power to release or restrain is one which belongs to the courts and not to the executive or administrative branch of government. Possibly a way can be found for meeting this objection on solid ground, by a slight modification in the organization and procedure of courts, and by the specialization of certain courts which may have continuous control of prisoners on parole.

It has sometimes been suggested that the *trial* court should have the power to control the paroled convicts and order their conditional release, their discharge or remand. But to this it seems to be a valid answer that after trial the judge and jury who have convicted the prisoner must lose all connection with his life and be ignorant of his conduct under discipline, which must be considered in relation to parole and discharge. Furthermore, the trial courts are scattered over a wide area in the larger states and there could be no unified and impartial administration of the parole system. The decisions would be contradictory and capricious, with all the marks of injustice and unfairness. In the case of minors sent to state reform schools the interference of trial judges, which is legal in Illinois, frequently works to demoralize the discipline of the school, and is sometimes quite without guidance from knowledge of the situation.

Judge John Franklin Fort, then justice of the Supreme Court of New Jersey, afterward governor of the state, before the National (American) Prison Association in 1902 made a powerful plea for the reformatory principle. He said of the indeterminate sentence:

"Given the right conditions and an impartial, non-partisan tribunal to control discharges, I would favor its application to all offenders. I would go still a step further. I would have neither the minimum nor the maximum term fixed by statute, and, possibly, not by the sentencing court. The proper way to cure those who are really criminal is as you cure other diseased persons; namely, keep them under treatment until they are cured, or at least, so nearly cured that they may be discharged safely." After this strong assertion of the reformatory principle he calls in question the present system of administration and proposes a substitute. "A board of managers of a penal institution is not always the safest body with which to leave the liberty of the prisoner. Even though it be constitutional and otherwise legal, to confer upon the managers of a penal institution* the power of discharge, is it not of doubtful wisdom under our form of government? Is it not a matter of serious concern whether a "court of discharge" should not exist in each state, having judicial power of inquiry and action? Would not both the public and the prisoner feel safer in the hands of an impartial tribunal in which was lodged the ultimate decision as to discharge; a tribunal with power to hear the whole matter and with the sole power to remand into custody for cause? Should not a man have the right to be heard on the question of his remand into custody? I would not take from the managers their power of initiative as to release. I would require all applications for release, before expiration of term, to come through them but, if they refused to permit an application for parole after a reasonable term of service, that the court might consider it, I would give the prisoner the right of review and of a hearing before the discharge court." He recommends that a judge should preside over such a court. "In the interests of absolute impartiality and assured public confidence—which are essential to

---

* Even when the parole board is not identical with the administrators of a prison it is still a part of the executive and not of the judicial organization of the state.

the permanence of the system—it seems clear that some such protection should be thrown around it."

Thus far a learned and far-sighted judge.

It is true that no American state has established a law which may be properly called an indeterminate sentence law. But it may fairly be claimed that many states have made great and rapid advance in introducing reformatory methods, and that the merely vindictive and retributive notion of punishment has been rejected by the most enlightened minds of the nation. In the treatment of the insane, of neglected children, and of delinquent youth, the re-educative purpose is dominant. In dealing with inebriates and others of imperfect mentality and will, the idea of cure and re-education is influential. The suspension of sentence and probation applied to adults gains friends and advocates. It remains only to show that a vast number of offenders are defectives in some degree to secure the extension of the same methods to them.

The discussions of facts and experiences found in these four volumes reveal a weak place in the administration of criminal law, not peculiar to the United States. We have no organization for the thorough and consecutive study of offenders. The trial by summary process is swift, superficial and bears on a few minor points. The trial in case of serious crime is usually only too prolonged, but has no scientific method of finding out the life history of the accused. The court papers sent to the warden of the prison give him scant information on which to base his plans of education and reformation. Indeed, the assumption of the court and law is, perhaps in a majority of cases, actually contrary to facts,—the assumption that the sane man did the criminal act of his own free will. Much time is spent to little real purpose in proving or disproving "intent." Some of the most progressive judges have learned a lesson from the experience of the juvenile court where the procedure is free from these unproved and false assumptions, and where a frank, patient and sometimes expert study is made of the nature, habits, life history and surroundings of the accused.

It begins to dawn on some of the judges that ordinary adult criminals are little more than youth; untaught, ignorant, perverted by their education, without the power to make moral distinctions clearly and sharply, and trained in social neglect to a false attitude toward law and order. Once establish this fact in the legal mind and we shall extend upward the methods which have already proved so fruitful with minors. Because we are too hasty, rapid and impatient with the half-shaped creatures who throng our courts of summary jurisdiction we are compelled to do our work over again—sometimes fifty or two hundred times. If we could persuade legislators, lawyers, judges and police that the present reckless, thoughtless method is sheer waste and tends simply to increase criminality, we might be able to establish colonies equipped for serious treatment of a vast number of the anti-social class. At this point America needs to make an earnest study of such colonies as those of Merxplas and Witzwil.

The metaphysical dogma of measured retribution for guilt clouds the judgment and blinds learned men to the real situation, even obstructs the efforts put forth already to take firm hold on dangerous delinquents and keep them under control until they can voluntarily walk in the way of rightness. In our most advanced juvenile courts we have the model;—a physician and a trained psychologist study the immature young person, and with the aid of the probation officers who know the home, lay before the judge all the data necessary for his choice of methods. This is plain common sense. That same judge, sitting in a "criminal" court, the next hour, has before him a young fellow who happens to be only one day over seventeen years of age, and the procedure becomes instantly a century behind modern science,—learns nothing from experience, forgets nothing of precedent. Good law becomes a synonym of bad method. Meantime the "Black Maria" moves like a shuttle back and forth between court and bridewell, full of the same unreclaimed rounders. If courts were free to decide according to real facts and not compelled to decide on unfounded assumptions, they would halt this procession and select at least a part of the helpless victims of vicious habit to recover their real "free will." The short sentence for this class is just as bad in our country as in any other and complaints have been sounded from unprejudiced and experienced citizens of all nations and states. The evidence collected and interpreted in these essays ought to help correct the vision of administrators of law and responsible framers of legislation. The establishment of scientific methods of studying all accused persons would force upon public attention some of the worst absurdities of a merely retributive and deterrent theory of criminal law.

THE ORDER OF DISCUSSION

In the first volume we have told the story of the development of thought in the United States by reciting the facts in biographical and historical form; we have shown how typical enlightened men, reflecting on the evils and abuses of the age and on the rational order and the criminal law, came to certain conclusions about fundamental principles. We have been exceedingly fortunate in securing for this historical sketch men whose memories are documents, the very primary sources of history; Mr. Sanborn and Mr. Brockway were influential in the first Congress at Cincinnati in 1870, and Dr. F. H. Wines, with a mastery of his theme gives a touch of filial admiration to his narration and interpretation. And who could have been chosen for the article on criminal law so properly as Mr. Eugene Smith, himself learned in the noble science of law, President of the renowned Prison Association of New York and identified with the progressive movement toward a more humane and effective administration of the law? Other leaders and prophets of a past generation are mentioned with praise and their chief contributions are characterized.

A brief biography of Dr. S. J. Barrows has been added, as all must confess to be appropriate. To the European members of the International Prison Commission, who hold him in affectionate and reverent esteem, this contribution of our gifted young journalist, Mr. Paul U. Kellogg, will be especially welcome.

To the second volume a number of the best representatives of the American prison and reformatory administration have contributed. Their papers may be regarded as the sincere and reliable expression of convictions and purposes which promise to control the future. They are men of long experience, and the fact that in a country where changes are so frequent and political appointments so uncertain, they have stood at their posts long enough to acquire professional skill and effect genuine reforms, gives promise of the near triumph of the "merit system" over the "spoils system" which has done our country so much harm. They are not the only men of this worthy class, but they are types of the kind we prefer and mean to have in office the country over.

Of the third volume, whose preparation was undertaken at the request of Dr. S. J. Barrows, it is not proper for the writer of the introduction to say more than is contained in the title, Preventive Agencies and Methods. It is, however, only justice to acknowledge the help of numerous specialists who generously and patiently furnished materials for its pages from their laboratories of social service. The names of the creditors are mentioned usually in connection with their works. The attempt was made to describe and interpret the "social policy" which is taking more definite shape in this country, from the standpoint of defense against all forms of anti-social conduct.

The author of the fourth volume on the treatment of delinquent and neglected children and youth has become known everywhere as a specialist in the best methods of helping homeless and neglected children. For many years he was secretary of the Board of Charities in Minnesota and then built up the Illinois Children's Home and Aid Society to be one of the most effective agencies of its kind in the land. As Secretary of the National Children's Home Society his wisdom, tact and skill have extended the usefulness of that national federation and gradually improved its methods. It is not probable that any really significant method could escape his attention, nor any abuse or error find aid and comfort from his pen.

We are grateful to many foreign writers who have visited our institutions and honestly sought to represent things as they are, and to interpret all sympathetically. Their cheer has encouraged us, their criticisms have made us more alert, their praises have been welcome. Probably their exposures of our mistakes have been most profitable of all.

At the same time Europe needs also to see how our methods look to those who are responsible for them, who are actually in the harness and are facing the problems as strangers do not. It is well to let the man speak who can tell us why he did not choose some course which to outsiders seems better but might be impossible under our circumstances.

We take this occasion to offer the cordial greetings of the members of the various societies interested in the social treatment of crime and delinquents, to the official delegates to the International Prison Congress, whom it is our privilege to meet on the soil of our beloved country. They are welcome among us. To them, first of all, we offer these volumes as a souvenir of a visit which brings to us great delight and profit, and which will long be remembered by the friends of prisoners and prison reform as an inspiration to do better work. In this story they will find much to criticize; the faults of a rapidly growing country whose development in material wealth has outrun its legislation and its institutions of culture; but we trust they will also find here a powerful and advancing movement to correct recognized evils, to promote order and security and to further general enlightenment. When they point out our defects, we are sure that this will be done with their customary courtesy and kindness, and that the severest criticisms will be made palatable by their appreciation of the spirit in which we have ventured on bold but promising experiments. If we fail we shall bear the burden and the cost; if we succeed the world will thank us for the trial.

ORGANIZATIONS FOR THE STUDY OF CRIME

For many years the American Prison Association has brought together the wardens, physicians and chaplains of prisons and reformatories, the representatives of state boards and interested students; and the discussions of this body, published in an annual volume, represent the best thought of practical men in the field in our country.

The National Conference of Charities and Correction approaches the subject rather from the side of prevention and education of the young; but it has also published valuable papers on prison science and criminal law.

The American Institute of Criminal Law and Criminology was organized in Chicago in 1909, in connection with the commemoration of the fiftieth anniversary of the founding of the law school of the Northwestern University. This Institute has already begun the publication of its Journal, whose initial number is dated May, 1910.

The following paragraphs by the editor-in-chief, Professor James W. Garner, make clear the motives and scope of the Institute and of its organ:*

"The American Institute of Criminal Law and Criminology is an outgrowth of the National Conference on Criminal Law and Criminology held in Chicago in June, 1909. The idea of a conference representing the various classes interested in the problems connected with the administration of punitive justice, including the treatment of criminals, was a happy conception of the law faculty of Northwestern University, and the holding of such a conference was adopted as an appropriate way of celebrating the fiftieth anniversary of the foundation of the law school of that institution. It was indeed a unique and fitting method of commemorating an anniversary of this kind, coming as it did at a time when there is an awakening of interest in legal reform and a crying need for co-operative effort among lawyers and scientists. The conference was composed of about one hundred and fifty delegates representing the various professions and occupations concerned directly or indirectly with the administration of the criminal law and the punishment of criminals, and included

* Journal of the American Institute of Criminal Law and Criminology. Vol. I, 1, pp. 2–5. (May, 1910.)

members of the bench and bar, professors of law in the universities, alienists, criminologists, penologists, superintendents of penal and reformatory institutions, psychologists, police officials, probation officers and the like. Delegates attended from every section of the country and the conference was a very representative gathering of those either actually concerned with the administration of the criminal law or interested in its problems as students and scientists. In character and purpose the conference was entirely without precedent in the history of the United States. It represented the first instance of co-operative effort among those interested in a better system of criminal justice, and marks, we venture to assert, the beginning of a new era in the history of American criminal jurisprudence. The conference afforded an excellent opportunity for the exchange of ideas among lay scientists and lawyers, and a sincere effort was made to reach a common understanding on certain points concerning which there has been a variance of opinion. Although the idea of such a gathering was new to America it was an old one in Europe, where congresses of criminologists have frequently been held for the promotion of criminological science and the consideration of practical problems connected with the administration of criminal justice. In Europe the value of co-operation among lawyers and scientists in promoting improvement in the criminal law and in methods of criminal procedure has long been recognized.

"An elaborate program covering almost every problem of criminal science was prepared for the Chicago conference mainly from the list of topics suggested by the delegates, and altogether it constituted a remarkable program of constructive effort looking to judicial and penal reform. For the systematization and dispatch of the work of the congress the delegates were divided into three sections, to the first of which were referred all topics relating to the treatment (penal and remedial) of criminals; to the second, those relating to the organization, appointment and training of officials concerned with the administration of punitive justice, and to the third, those having to do with criminal law and procedure. To the conference as thus organized one hundred and thirty-five topics were submitted for consideration. They included such questions as the indeterminate sentence, rehabilitation, procedure of juvenile courts, treatment of accused persons under detention, indemnification for wrongful detention, the employment of prisoners, bureaus of identification, probation and parole, the insanity plea, public defenders, the selection and treatment of jurors, means of increasing the effectiveness of the jury system, the unnecessary multiplication of criminal laws, the examination of accused persons, the simplification of pleading, the need of efficient agencies for collecting and publishing criminal and judicial statistics, restrictions on the right of appeal, reversals for technical errors, enlargement of the power of the judge, the constitution and procedure of municipal courts, laboratories for the scientific study of criminals, the individualization of punishment, the use of medical expert testimony, and many others. Realizing the impossibility of dealing adequately with such a variety of questions the conference wisely decided to restrict its deliberations to the consideration of a small number of topics which are to be made the subjects of investigation by committees and upon which reports are to be presented at the next conference. Among those topics were: (1) an effective system for recording the physical and moral, hereditary and environmental conditions of offenders; (2) the most effective methods of probation and parole for adult offenders; (3) the indeterminate sentence; (4) the organization and training of pardon and parole boards and the correlation of such boards with one another and with the courts; (5) the practicability of establishing commissions of specialists for giving expert testimony; (6) the possibility of unifying state and local courts so as to diminish the cost of transcripts, bills of exception, writs of error, etc., in accordance with the suggestion of the Committee of Fifteen of the American Bar Association; (7) the simplification of pleading in criminal cases and the elimination of technical errors. A committee was also appointed to investigate and report on the methods of criminal procedure in Europe and particularly in Great Britain, where the administration of justice is frequently asserted to be a model of efficiency and dispatch. Dean John D. Lawson of the University of Missouri School of Law, and editor of the American Law Review, and Professor Edwin R. Keedy, of Northwestern University Law School, as members of this committee, are now in England studying British criminal procedure, this mission having been undertaken with the approval and good wishes of President Taft, who is a great admirer of the English system and deeply interested in the outcome of the proposed inquiry. These gentlemen, it is understood, will be joined by other members of the committee at an early date and the result of their investigations will be awaited with interest by all those who desire impartial and first-hand information regarding the methods by which the administration of criminal justice in England has been brought to such a high degree of efficiency.

"An encouraging feature of the Chicago conference was the practical unanimity among lawyers and laymen alike that certain of our rules of criminal procedure and penal methods are antiquated, inadequate and unworthy of the high standard of civilization that we have attained in other respects, and should be modified in the interest of justice and social security.

"The conference adopted resolutions calling attention to the popular dissatisfaction with the results of our present methods of administering criminal justice; declared that reliable and accurate information regarding the actual administration of the criminal law was necessary to efficient legislation and administration; appealed to Congress to provide through the agency of the Census Bureau for the collection of full and accurate criminal and judicial statistics covering the entire country; and urged the enactment of legislation by the states, requiring prosecuting attorneys and magistrates to report to some state officer full information regarding crime committed within their jurisdictions and the punishment of offenders. Recognizing the desirability of making readily accessible in English the more important treatises on criminology published in foreign languages, steps were taken looking toward the translation and publication of such treatises, to the end that the principles of criminal science may be more generally studied and the criminal law improved. Finally, impressed with the advantages of uniting the efforts of lawyers, criminologists, sociologists and all others in the cause of a better criminal law, the conference resolved to effect a permanent national organization, to be known as the American Institute of Criminal Law and Criminology, whose purposes shall be to advance the scientific study of crime, criminal law and procedure, to formulate and promote measures for solving the problems connected therewith, and to co-ordinate the efforts of individuals and of organizations interested in the administration of certain and speedy justice. Mr. John H. Wigmore * of Chicago was elected president of the new organization and it was decided to hold the next meeting in Washington in October, 1910, in connection with the International Prison Association. The proceedings of the Chicago conference will be published for distribution among the members."

The organization of this Institute and the establishment of the Journal are the most significant events in the development of a really scientific study of the social treatment of crime in this country.

* Professor Wigmore, Dean of the Northwestern School of Law, deserves highest honor for the initiation of this enterprise.

RUSSELL SAGE
FOUNDATION

PRISON REFORM

EDITED BY

CHARLES RICHMOND HENDERSON, Ph.D. (Leipsic)

PROFESSOR OF SOCIOLOGY IN THE UNIVERSITY OF CHICAGO
COMMISSIONER FOR THE UNITED STATES ON THE INTER-
NATIONAL PRISON COMMISSION

CORRECTION AND PREVENTION

FOUR VOLUMES PREPARED FOR THE
EIGHTH INTERNATIONAL PRISON CONGRESS

NEW YORK
CHARITIES PUBLICATION
COMMITTEE . . . . . MCMX

TABLE OF CONTENTS

PAGE

I. Historical Introduction 3
By Frederick Howard Wines, LL.D.

Declaration of Principles Promulgated at Cincinnati, Ohio, 1870 39

II. E. C. Wines and Prison Reform 64
A Memoir by F. B. Sanborn

III. The American Reformatory Prison System . . . 88
By Z. R. Brockway

IV. Possible and Actual Penalties for Crime 108
By Frederick H. Wines

V. Samuel June Barrows 123
By Paul U. Kellogg

VI. Gen. Rutherford B. Hayes 140
By W. M. F. Round

VII. Biographical Sketches 145
Francis Lieber 145
Theodore W. Dwight 150
Edward Livingston 151
Dorothea Lynde Dix 158
Ellen Cheney Johnson 159
Gardiner Tufts 159

INDEX 161

LIST OF ILLUSTRATIONS

FACING PAGE

E. C. Wines . . . . *Frontispiece*	
Theodore W. Dwight	16
John L. Milligan	24
Count Sollohub	32
Front cover of a Japanese book on Prison Reform . . .	36
Back cover of the same book	37
F. B. Sanborn	64
Richard Vaux	70
A. G. Byers	78
Ellen C. Johnson	86
Z. R. Brockway	90
Gardiner Tufts	98
Frederick H. Wines	110
Samuel J. Barrows	124
Rutherford B. Hayes	140
Francis Lieber	146
Edward Livingston	152
Dorothea L. Dix	158

PRISON REFORM

HISTORICAL INTRODUCTION

By FREDERICK HOWARD WINES, LL.D.

THE remarkable progress made in criminal law and prison reform, both at home and abroad, since 1870—the date of the Cincinnati Prison Congress—justifies the characterization, by Count Sollohub, of America as "the home of penitentiary science." That eminent statesman, director of the house of correction in Moscow, said also, speaking of Russia, "The idea that the same system can be applied indiscriminately to all countries is an idea incapable of realization. . . . It results that, while preserving the immutable principles of justice, the penitentiary system of each country should maintain its distinct physiognomy." This he denominated "the application of the principle of nationality."

In the preparation of this series of volumes, the principle of nationality, thus defined, has been ever kept in mind. Our foreign friends will find in them much that is inapplicable, or impossible of adoption or imitation, in countries differing widely from the United States in many ways. A young nation, comparatively free from the entanglement of precedent and prejudice, with popular, democratic institutions, may have gone faster and farther in reducing theory to practice than may seem desirable to a more conservative people; but after all, the test of experiment is experience.

The most complete and authoritative compendium of American belief with reference to all the elements that enter into the prison question is the "Declaration of Principles," which was adopted by the National Prison Congress of Cincinnati. It was formulated by Dr. E. C. Wines, but slightly, though not materially, modified by the committee to which it was referred for revision. Every section of this paper was separately voted upon by the Congress. It is reprinted at the close of this article.*

Professor C. R. Henderson, who succeeds the lamented Dr. Samuel J. Barrows as president of the International Prison Congress, has assigned to me the congenial task of tracing the genesis of this famous Declaration in the mind of my father.

No man that ever lived would be less inclined than he to claim the credit of having originated ideas which had floated for centuries through the minds of many men in many lands. When, in 1862, he became the secretary of the New York Prison Association, he knew no more about crime and criminals than any intelligent man the vicissitudes of whose life have not brought him into contact with either. Eight years later, he was the acknowledged leader of leaders in prison reform throughout the world. The study of his career, interesting in itself, cannot fail to shed light upon the history of a movement that is in the highest degree characteristic of modern civilization.

The remarkable impulse given, in the latter half of the nineteenth century, to the cause of prison reform in the United States, is chiefly attributable to three men, of whom two—Messrs. F. B. Sanborn and Z. R. Brockway—survive to rejoice in the abundant harvest from seed planted in what then appeared to be sterile and unpromising soil. Dr. Wines has long been "where the wicked cease from troubling." Dissimilar as were these three in temperament, experience, and habits of thought, their fundamental agreement as to the nature of the changes demanded in criminal law and its administration, and their mutual regard and affection, so united them in purpose that they constituted a threefold cord not quickly broken.

The New York Prison Association was the youngest of three similar organizations. Between the other two—the Philadelphia and the Boston prison discipline societies—a bitter controversy was waged for many years over the question whether the Pennsylvania system (isolation of the convict by day and night) or the Auburn plan (isolation by night only, and compulsory silence in association) was preferable. That issue no longer agitates the American mind. Echoes of the controversy still reach our ears from across the sea, but in the New York reports it is scarcely mentioned. They are filled with denunciation of political control of prisons, and attacks upon the con-

* See page 39.

tract system of convict labor. In New York, and in other states as well, though not in all, these were at that time crying evils; and they were attended by their natural sequence, unnecessary severity of discipline, as it affected the amount and character of disciplinary punishment.

This is a painful subject to discuss, and it ought not, for obvious reasons, to be here dwelt upon at length. Some allusion to it cannot be avoided, since the starting-point of Dr. Wines' labors in behalf of a better system was his hostility to the system which stood in the way. It is difficult to discuss this older system fairly and in such a way as to convey no false impression to the reader's mind. Every successive stage of social evolution is of necessity transient and transitory; it may be contrasted with what went before, or with what follows. From the former point of view, each is an advance. Thus it has been truly said, that the history of civilization has been characterized by no single step in advance so radical as the institution of human slavery as an alternative for the massacre of captives taken in battle. The feudal system prepared the way for constitutional government. Without the legal fiction of corporate personality, few of the great enterprises of our own times could have been carried to successful completion. But the time arrived when feudality and slavery became stenches in the nostrils of those who saw and felt the burden of the wrongs perpetrated in their name. Something analogous has occurred in the evolution of the American prison system.

For instance, the centralization of control of the state prisons of New York, in 1847, partly at the instance of the New York Prison Association, was an advance. The prison inspectors of that state are believed to have constituted the first central board of administration of state institutions, of any class, in the United States. The introduction of productive and profitable convict labor into American prisons, even under the contract system, was a vast improvement on the compulsory association in idleness which characterized their former administration; and it may even be said to have been one of the chief roots of modern prison reform. As to disciplinary punishments in prisons, they are essential to the order and security of these establishments; the refusal of prisoners to perform the tasks assigned them is of course one principal occasion for such punishments.

It should also be said, by way of caution against misapprehension, that political appointments are not necessarily bad appointments. In a free country, which depends for its very existence upon the action of political parties of some sort, it is impossible wholly to

5

divorce the conduct of public affairs from political considerations. The attempt to do so would be unwise, and it would be futile. It must not be imagined that the prison inspectors, or even the prison contractors, were worse men than the average citizen—less intelligent, more corrupt or more cruel. Nevertheless, the system as it existed in New York about the time of the Civil War was very bad.

Perhaps no better statement of the influence of political control upon prison discipline has ever been formulated than that found in the testimony of Gaylord B. Hubbell, warden at Sing Sing. "The inspectors are nominated by political conventions, and elected by party votes. The party in power claims all the patronage to be dispensed in the prisons, and that patronage is used irrespective of the qualifications of persons applying for and appointed to office. The board of inspectors has the appointment of all the officers in the prisons. Whenever the majority of the board is changed from one political party to another, it is the practice to remove nearly all the officers, and fill the vacancies so made with others, who in most cases have had no experience at all in prison management. The subordinate officers are frequently appointed without having ever been seen by the inspectors, and solely on the recommendation of politicians. When a new inspector comes in without changing the political character of the board, he usually claims a certain share of the patronage by a redistribution of offices. The list of officers of any one prison, being taken up, is carefully canvassed, and it is generally found that if considerations of personal or political friendship alone prevailed all would be retained. But the changes must be made, and some principle must be found on which it can be done. The principle usually adopted is that of removing the officers who have served the longest, till the requisite number of vacancies has been made. These vacancies are then filled by the nomination of the new inspector. This system of political appointment disturbs the whole arrangement of the prisons, by taking away their best and most experienced officers and replacing them with untried and not infrequently worthless men. . . . On one occasion, when a number of removals had been made on party grounds, I peremptorily declined to be responsible for the safety of the prison unless the inspectors reversed their action. . . . The changes are so constant, and the tenure of office so short, that the best men will not become candidates; and even though an officer may possess good natural abilities, he will lack the indispensable quality of experience."

The chaplain at Sing Sing testified that in eighteen years he had served under nine different wardens.

Under the contract system, in the words of Dr. Theodore W. Dwight, "Convict labor becomes substantially slave labor, with many of its concomitant evils. Its rule is the same; the largest amount of work for the smallest return." The objections to that system may be tersely stated, as follows:

(1) The farming-out of governmental rights and powers to private parties is contrary to public policy. What the government undertakes to do, it alone should do. The presence of the contractor in the prison leads to divided responsibility.

(2) The financial interest of the contractor is a selfish interest. The prison wishes to sell its labor at a high rate; the contractor desires to buy it at the lowest possible price. The state wants a fair division of the profits of the establishment; the contractor cares little whether the state makes or loses money on the deal, if he can enrich himself.

(3) The political connections and power of the contractor are often such as to enable him to dictate the selection of the managers and warden of the prison. The tenure of his position, under contract, is more secure than theirs, under election or appointment. It therefore not infrequently happens that he becomes the real head of the prison.

(4) The internal economy of the prison, under the contract system, is apt to be shaped, if not with exclusive reference, yet with a predominant reference, to pecuniary results.

(5) The system is incompatible with proper regard to the reformation of prisoners. The New York law of 1847 declared the reformation of the prisoner to be one of the ends sought in his incarceration. That law was far in advance of popular sentiment; it was little more than a counsel of perfection. The prevailing opinion in the community, as one of the New York judges well phrased it, seemed to him to be "that offenders against the law should be caught, condemned, imprisoned and punished at the smallest expense. Improvements in prison discipline, as connected with judicious state policy, and with considerations applicable to the plea of humanity or the precepts of religion, do not appear to enter into the thoughts of most of our citizens." In a report of a visit to Sing Sing by a committee of which Dr. Francis Lieber was a member, it is said: "The opinion seems to prevail among the officers, that efforts to reform are incompatible with discipline." Before a special com-

7

mittee authorized to inquire into the management of the prisons, the physician of the Auburn prison testified: "I have served under five different administrations. During that time, the main object of them all, as far as I can judge, has been to make the prison pay its way, and earn a surplus if possible. I think there has been a desire on the part of those who have governed it, for the improvement of the prisoners; but there has been little faith in the reformation of the criminal class, and consequently little effort put forth directly to that end." The clerk of the same prison said: "Reformation cannot be made the chief design, with the contract system in operation; that system, by the very law of its being, sets itself too directly and strongly against such a purpose." The chaplain at Sing Sing said: "Reformation is made a very secondary matter in the management of this prison. The public demands that institutions of this kind, in this state, should be made to pay their way, and if possible earn a surplus, or come as near this point as may be; and the gentlemen who administer the affairs of this prison, both inspectors and officers, aim to gratify the public in this respect."

Against the retention of this system the New York Prison Association waged relentless war.

In 1866, a joint resolution was adopted by the legislature, which conferred authority upon the executive committee of the Association to appoint a commission of their own members, which should have, "in addition to the power now possessed by them of examining on oath all prison officers in actual service," the right to "invite any former prison officers of the state, and any officers now or heretofore connected with prisons of other states, to appear before them," in order that the commission might take sworn testimony regarding "the management of the prisons of New York and the general subject of prison discipline and government."* One of the main results of this special inquiry was to bring into bold relief the evil effects, as they were known to the present and former officers of New York prisons, of the contract system of labor, in connection with the political control of these institutions. The interrogatories put to the witnesses upon the stand were searching, and the replies given by them were fearlessly frank. Among other admissions, the fact was clearly brought to light that under that system corrupt collusion between the prison guards and the contractors' men is possible, and that where it exists it is most demoralizing. Warden Hubbell was

* The report of this commission is signed by Theodore W. Dwight, E. C. Wines, John H. Griscom, F. W. Ballard, John A. Bryan, and Edmund Coffin.

asked, "How did the system of overwork originate?" He replied: "The system in Sing Sing had no formal or designed beginning; it grew up gradually, and I may say almost imperceptibly. The contractors received special permits to give the prisoners tobacco, and sometimes medicines. The prisoner in return, as an act of gratitude, would do work beyond his required task. Further permits were afterwards received by the contractors to give the prisoners some little delicacies on public holidays. This stimulated a desire on their part for further indulgence. They would intercede with contractors' foremen to bring them various articles of food privately, for which they would pay money* which they managed to secrete about their persons when they came to prison, or which they had received from friends at their periodical visits. But some prisoners do not have money, and could not do this; consequently they would offer to pay for these things in overwork. The foreman seized upon this as a favorable opportunity for making some money by bringing in contraband articles and selling them to convicts at exorbitant prices. This system gradually enlarged its dimensions, until little stores, almost, were formed inside the prison, which were daily replenished from the village groceries." This testimony should be read in connection with that offered by an ex-keeper in the prison at Auburn: "These contraband articles are, I think, usually sold at an advance of not less than 400 per cent on what the same could be obtained for on the outside. . . . Where the state receives fifty cents per day for a convict's labor, and his labor is worth to the contractor one dollar, if he does half a day's work over his assigned task, thus earning for the contractor a dollar and a half, and the contractor pays him twenty-five cents for his extra work, the difference between seventy-five cents and one dollar and fifty cents will be divided between the contractor and the keeper. A keeper has stated to me that he received more from the contractors than he did from the state in the shape of salary. . . . A contractor can allow overwork or not, at his discretion. . . . Those who allow it, permit only certain men to do it. . . . Contractors will sometimes prohibit men from doing overwork, as a means of punishing them. They thus assume to exercise, and in fact do exercise, discipline within the prison. . . . There is a rule requiring money earned by overwork to be paid to the keeper or the clerk, but it is constantly evaded,

* A former warden of Sing Sing prison said that he had no doubt that, if all the money hidden away by the inmates could be reached in any way, "five thousand dollars could be picked up there any day."

and the money is paid directly to the convict; with it he buys the contraband articles referred to in a former answer."

The brutality of the administration of the state prisons of New York, when Dr. Wines first made their acquaintance, was revolting to a man of his sensibility and good sense. I shall not dwell upon it at length. It is enough to say that the abuses practised were so great, that the legislature was twice compelled to intervene for their suppression: first by prohibiting the use of the lash, and afterwards, in consequence of the death of a prisoner at Sing Sing from the effect of a shower-bath, it also forbade the punishments of ducking, showering and the yoke, also known as crucifixion. These cruelties grew naturally, and almost inevitably, from the alliance between greed for office and greed for gain, which exerted so malign an influence upon the organization and operation of the old system, now (happily) only a memory.

All the opponents of the system agreed that the only way to clear the ground of this unsanitary rubbish was to secure the adoption of a constitutional amendment divorcing the prisons from the politicians. In the autumn of 1866, the people of the state voted to hold a convention for the purpose of revising the constitution, and elected representatives to membership in it. The New York Prison Association prepared the draft of an article on prisons and submitted it to the convention, accompanied by a memorial which was in substance an argument and a prayer for its incorporation into the fundamental law.* This article as originally drawn and presented provided for the appointment by the governor of a board of five governors of prisons, with power to appoint and remove (for cause) all state prison officials, and to visit and inspect all institutions for the reformation of juvenile delinquents and the prevention of crime. Its relations to the county jails and penitentiaries were left to the determination of the legislature. The committee on prisons, to which this paper was referred, reported a substitute providing for the appointment of a single superintendent instead of a board of governors, "and otherwise differing materially from the plan proposed by the association." One member of the committee made a minority report, favoring that plan. Dr. Wines was instructed to use his best efforts to conciliate the convention to the measure. He was at the time confined to his

---

* The memorial was signed by Theodore W. Dwight, William F. Allen, Francis Lieber, John Stanton Gould, John H. Griscom, Gaylord B. Hubbell, and E. C. Wines. Judge Allen was the author of the article, "which was variously amended by Mayor Hoffman, Dr. Lieber, and the Honorable Charles J. Folger," before receiving the endorsement of all the gentlemen named.

room by a broken leg, and could do no more than address a letter to the president of the convention* on the subject, which accomplished its aim. The article as adopted was almost identical in substance with that drafted by Judge Allen; but the word "managers" was substituted for "governors," provision was made for a secretary of the board, and the wardens were authorized to appoint all officers other than the clerk, chaplain and physician, and to remove them at their pleasure. In 1869, the people rejected the proposed constitution, including of course this article with the rest.

In 1876, however, a vote was separately had on a proposed amendment to article five, section four, which was adopted. This amendment was in the following words:

"A superintendent of prisons shall be appointed by the governor, by and with the advice and consent of the senate, and hold his office for five years unless sooner removed; he shall give security in such amount and with such sureties as shall be required by law for the faithful discharge of his duties; he shall have the superintendence, management and control of state prisons, subject to such laws as now exist or may hereafter be enacted; he shall appoint the agents, wardens, physicians and chaplains of the prisons. The agent and warden of each prison shall appoint all other officers of said prisons, except the clerk, subject to the approval of the same by the superintendent. The comptroller shall appoint the clerks of the prisons. The superintendent shall have all the powers and perform all the duties, not inconsistent herewith, which were formerly had and performed by the inspectors of state prisons. The governor may remove the superintendent for cause at any time, giving to him a copy of the charges against him and an opportunity to be heard in his defence."

The protracted struggle was at an end, and responsibility in prison management was henceforth insured. There remained the important and difficult work of reconstruction, to which Dr. Wines addressed himself with characteristic vigor and ability.

There always have been, and probably always will be, two opposing theories as to the nature of government current in the world —in the family, in the church, and in the state. The ideal of those who hold to the one is submission to authority, implicit obedience; of those who hold to the other it is individual freedom and responsibility. Can the will be trained? or must it be broken? Is the force which moulds an untrained will, like that of the child, or which

* William A. Wheeler, afterward Vice-President of the United States during the Hayes administration.

brings a perverted will into harmony with law (human and divine) material or spiritual? Nowhere has the conflict of sentiment here indicated been more palpable than in the history of the effort to suppress crime. The criminal is a man with a weak, an abnormal, or a perverted will. Shall we deprive him of the power of resistance? or shall we seek to develop in him the power of self-control? That is the problem of the prison.

Corporal punishment is the application of physical force; an endeavor to coerce the spirit of a man through arguments addressed to his body alone. It is an appeal to his lower nature, to his fears; its tendency is to make of him a coward and a brute. It is irrational and ineffectual, in the vast majority of instances. It is a last resort, when all other means fail to produce the desired result. Incompetent men are far more apt to fly to it than are the brave and the intelligent. A prison governed by force and fear is a prison mismanaged, in which hope and love, the two great spiritual, uplifting, regenerating forces to which mankind must ever look for redemption, are asleep or dead.

When, therefore, the employment of physical pain as a stimulant to righteous living is forbidden, the question at once arises, what motive must be stirred into activity? Hope is the antithesis of fear. Why not try the effect of rewards upon the prisoner? Rewards, as truly as punishments, appeal to the inextinguishable principle of self-interest in his breast. The negative pole of a battery repels; the positive pole attracts. Teach him that if wrongdoing is sometimes pleasant, the only road to happiness is by doing right. Let him learn this lesson in the school of personal experience.

So thought and felt Dr. Wines and his friends. They rejoiced for a time in the introduction into the prisons of the system of over-work, because they seemed to see in it an inducement to convicts to labor for their own benefit and that of their families. It appeared to them to open a door of hope for the future to men who were before without hope. They thought that it would obviate the need for so great severity in the discipline of the prisons. As it was carried on in New York, on the contrary, it was the source and occasion of new and unlooked-for ills. Its application was too limited and too unequal. It was the cause of intense jealousy on the part of men who did not enjoy a privilege arbitrarily accorded to their fellows in misfortune, no more capable, no more deserving than they. The introduction of money into the prisons, where it was directly paid to the overworker, led to surreptitious contempt for the rules by which they were ostensibly governed. The money itself was largely wasted. The family of the prisoner got very little of it, if any. Much of it was spent in betting on the elections. It was paid out in the vain hope of purchasing influence as a means of securing a pardon. A large percentage of it went into the pockets of the keepers and of the contractors' men, in return for illicit favors and indulgences. Prisoners were continually scheming and manœuvring to secure a transfer from a shop in which no money was paid for overwork into some other, or into a shop in which their earnings would, they believed, be greater. The contractors' men often played tricks designed to reduce the earnings of the prison under a contract, in order to admit of larger earnings by overwork, by which they themselves would pecuniarily benefit.

When the actual results of the system became apparent, the Prison Association changed its attitude somewhat. It still believed in allowing to prisoners a share of their earnings, but upon a different plan. Instead of giving to a favored few an uncertain share of the earnings of the contractor by this method of payment, never of what overwork was really worth, but always in accordance with the terms of an individual agreement in which the convict invariably got the worst of the bargain, it desired to see every man in the shops employed "from bell to bell," and to have a fund created, to consist of a fixed percentage of the amount due to each contractor, for distribution to all the inmates of the prison on some equitable basis, taking into account the diligence and good conduct of each prisoner, on the one hand, and the value of the product of his labor, on the other. It finally succeeded in this endeavor.

But if men are influenced by the hope of gain, much more is the average prisoner influenced by the desire to regain his freedom. Visions of a possible pardon haunt his dreams. He is perpetually on the watch for an opportunity to make his escape. It was accordingly a long step in advance, in the direction of humanity and good order in prisons, when the commutation acts began to be passed by state after state.

The abbreviation of terms of sentence imposed by the courts, as a reward for good conduct while in prison, was first embodied, so far as is known, in a New York statute of 1817, which conferred authority upon the prison inspectors to release, at the expiration of three-fourths of his term of sentence, any convict sentenced to imprisonment for not less than five years, provided that he could produce a certificate from the principal keeper showing that he had behaved well, and that the portion of his net earnings set aside and invested for his personal account had amounted in all to not less than fifteen dollars per annum. Dr. Wines says of this law that "it remained a dead letter on the statute-book—a monument at once to the wisdom of the legislature that enacted it and the folly of the state that neglected to enforce it."

Nearly twenty years later, in 1836, Tennessee made it the duty of the governor, whenever the conduct of a prisoner had been exemplary and unexceptionable for a whole month together, to commute his term of imprisonment for any period of time not exceeding two days for each and every month that he should have so conducted himself.

Another twenty years had elapsed when, in 1856, Ohio granted a deduction of five days in each month during which any prisoner "shall not be guilty of a violation of any of the rules of the prison, and shall labor with diligence and fidelity."

It is a noteworthy circumstance that these were original and independent acts, not copied from one another. But the example of Ohio at once provoked imitation. Statutes drawn on similar lines were passed by other states in rapid succession, as follows: In 1857, Iowa and Massachusetts; in 1860, Wisconsin; in 1861, Michigan and Pennsylvania;* in 1862, New York and Connecticut; in 1863, Illinois; in 1864, Oregon and California; in 1865, Missouri and Nevada; in 1866, Maine; in 1867, New Hampshire, Minnesota, Kansas and Alabama; in 1868, New Jersey, Vermont and Rhode Island. In Missouri, for faultless conduct maintained for eighteen years, even a life prisoner was entitled to his release. Warden Haynes, of Massachusetts, regarded the passage of the commutation act by that state as "the most important step in prison discipline that has been taken in this country in the last forty years."

Before the war of 1861–65, the United States maintained a penitentiary at Washington, D. C. It was needed for use as a military prison, so that in September, 1862, the government contracted with the authorities of Albany county, New York, to receive federal prisoners and care for them in the Albany penitentiary. In the absence of a federal commutation law, the prisoners transferred to Albany from Washington were at a disadvantage in comparison with those committed by the state courts. The same was true of federal prisoners generally, who were serving sentences in prisons owned and

---

*In Pennsylvania, the act was held by the supreme court, upon technical grounds, to be unconstitutional.

controlled by the states. The federal government had no prisons of its own in which to confine them. In November, 1866, a federal prisoner in Sing Sing wrote to the United States district attorney for the southern district of New York, asking him to secure his release, on the ground that he was entitled to the benefit of the state commutation act. This letter was referred to the executive committee of the New York Prison Association, which deputed two of its members to proceed to Washington and intercede with the President for the exercise by him of executive clemency on behalf of all federal prisoners serving time in any state prison.* President Johnson at once issued an order, in which he pledged himself to "extend to them the same clemency and abatement of time, upon the same terms, as provided for the convicts under sentence of the courts of the state." The Association then secured the introduction of a bill in Congress, giving to federal prisoners the benefit of the commutation law of the state, whatever it might be, in which any such prisoner was confined. In 1867, a substitute measure was enacted granting a deduction of one month in each year in which no charge for misconduct is sustained against him.

The operation and effect of these laws has been most happy.

It would, nevertheless, be futile to imagine that any system of rewards can do more than conciliate the good will of a prisoner and enlist his co-operation with the authorities placed over him in carrying out their plans for the maintenance of order, and possibly for his own improvement. The purpose of the prison is the reconstruction of the prisoner, which is a positive work and demands positive measures for its achievement. He has proved himself to be a menace to social order and security. He regards society as his natural enemy. He must be convinced that the state is his best friend, and persuaded to respect and obey its laws.

When Dr. Wines became the secretary of the Prison Association, among the duties assigned him were these: "To carry on an extended correspondence both in our own country and Europe with gentlemen connected with the administration of penal justice, to collect and examine reports of penal institutions at home and abroad, to inspect and examine prisons, to make himself familiar with the doings of other organizations similar to our own and with the whole range of penal literature."

How faithfully he obeyed these instructions, his published re-

---

* There were at that time about 500 federal prisoners in the various prisons of New York.

ports clearly show. He neglected no opportunity to inform himself of the views of students of penology, living and dead, in all nations, especially of such as had acquired their knowledge of the subject by practical experience in the administration of prisons and of the criminal law. Among his correspondents were Sir Walter Crofton, of Ireland; Sir John Bowring, Messrs. Frederick and Matthew Davenport Hill, and the Misses Florence and Joanna Hill, Florence Nightingale, and Mary Carpenter, of England; Messrs. A. Corne and Bonneville de Marsangy, of France; Baron Franz von Holtzendorff, of Prussia; the Marquis Martino Beltrani Scalia, of Italy; Count Sollohub, of Russia; and many others of equal ability and distinction. Among those from whom he derived valuable counsel and support in his own country may be named some of the leading wardens of prisons, particularly Gaylord B. Hubbell, of Sing Sing, Charles E. Felton, of Buffalo, and Amos Pillsbury, of Albany; Gideon Haynes, of Massachusetts; Z. R. Brockway, of Detroit; and Henry Cordier, first of Wisconsin and later of Pennsylvania. Other collaborators in the same field were Mr. F. B. Sanborn, of Massachusetts; Mr. Richard Vaux, of Philadelphia; the Rev. John L. Milligan, chaplain of the Western Penitentiary of Pennsylvania (his former pupil, whose love for him was like that of a son for a father); the Rev. A. G. Byers, former chaplain of the Ohio State Prison, and afterward secretary of the Ohio State Board of Charities; and many more. The executive committee of the New York Prison Association numbered among its members some of the best and ablest men of the city and state of New York, with the celebrated Dr. Theodore W. Dwight at their head.

The exhaustive study made by Dr. Wines (assisted by certain of the members of the executive committee) of the prisons of New York, convinced the Association that the whole prison system of the state required careful and thorough revision. A committee was therefore appointed* to prepare a plan for its reconstruction. The defects of the existing system were obvious, but the remedy obscure. With a view to profiting by the experience of other states, the executive committee applied to the legislature for a grant of funds to enable it to appoint two commissions, one to visit prisons in this country and the other abroad. Failing to secure an appropriation from the public

---

* The members of this committee were Theodore W. Dwight, LL.D., Francis Lieber, LL.D., William F. Allen, John T. Hoffman, Rensselaer T. Havens, John H. Griscom, M.D., John Stanton Gould, Thomas W. Clerke, John Ordronaux, M.D., and E. C. Wines. There were subsequently added to it J. W. Edmunds and Warden Hubbell.

Theodore W. Dwight

treasury, resort was had with better success to a private subscription, and Dr. Dwight and Dr. Wines, who were respectively the president and the secretary of the Association, were commissioned to make a tour of the United States and report their observations and conclusions. They visited the states of Maine, New Hampshire, Vermont, Massachusetts, Rhode Island, Connecticut, New Jersey, Pennsylvania, Delaware, Maryland, West Virginia, Kentucky, Missouri, Michigan, Ohio, Indiana, Illinois and Wisconsin, and even crossed over into Canada. Their report was printed in 1867, at the expense of the state, by order of the legislature.

In this remarkable and epoch-making report they say, among other things worthy of quotation: "Whatever differences of opinion may exist among penologists on other questions embraced in the general science of prison discipline, there is one point on which there may be said to be an almost if not quite perfect unanimity, namely, that the moral cure of criminals, adult as well as juvenile, their restoration to virtue and the 'spirit of a sound mind,' is the best means of attaining the end in view—the repression and extirpation of crime; and hence that reformation is the primary object to be aimed at in the administration of penal justice. We have only, then, to ask ourselves the question, first, how far any given system aims at the reformation of its subjects, and second, with what degree of wisdom and efficiency it pursues that end, to have an infallible gauge wherewith to mark its approach to or recession from the standard of perfection.

"There is not a prison system in the United States which, tried by either of these tests, would not be found wanting. There is not one, we feel convinced, always excepting the department which has the care of juvenile delinquents, which seeks the reformation of its subjects as a primary object; and, even if this were true of any of them, there is not one, with the exception above noted, which pursues the end named, by the agencies most likely to accomplish it. They are all, so far as adult prisoners are concerned, lacking in a supreme devotion to the right aim; all lacking in the breadth and comprehensiveness of their scope; all lacking in the aptitude and efficiency of their instruments; and all lacking in the employment of a wise and effective machinery to keep the whole in healthy and vigorous action."

Space may be allowed for one further extract from their report: "The whole question of prison sentences is in our judgment one which requires careful revision. Not a few of the best minds in Europe and America have, by their investigations and reflections, reached the conclusion that time sentences are wrong in principle, that they should be abandoned, and that reformation sentences should be substituted in their place. Among the advocates of this view abroad we may mention Mr. Commissioner Matthew Davenport Hill, for nearly thirty years recorder of Birmingham, and one of the ablest criminal judges of Great Britain; and his brother Frederick Hill, for many years inspector of prisons in England and Scotland, and the author of a judicious and valuable treatise under the title of Crime; its Amount, Causes and Remedies. . . . Our own convictions are well and forcibly expressed by the several writers from whom we have taken the foregoing extracts. When a man has been convicted of a crime—burglary, arson, forgery, or any other—we would have the judge address him somewhat after this manner: 'John Doe, . . . until you show, to our satisfaction, that you can be restored to freedom with safety to the community, your imprisonment must continue; and if you never give us such satisfaction, then you can never be discharged; your imprisonment will be for life. . . . We put your fate in your own hands; and it is for you to determine the period, within certain necessary limits, during which the restraint upon your liberty shall continue. You may either prolong it to the close of your life, or restrict it to a duration which you yourself will allow to be but reasonable and just.'"

Dr. Wines held that the three fundamental principles that must underlie and interpenetrate every reformatory system of prison discipline deserve to be called moral axioms, and he stated them as follows:

"1. It must work with nature, rather than against it." This rule is the condemnation of both the so-called Pennsylvania and the so-called Auburn systems: the former ignores man's social nature, and the latter seeks to enforce the impossible rule of absolute silence.

"2. It must gain the will of the convict." This is done by uniting the maximum of kindness with the minimum of severity: large use must be made of the granting and withdrawal of privileges. The promise which appeals most strongly to the mind of the prisoner is that of speedier release, either an absolute discharge by virtue of the commutation act, or a conditional release under the indeterminate sentence.

"3. It must supply a system of reliable tests, to guarantee the genuineness of the reformation claimed for the liberated prisoner." It is precisely at this point that our new American reformatory prisons have failed to accomplish all that was expected from them. This is an error in administration, which time and experience will no doubt correct.

The most formidable obstacles to the successful application of these principles are found not so much in the character of the subjects of reformatory discipline as in that of the officers by whom it is administered: disbelief in the possibility of reformation, lack of interest in the work, want of adaptation to it, and non-conformity to a sufficiently high standard of moral character and conduct.

Dr. Wines believed in the reformability of criminals, as he believed in the curability of lunatics or the salvability of sinners—with this reservation of course, that neither of the three great hindrances to their restoration (depravity, physical degeneracy and bad environment) is in any given instance insuperable or irremovable. With his whole heart he desired their reformation. But he also believed that the first step to that end must be the reformation of prisons.

The agencies upon which he relied for subduing evil tendencies and dispositions were two, education and labor. Or, if a distinction should be made between the culture of the intellect and of the heart, these agencies are three: religion, education and labor. In other words, since the nature of man is threefold, the treatment to be given to the abnormal or the perverted must be directed at once to soul, mind and body. And, since labor has an educational value, the entire process may be said to be one of education.

As a Christian man and a clergyman, he placed chief stress upon the regenerating influence of religion. He believed in the healing power of the personal touch, and in the need for quickening and quieting the conscience. "As a man thinketh in his heart, so is he."

As a teacher, he set a high value upon the potency of education. "I think," he said, "that a penal establishment—especially in the later stages of imprisonment, which should have less of a punitive and more of a reformatory character impressed upon it— ought to be as it were a great school, in which almost everything should be made subservient to instruction in some form—mental, moral, religious or industrial. Of course I would have school rooms fitted up and classes formed, into which should be gathered such convicts as are in similar stages of advancement. In addition, I would have libraries,* lectures, competitive examinations, and all other needed appliances suited to create and gratify a rational curi-

---

* It is an interesting historical fact, that the first prison library in the state of New York, if not in the United States, was purchased with a gift of three hundred dollars by William H. Seward, then governor of New York, who was afterward secretary of state under President Lincoln.

osity. In a word, I agree in opinion with Mr. F. B. Sanborn, the late intelligent secretary of the Massachusetts Board of Charities, who, in his evidence before a commission of the Prison Association in 1866, said: 'I doubt if the instruction of prisoners has ever been carried far enough anywhere. Even in Ireland it would be possible to improve it. I would have all convicts taught something, and put in the way of teaching themselves. As a class, they are wretchedly ignorant, and have sinned through some form of ignorance conjoined with vice. To educate them is the plain duty of the state; and, when seriously undertaken, such efforts would show important results. A portion of each day, as well as the evening, should be given to this duty; and those not compelled to labor should be stimulated to some mental occupation, as a defence against bad habits and evil thoughts.' "

One of the arguments against the contract system is that it renders the education of prisoners difficult, if not impossible. In the first place, the contractor buys all the time of the convict; no time is left for school. Moreover, the educational value of most trades pursued in prisons conducted for pecuniary gain, is comparatively slight. They should be chosen with direct reference to their effect upon the mental and moral development of the prisoner and his economic status after his discharge. The contractor, by bidding, selects them with exclusive reference to his own profit. Probably from two-thirds to three-fourths of those convicted of crime have learned no trade, which is one cause of their downfall. If they are not qualified, while in custody and under control, to earn an honest living, the temptations that they were unable previously to meet will return upon them with added power, and the chances of their falling again by the wayside are greatly multiplied.

The entire literature of philanthropy contains perhaps no nobler presentation of the value of manual training in a reformatory institution than the remarkable address on The Influence of Manual Training on Character, delivered in 1888, at the annual session of the National Conference of Charities and Correction in Buffalo, by Dr. Felix Adler, in which he traced the effect of industrial education in strengthening and disciplining the will, in developing the property sense, and establishing a just balance between human faculties. One paragraph of that address is so pertinent to the present discussion, that it may advantageously be cited:

"There are influences in manual training which are favorable to a virtuous disposition. Squareness in things is not without relation to squareness in action and in thinking. A child that has learned to be exact—that is, truthful—in his work, will be inclined to be scrupulous and truthful in his speech, in his thoughts, and in his acts. The refining and elevating influence of artistic work I have already mentioned. But, along with and over and above all these influences, I need hardly say to you that, in the remarks which I have offered this evening, I have all along taken for granted the continued application of those tried and excellent methods which prevail in our best reformatories I have taken for granted the isolation from society, which shuts out temptation; the routine of the institution, which induces regularity of habit; the strict surveillance of the whole and of every individual, which prevents excesses of the passions, and therefore starves them into disuse. I have taken for granted the cultivation of the emotions, whose importance I am the last to under-value. I have taken for granted the influence of example, good literature, good music, poetry and religion. All that I have intended to urge this evening is that between good feeling and the realization of good feeling there exists, in persons whose will power is weak, a hiatus; and that manual training is admirably fitted to fill that hiatus."

The moral influence of labor in any institution is *nil*, unless it is productive labor. The workman must make something into which will have entered a portion of his being, and for which he will there-fore have a certain affection. There can be nothing more senseless than the "hard" labor to which it was once the fashion to sentence criminals, meaning thereby such ingenious devices for wasting human life and energy as the crank, the treadmill, the shot drill, and (as practised in prisons) the picking of oakum. Their sole purpose was punitive or preventive, or both. Their influence was to deaden and uproot every finer feeling of the soul.

There is a distinction, of which we must not lose sight, between productive labor and profitable labor. The root of all the evils in the New York prison system was the desire to make money out of convicts. Dr. Wines says: "The idea obtained early among our prison officers that the convicts were sent there to be punished, and to that end they must be made to suffer in every form which the law did not expressly forbid, and which a mistaken sense of duty or the dis-torted ingenuity of cruelty or cowardice could devise. Hence arose the idea, among others of a cognate character, that their labor must be unavailing to them; they must work for nothing, so far as they and their families were concerned. The law nowhere said this.

It was not made any part of the officers' duty, yet they assumed it and acted upon it. After a while it was found that this labor might be made productive of profit. Then the contract system was invented, to the increase of those profits and greatly to the relief of the officers from anxiety and toil. Then the hope was entertained, and its realization aimed at, that the prisons might be made to pay all they cost, and the state be relieved from any expense for the punishment of offenders against the laws; and, finally, that it might be carried so far as actually to be a source of net profit to the state." In the same connection he showed that, after deducting the amounts paid for salaries and wages, the earnings of the three New York state prisons were in a single year $58,740.97 in excess of the cost of their maintenance and all other incidental expenses. He asks: "Cannot the time of the prisoners be put to a better use for the community than in earning the pay of the officers?" The answer to his question depends upon the answer to be given to another: What is the object of a prison? Is it to make money or to make men?

It is not surprising that honest workingmen should have rebelled against the disturbance of the labor market engendered and fostered by competition of this nature. They may possibly be excused for carrying their hostility to profitable prison labor to the point where it assumed the form of a bitter war upon productive prison labor, as well. The contractor had no more consideration for the rights of honest workingmen than he had for the well-being of convicts. Had prison labor never assumed the shape it did, it may be that the outcry against it would not have arisen.

None the less, the opposition to productive labor in prisons is irrational, cruel and wicked. It must be attributed more to pride and avarice than to patriotism or philanthropy. The reasons assigned in support of the contention that an end should be put to the competition of convict labor with "free labor outside" are more specious than convincing. Prisoners cannot be allowed to rot in idleness. Apart from the demoralizing influence of idleness, its tendency is to mental deterioration, insanity and death. No form of labor can be devised, other than trade education, which does not result in competition. Production is the source of national wealth, which benefits all classes of citizens alike. Restrictions upon production are usually contrary to public policy. If prisoners are not permitted to earn their own support, they must be supported from the public treasury, at the cost of the taxpayers; but a large share of the taxes is paid by workingmen. The substitution of trade education as a means of occupying the hands and diverting the minds of men in confinement upon a criminal charge merely changes the form of competition; it results in an increase in the number of skilled workingmen, and so affects the rate of wages. Besides, the unconvicted man has a right, and it is his duty, to support himself; how does his change of status relieve him of that duty or deprive him of that right?

The agitation of this question resulted in the introduction, in 1866, of a bill for "an act for the better protection of the mechanics of this state, by regulating the use of convict labor in the several state prisons." It contained a provision forbidding all such labor in any of them as might compete with the labor of mechanics outside. In the year following its defeat, the doctrine was proclaimed that "no trades must be taught to convicts in prison."

Naturally and logically, Dr. Wines did what lay in his power to stem the tide of opposition which threatened to convert the prisons of New York into costly abodes of helpless, hopeless misery, hotbeds of disease and vice, the disgrace of the century, from which no man could go forth without having been rendered worse instead of better by his enforced sojourn within prison walls. He expressed himself in this regard with vigor, but without loss of temper, though his spirit must have been sorely tried. He said: "The products of labor in prisons, thrown into the general mass of merchandise in the market, interfere with the mechanical and manufacturing interests of free labor about as much as the abstraction of a bucket of water from the Hudson would interfere with the navigation of that river. . . . If it be wise to maintain prisoners in idleness or in unproductive labor, it must be equally wise (and if not, why not?) to maintain certain other classes of people in idleness; those, for instance, who live in a certain street of every town, or whose names begin with a certain letter of the alphabet. . . . The only effect would be to throw upon other persons the labor by which the profit is earned, instead of the labor being performed by the prisoners. . . . If the labor of prisoners in prison is mischievous, their labor out of prison must have been equally so. . . . It would, we think, puzzle any chopper of logic to show how the state is at once benefited by the industry of all her free citizens and injured by that of the small fraction who have been convicted of crime. . . . Even if it were proved that the supplies from prison labor do tend to lower prices, that can hardly be deemed a calamity." He added: "Work— steady, active, honorable work—is the basis of all good, and especially all reformatory, systems of prison discipline. It not only aids reformation, but is an essential condition of it. . . . Unless a prisoner acquire the knowledge of some handicraft, the taste for work, and the habit of steady industry; in other words, unless he gain the power, as well as the wish, to live honestly, it is all in vain; sooner or later, he will return to criminal courses. . . . We entreat the present legislature to turn a deaf ear to all petitions, come from what quarter they may, which ask for restrictions upon the industries of our prisons."

In 1870, a new bill was proposed, containing four provisions: (1) the abolition of contract labor in all the state penitentiaries, the county penitentiaries, and the reformatories of the state; (2) the prohibition of the manufacture, in any of them, of articles other than such as are exclusively imported from abroad or will least conflict with New York workingmen; (3) forbidding the sale, at prices below their actual market value, of goods manufactured in the prisons of the state; (4) requiring the county penitentiaries to pay their earnings into the state treasury, the legislature to make the appropriations requisite in order to carry on their manufacturing and business operations.

It was apparent that a measure so radical and possibly so far-reaching in its consequences ought not to be enacted without preliminary investigation. The governor was accordingly authorized to appoint a special commission for the performance of this duty. He named Dr. Wines and two other gentlemen, Messrs. Myers and Fencer.

Their conclusions, after visiting all the prisons and taking much sworn testimony (which they submitted with their report), were summed up in ten formal propositions, beginning with a declaration that the contract system should be abolished. Other principles enunciated by them were: that the industries of a prison, as well as its discipline, should ordinarily be managed by its head; that the successful management of these industries requires business experience and tact; that it is unwise to entrust the head of the prison with such management, so long as he is sure to be displaced on every transfer of power from one political party to another; that it would therefore be unwise to change the system of labor without changing the system of government of the prisons; that political control must be eliminated from their organization and administration; that the only way in which that could be accomplished was by means of an amendment to the constitution; that the disturbance of the labor

24

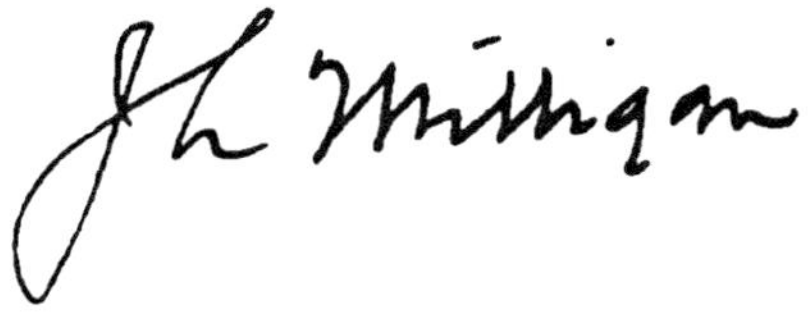

John Milligan

market resulting from the competition complained of was local rather than general, and it might be obviated to some extent by the multiplication of industries in the prisons; that the opposition of the workingmen was not to productive labor as such, but to the manner of it, in other words, to the contract system; and that the abolition of productive industries in the county penitentiaries and reformatories would involve and necessitate so many and such radical changes, that the question of their relations might wisely be postponed, "to await the result of the movement now in progress to secure the reform of the whole penal system of the state."

The report closed with the recommendation that the amendment to the constitution originally proposed by the Prison Association and incorporated (in a modified form) in the rejected draft of a new constitution proposed by the constitutional convention of 1867, be submitted to the people at the next election, for separate consideration and adoption.

This was the last service offered by Dr. Wines to the cause of prison reform in his adopted state. All his efforts had been crowned with victory, or were in a fair way to it. In the final outcome, he vanquished the prison inspectors, freed the prisons of New York from the strangle-hold of the politicians of both parties, drove out the prison contractors, and prepared the way for the signal reforms that have followed, all or nearly all of which he advocated by his voice and pen, compelling attention to his words by his ability, his character, his singleness of purpose, and his untiring persistency and courage. He had, too, a certain power vaguely described as magnetism, which attracted men to him, even where they were not ready to accept his views, and disarmed opposition. I remember the deep feeling with which Mr. Richard Vaux, the president of the Pennsylvania State Penitentiary, a champion of the strictly cellular system, and a disbeliever in the indeterminate sentence, once said to me, "I would do anything for Dr. Wines."

It remains to relate the story of his connection with the establishment of the Elmira Reformatory.

As far back as 1863, Mr. A. B. Tappan, then a member of the board of state prison inspectors,* and afterward a judge of the supreme court, in a letter to the Prison Association, urged the establishment of a new prison to be called a state penitentiary. The Association approved this suggestion, and memorialized the legislature to carry it into effect, assigning two reasons for its acceptance. The

---

* Which goes to show that there were good inspectors as well as bad.

first was that it would be of a grade intermediate between the state prisons and the county jails, and thus adapted for the reception of offenders not charged with the major felonies; the second, that it would afford the Empire State an opportunity to erect and organize a prison with all the modern appliances for the health, the discipline, the labor, the instruction, and the reformation of its inmates; "in short, an institution which shall be a model of its kind." In 1868, the Association renewed the effort to secure its creation, giving, as an additional reason why the legislature should grant their request, that it "would afford an opportunity to test, on a small scale and under the most favorable circumstances, what is now generally known as the Irish system of prison discipline." The legislature responded to this appeal by directing the governor to name a commission to select a suitable site and frame a plan for the proposed industrial reformatory.

At what precise date Dr. Wines first had his attention directed to the work of Sir Walter Crofton in Ireland is uncertain. It may have been as early as 1863; it was not later than 1864, for in that year he prepared an article for publication in the *North American Review*, entitled Progress of Prison Reform in England, which was accepted, and was to have appeared in the January number, 1865, but was crowded out by the pressure of other matter. He thereupon withdrew it, in order to include it in the report of the Association for 1864, printed in 1865, where it may be seen. In it he thus refers to the work of Captain Maconochie in Australia: "The discipline originated by this gentleman is known to penologists under the denomination of the 'mark system.' It rests on four chief principles: 1. Instead of a time sentence, it inflicts a labor sentence, thus setting the convicts to win back their freedom by the sweat of their brow. 2. It teaches the prisoners self-denial, by enabling them to purchase a speedier termination to their slavery by the sacrifice of present animal indulgence. 3. It appeals to their social qualities, and makes the prisoners themselves coadjutors in the preservation of discipline, by giving them an interest in each other's good behavior. 4. It prepares them for restoration to society, by gradually relaxing the restraints on their conduct and training their powers of self-governance. To carry out these principles, Captain Maconochie treated the convict as a laborer, with marks for wages, and required him to earn a certain number as the condition of his discharge. These marks had an alternative value; they could either purchase extra food, or the deduction of so many days from the sentence. He fixed on ten marks as a fair day's wages, the men being paid by piece-work, and not by time, and for every ten marks he saved, the convict shortened his time by a day. At the stores he purchased daily his necessary supplies, paying for them in marks. . . . The marks, too, furnished the means of disciplinary punishment, a proportionate fine being the penalty for every act of misconduct. And while, by this machinery of marks, Captain Maconochie trained his convicts to self-denial and industry, he secured his other objects by different means. He divided the convicts' sentences into three periods," the penal, the social, and the individual, each of which Dr. Wines describes. These were administrative measures; they afford no more than a hint, and hardly that, of the indeterminate sentence as part of a penal code of law.

Between this system and that invented by Sir Walter Crofton there are marked resemblances, although justice to him demands that notice should be taken of his declaration, in a letter written to Dr. Wines in 1867: "There are many mark systems which have no reference to Captain Maconochie's plan. The Irish system is not on his plan, neither is the English. I had not seen his plans until the Irish system had been carried out some time." Of the Irish system Dr. Wines says, in the article cited: "The Irish penal system has a scheme of discipline peculiar to itself, which it owes to the genius of Sir Walter Crofton, a prison disciplinarian of the school of Captain Maconochie," and he intimates his purpose to give an account of it in a later contribution to the *Review*.

Mr. Gaylord B. Hubbell became the warden of Sing Sing prison in the year 1862. He was an enthusiastic admirer of the Irish system, and in 1866 he paid a visit to Ireland for the purpose of seeing it in operation. In his report to the Prison Association he said: "The convict system of Ireland claims to be, and in point of fact is, reformatory in its design and operation. It rests upon two simple principles, but they are broad enough and strong enough to support firmly the entire structure. The first of these is the subjection of the convict to adequate tests prior to his discharge, whereby his reformation can be determined with a reasonable degree of certainty. The second is individualization; that is, such an arrangement of the discipline that each man's case may be separately handled with reference to his antecedents, character, actual state of mind, and the necessities resulting from a combination of all these elements. Of imprisonment proper in the Irish system, there are three distinct stages. The first of these has a strongly punitive character; the second is also in a high degree penal; while the third, which affords the principal theatre for the operation of those tests of reformation to which reference was just made, loses the penal element almost wholly. There is a fourth stage, which precedes complete liberation from the grasp of the law; namely, release on ticket of leave, a conditional pardon to those who prove themselves worthy of it, in which there is an entire absence of the punitive element. . . . The distinctive feature of the Irish convict system, in the second stage, is the employment of marks to determine the classification. The maximum number of marks attainable by a convict each month is nine, namely, three for discipline, that is, general good conduct; three for school, that is, the attention and desire for improvement shown, and not the absolute proficiency made in the attainment of knowledge; and three for industry, that is, diligence and fidelity in work, and not the mere skill shown therein. . . . Can the Irish system be adopted to advantage in our own country? For my own part I have no hesitation in returning an affirmative answer, with emphasis, to this question. There are, to my apprehension, but two obstacles in the way. These are the vastness of our territory and the inefficiency of our police." Mr. Hubbell proceeds to define in outline a practicable scheme for its introduction into New York. "Let a farm of two or three hundred acres be purchased, situated (say) on the line of the Erie railroad. . . . I would erect a new prison, having three distinct divisions, near to each other, and on the same farm. . . . In the first division, the prisoners, being kept in solitude, would of course take their meals in the cells. In the second division, a comfortable dining hall should be prepared. In the third division, all the arrangements should be such as to give as much freedom as possible to the inmates. . . . Throughout the entire period of imprisonment, all the moral appliances of chaplains, schoolmasters, lecturers, libraries, etc., should be liberally provided and faithfully and zealously used. . . . A careful system of classification of prisoners should be made, based on marks, honestly given according to their character, conduct, industry and obedience. For it must be remembered, and never forgotten, that a classified system of association without impressing on the prisoner's mind the necessity for progressive improvement is of little or no value. . . . All prisoners sent to the proposed establishment should, under proper restrictions, be allowed to work their way out."

These were the views in general entertained by Dr. Wines and by many others in the United States; for instance, by Mr. Sanborn, who testified before the New York commission appointed to take evidence as to prisons and prison discipline, in 1866: "My knowledge of the Irish system is derived from reading, and not from observation. The principle of the Irish system seems to be to make punishment subordinate to reformation. This principle is carried out by allowing the prisoner to shorten his own sentence, it being supposed that the power of shortening his own sentence is one of the strongest aids to reformation. . . . It can be introduced into any of the states."

The commission appointed by the governor (which numbered among its members Dr. Dwight and Warden Hubbell) reported in 1870 that they had selected a site of two hundred and fifty acres in the city of Elmira, and recommended the erection of buildings to accommodate five hundred prisoners, one in each cell, to be so constructed as to admit of the necessary classification of inmates. Political control was to be obviated—measurably at least—by placing the institution in the hands of a board of managers to be appointed by the governor. The contract system of labor was to be forbidden by law. No prisoners were to be received under the age of sixteen or over that of thirty. The discipline was to consist largely in the bestowal and withdrawal of privileges. But the new and distinguishing feature of the report was its inclusion of the principle of the indeterminate sentence. "We propose to carry out this principle (of rewards) so far, in the felonies for which minor punishments are inflicted, as to make the sentences substantially reformation sentences. It has been a favorite theory of that distinguished criminal judge and philanthropist, Mr. Recorder Hill, of England, that criminals should be sentenced, not for a definite term of years, as at present, but until they are reformed, which may of course be for life. While we do not propose to recommend this rule in full, yet we think that it has much to commend it in principle, and that it may safely be tried in a modified form. A sentence to the reformatory for so short a term as one or two years, with the commutation laws now in force, is not sufficiently long for the efficient action of reformatory agencies. We therefore propose that, when the sentence of a criminal is regularly less than five years, the sentence to the reformatory shall be until reformation, not exceeding five years. . . . This provision is confessedly in the nature of an experiment, and, should it work well, it can easily be extended to other sentences." They were not prepared to recommend conditional liberation, for the reasons stated by Mr. Hubbell, which have been already cited. They remark that "an institution such as we have sketched will meet with no success, unless under the control of men imbued with reformatory ideas;" but express their confident belief that "the practical working of this scheme will open a new era in prison discipline," and that "its results will lead in time to a reorganization of our state prisons, and will furnish suggestions to other states, whereby the increase of the dangerous classes in society will be checked, and the great problem respecting the disposition of our criminals will be substantially solved." Prophetic words!

Dr. Wines had already printed, in his report for 1866, a translation of the memorable address by Bonneville de Marsangy, delivered in 1846 before the civil tribunal of Rheims, nine years before the initiation of the Crofton experiment, on Preparatory Liberation. M. Charles Lucas, of France, had said that "the end of imprisonment being the reformation of the criminal, it would be desirable to be able to discharge every convict when his moral regeneration is sufficiently guaranteed." Taking this declaration for his text, Marsangy argued that the administration should have "the right, upon the previous judgment of the judicial authority, to admit to provisional liberty, after a sufficient period of expiation, and on certain conditions, the convict who has been completely reformed, reserving the right to return him to prison on the least well-founded complaint." He said that the practice of granting conditional liberation had existed for ten years in France, not merely in the case of young prisoners in Paris, but in the penitentiaries of Lyons, of Rouen, and of Strasburg.*

But conditional liberation is not the indeterminate sentence, any more than the indeterminate sentence is the ticket-of-leave. The two may be conjoined, or either may exist alone.

In a letter to Dr. Wines from Recorder Hill, in 1868, I find the following: "The subject you propose for a paper in your next report —the substitution of reformation sentences for time sentences—is

---

* This deliverance by M. de Marsangy is generally believed to have been the first public proclamation of the principle of conditional liberation. Singularly enough, an American philanthropist, Dr. Samuel G. Howe, of Boston, in a letter written that self-same year (1846), said: "The doctrine of retributive justice is rapidly passing away, and with it will pass away, I hope, every kind of punishment that has not the reformation of the criminal in view. One of the first effects will be, I am sure, the decrease of the length of sentences, and the adoption of some means by which the duration and severity of imprisonment may in all cases be modified by the conduct and character of the prisoner. What we want is the means for training the prisoner's moral sentiments and his power of self-government by actual exercise. . . . It will be difficult to contrive any system by which any considerable amount of self-government can be left to prisoners, without running the risk of escape. Nevertheless, I do not think that it is impossible to do so; and I believe that there are many who might be so trained as to be left upon their parole during the last periods of their imprisonment with safety and with great advantage to themselves."

one the importance of which cannot be overestimated. . . .
It is quite clear that to fix a period for discharge in the sentence is
calling on the judge to take upon himself the attributes of a prophet.
In short, the reformatory system of treatment by necessary implica-
tion calls for the abrogation of time sentences."

Dr. Wines induced Mr. Brockway to furnish a paper for the
report submitted to the legislature in January, 1869, in which the
able and successful superintendent of the Detroit House of Correction
(a municipal prison) discussed the subject of Intermediate or Municipal Prisons. From this paper the following extracts may properly
here be quoted: "Legislation is needed to abolish the peremptory
character of the sentences imposed upon persons committed to these
establishments. The work of reformation is hindered by the sentence
to imprisonment for any definite term. . . . Persons whose
moral deformity makes them a public offence should be committed
to properly organized institutions until they are cured. . . .
When a relapse occurs, the patient may be placed under treatment
again, as would be the case if he were afflicted with a relapse of con-
tagious disease or mental malady." Among the rewards specified by
him as appropriate to a reformatory discipline, he gave the first place
to "the hope of release from imprisonment upon the one and only
condition of improved character, which condition may be supplied
by legislation in connection with the organization."

Mr. Brockway, in his own prison report in 1868, requested his
board of managers to procure an act from the legislature of Michigan,
"authorizing or directing courts of competent jurisdiction to commit
persons from one or all of the classes mentioned," namely, prostitutes, vagrants, confirmed pilferers, etc., "when convicted of misdemeanor, to the house of correction until discharged by the circuit
or other judge, on recommendation of the superintendent or inspectors, upon the ground of their improved character." In 1869, the
legislature passed the "three years law," on these lines; but it applied
solely to prostitutes, and the supreme court held that its provisions
were in force only in Wayne county. This was the first indeterminate sentence act in the United States.

In their report for 1869, the directors of the Ohio penitentiary
said: "It may seem to be in advance of the present day, but it is,
we believe, but anticipating an event not far distant, to suggest that
sentences for crime, instead of being for a definite period, especially
in case of repeated convictions, will, under proper restrictions, be

made to depend upon the reformation and established good character of the convict."

In 1870, the governor of New York appointed a building commission for the Elmira Reformatory, of which General Amos Pillsbury was chairman. In 1876, the building was ready for occupancy; and on the sixth of May, the board of managers conferred the superintendency of the new institution upon Mr. Brockway, than whom no better choice could have been made. He was fitted for it by experience, by wide acquaintance with the literature of penology, by an open mind and the sort of audacity required for such an experiment, by remarkable ingenuity and fertility in expedients, and above all by hearty sympathy with the avowed purpose of the projected enterprise. In the language of Dr. Dwight, he was "a man imbued with reformatory ideas."

The students and theorists had assiduously and thoroughly prepared the ground. Mr. Brockway, in his first report, laid the corner-stone of the structure thereon to be erected. It was the indeterminate sentence. He prepared the draft of a bill for an act incorporating it into the criminal jurisprudence of the state and of the United States, which his board of managers accepted and recommended to the legislature for adoption. The legislature passed it substantially as drawn, with some unimportant amendments, but with one notable difference. In its original form, it mentioned no maximum term of imprisonment. The second section provided that sentences to Elmira should run "until released therefrom by due process of law." Instead of this, the law, as signed by the governor, reads: "Every sentence to the reformatory of a person hereafter convicted of a felony or other crime shall be a general sentence to imprisonment in the New York State Reformatory at Elmira, and the courts of this state imposing such sentence shall not fix or limit the duration thereof. The term of such imprisonment of any person so convicted and sentenced shall be terminated by the managers of the reformatory, as authorized by this act; but such imprisonment shall not exceed the maximum term provided by law for the crime for which the prisoner was convicted and sentenced." The managers were directed to organize the new prison upon the mark system, and were granted power to release prisoners on parole, without relinquishing custody and control of those so liberated, who could at any time be arrested and re-imprisoned for violation of the law or of the conditions imposed.

This was the culmination of the labors of all who had in any

Sollohub.

measure contributed to the final result, but it was also the dawn of a new era in the history of prisons in this country.*

We must now go back to 1870 and the Cincinnati Congress. Dr. Wines has left the record of the steps that led up to it and its work.† It will add life to this narrative, to give it in his own words, as follows:

"Count Sollohub, the originator, organizer, and successful conductor of a remarkable experiment in prison discipline at Moscow, in replying in 1868 to a request for information on the state of the prison question in Russia, closed a very able report on that subject with the suggestion that an international congress be convoked for a broader study of the question. The thought struck me as both timely and practicable. I was at that time, and had been for a number of years, secretary of the Prison Association of New York, which was then largely national and to a certain extent international, in the sense that it published and circulated information gathered at home and abroad in relation to penitentiary matters, so that its reports‡

* Mr. Brockway, who added extraordinary executive ability to his intellectual courage, candor and originality, demonstrated at Elmira the practicability of administering a prison successfully under the indeterminate sentence, and the value of this adjunct to a truly reformatory discipline. He had had long and varied experience in prison administration, and possessed a peculiar insight into criminal character and conduct. He saw clearly what many were unable to see: the physical basis of thought and of character, and the necessity for reaching the mind through the body; the power of habit, in rendering thought and volition automatic; the psychologic and ethical error of basing reformatory treatment on the retributive principle; the vital connection between crime and economic conditions, so that the economic status of the majority of criminals must be changed, as a condition of their permanent restoration; and the true nature of the entire process of reformation, as one of education, including physical culture, mental development, trade instruction, and moral suggestion. He was a daring experimenter. No popular beliefs, no beliefs which he had himself formerly entertained, could stand before the intensity of his desire to know the truth, or prevent him from speaking the truth, as he saw it. The world has never seen a prison officer like him. A special literature, in many languages, treats of his effort to rebuild the social institution of the prison on a sane, sound and safe basis. His success led to the adoption of his principles and methods, though not without bitter opposition, in most American states, and his influence will outlive him and affect the history of prisons in all lands, for all time to come.

Whether he would have had the opportunity to prove the truth of his theories, but for the preparatory labor, in the state of New York, of Dr. Wines and his colleagues, must forever remain a matter of speculative opinion. They conciliated public opinion in advance, formulated the plans of the Elmira Reformatory, secured its creation, and freed it from political control, leaving to Mr. Brockway a free hand in its subsequent development.

† The State of Prisons and Child-Saving Institutions in the Civilized World. Cambridge, Mass., Wilson, 1880. Pages 45–56.

‡ Baron von Holtzendorff wrote him (in 1868): "The last report of your prison association is excellent work, of uncommon and methodically unprecedented merit. No attempt has hitherto been made to collect within such a report all the materials having reference to the same object in foreign countries. Therefore your idea of printing short reports on foreign prisons, together with those of your New York Association, may lead to a centralization of prison experience."

were sought from all parts of the world by governments as well as by individuals. Accordingly, at the stated meeting of the Association, which constitutes in fact its board of managers, I submitted a proposition that the Association should undertake the convocation and organization of a congress of nations, as suggested by Count Sollohub, for the study and promotion of prison reform.

"This proposition was held under advisement for six months, and finally negatived. But the project had received so much sympathy and encouragement from distinguished friends of the cause on both sides of the Atlantic, that I was unwilling to let it drop without further effort. Consequently, a call was drawn up and issued for the convocation of a national prison reform convention, to meet in October, 1870, at Cincinnati, Ohio, which call was signed by one hundred persons, including a large proportion of the governors of states and the heads of nearly all the principal prisons and reformatories in the country. The result was a congress at the date and place named, composed of some hundreds of members drawn from nearly all the states of the Union.

"The president of the congress was Rutherford B. Hayes, then governor of Ohio, now (1879) President of the United States. And let it be stated here, parenthetically, that Mr. Hayes had determined to attend and take part in the prison congress of Stockholm, which intention was defeated only by his election to the chief magistracy of the nation. This statement will explain the warmth with which he referred to the Stockholm gathering in his first message to the Congress of the United States.

"The sessions of the Congress of Cincinnati continued for six days, with unabated interest from the beginning to the end. It was a hard-working body. Nearly forty papers were read and discussed. Eleven of these were communicated from foreign countries, namely, six from England, two from France, one from Italy, one from Denmark, and one from British East India. The project of organizing a national prison association was considered and adopted, and the preliminary steps to that end taken. A vote was passed to the effect that the time had come when an international congress might be summoned with good hopes of success, and I was honored with an invitation to take charge of the work. Finally, a declaration of principles, thirty-seven in number, was considered, debated, and adopted with, I think, absolute unanimity."

As has been said, Dr. Wines was the author of this Declaration,* which was the mature result of eight years of continuous study of the

* See page 39.

subject. An analytical index to it may be of service as an aid to its comprehension. The numbers in parentheses are the numbers of the articles.

Crime and punishment defined (1).

Responsibility of society for the prevalence of crime (12).

Reformation the supreme end of prison discipline (2, 15).

Classification of prisoners (3, 18) and of prisons (19, 31).

Centralized control (36).

Reformatory agencies: religion (9), education (10), moral training (15), industrial training (16), rewards and privileges (4).

Obstacles to reformation in prisons: degrading punishments (14), short sentences (20).

The indeterminate sentence: inequality of sentences (28), reformation sentences (8), their influence upon the prisoner (5).

Pardons (27).

Probation, the Irish system (18).

Prison officials should be trained for their work (7), must be in sympathy with reformatory aims of the prison (11, 12), must cultivate manhood and self-respect of the prisoner (14).

Politics in prisons (6).

The contract system and its evil effects (17).

Earnings of inmates (32).

Criminal lunacy (25).

Discharged prisoners (22).

Indemnification (24).

Prison statistics (29).

Prison architecture (30).

Prison hygiene (33).

Preventive measures: preventive institutions (21), war on capitalists of crime (23), compulsory education (35).

Responsibility of parents for support of offspring in juvenile reformatories (34).

Women on prison boards (37).

At the congress of London, the American delegates submitted a revised version of these propositions, changing their order, but following closely their substance and expression. As Dr. Wines says, the congress did not adopt them *eo nomine*, but, in an epitome of the sense of the attending delegates, they were reproduced in an altered and abbreviated form. The Americans themselves omitted such as had merely a national interest, like those relating to politics in prisons and the contract system; also some principles not likely to be acceptable to some from other nations, particularly those about the Irish system and the indeterminate sentence.

At an American conference at Newport, Rhode Island, in 1877, preparatory to the Stockholm congress, they were reaffirmed, with extensive additions.

The relation of Dr. Wines to the international congress apparently warrants carrying this account of his life and labors a little farther. The special subject assigned to the author ends with the Cincinnati congress.

To return to his narrative, Dr. Wines says: "In studying the problem how best to set about the task assigned me,* this thought had great force: If ever true and solid penitentiary reform is had, it must in the end be through the action of governments; therefore it would be desirable to enlist the interest and co-operation of governments in this international study, so that their delegates might keep them *au courant* of both experiment and opinion. This idea was the keynote of my work. My first endeavor was to gain my own government, which was done without difficulty. An act was promptly passed, authorizing the President to appoint a commissioner to the proposed congress, which appointment was placed in my hands, together with a circular letter from the secretary of state addressed to all the diplomatic and consular officers of the government abroad, requesting them to lend their aid in my negotiations with the several governments to which they were accredited, with a view to the organization of the congress. My next step was to call upon the foreign ministers resident in Washington and lay the matter before them, all of whom readily yielded their adhesion, and gave me letters to their respective governments. Thus armed, I visited Europe, and spent the summer and autumn of 1871 in negotiating with the European governments, most of them in person, and the remainder by correspondence through our American ministers. The success of this mission was beyond what could have been anticipated; and when the congress convened in London in the summer of 1872, it was found that all but one of the states of Europe were officially represented in it, the greater part by several delegates. A considerable number of the governments of both North and South America also sent commissioners to take part in the proceedings, as well as many of the individual states of the German Empire and of the American Union. Altogether, the number of official delegates must have reached nearly one hundred.

* The organization of the international congress.

THE LAW OF LOVE AND LOVE IN LAW

獄事叢書

明治廿八年一月三日發行　同情會

第十號

FRONT COVER OF A JAPANESE BOOK ON PRISON REFORM CONTAINING A
PORTRAIT OF DR. E. C. WINES AND AN ACCOUNT OF HIS WORK

（明治廿七年四月十六日逓信省認可）

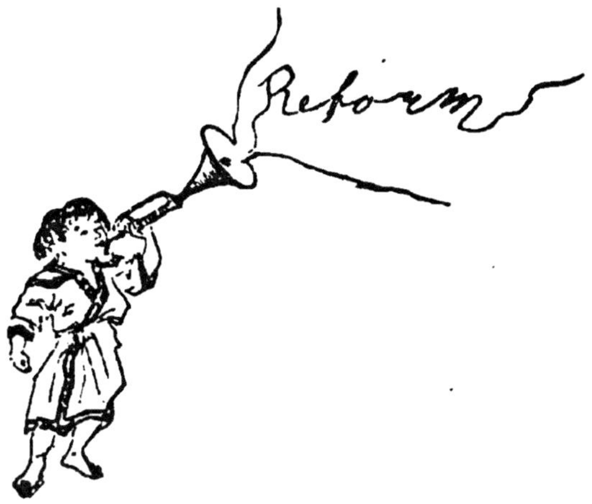

Back Cover of the same Book

"But it seemed equally clear that a congress composed wholly of representatives of governments would have a character too exclusively official, and therefore it was determined to combine a non-official with the official element, so as to give greater freedom and breadth to the discussions.

"The union of these two elements in the same body stamped a character of originality on the congress of London. There had been international congresses of governments and international congresses of private citizens, the one wholly official, the other wholly non-official; but the London congress was unique in that it combined both these elements. It was an illustrious body. Lord Carnarvon was its president. The Prince of Wales honored it with his presence. The British Secretary of State for the Home Department gave official welcome to the foreign delegates in a speech at once cordial and eloquent. . . . The discussions of the congress continued ten days. The questions considered were many and weighty, the discussions able and earnest. . . . Before the congress adjourned without day, it appointed a permanent international penitentiary commission to replace the congress during its recess, to collect and publish international prison statistics, to fix upon the time and place for convoking another congress, and to make all needful preparations for the same."

Of this international commission Dr. Wines was chairman, and he organized the second congress of the series, at Stockholm, of which he was made honorary president. His duties required him to visit Europe on several occasions, when he continued his favorite occupation of visiting and inspecting prisons; probably John Howard himself was never in so many.

His life and work remind one of that saying of Solomon: "Seest thou a man diligent in his business? He shall not stand before mean men, he shall stand before kings." The Emperor of Brazil, when in this country, spent half a day or more in private conversation with him at his own home. Leopold of Belgium talked familiarly with him, seated by his side upon a sofa in the palace at Brussels. Oscar of Sweden toasted him personally at a public banquet. Victor Emmanuel of Italy provided for his entertainment in Rome, as the guest of the government. President Thiers of France called upon him at his hotel in Paris. The French Academy of Moral and Political Sciences invited him to address that body. None of these honors disturbed the sweet simplicity of his soul. He accepted them as tokens of interest in the cause and of admiration for the country which he represented. He could truly say, with the great apostle, "This one thing I do."

He could not foresee all the logical fruits of his teaching and his example: the blossoming out of the indeterminate sentence, for instance, into the practice of probation, before or after trial, but without imprisonment, of children and adults; and the institution of the juvenile court. His mind did not foreshadow the identification of criminals by the Bertillon system of measurements and by their finger prints, though he approved the plan of criminal registration advocated by Bonneville de Marsangy. Doubtless there are other changes impending, traceable to the same root.

His final gift to the world was his book entitled The State of Prisons and of Child-saving Institutions in the Civilized World, printed by private subscription, which did not appear until after his death, in December, 1879, although he had very nearly completed the task of revising it in the proof-sheets.* It is a treasure-house of information, and its statements are based in large part on written evidence furnished him by the governments with which he had formed relations.

If any apology is needed for the form of this historical sketch of the rise of the new criminology this side of the sea, it is that the great share which one man had in its development and in conciliating public opinion in its favor impart to the story a certain dramatic unity and vital human interest. A full history of the movement would call for the mention of many other names, some of them of still greater distinction; but want of space forbids. Much of that history will be recorded in the various volumes of the present series, to which the reader is referred, with confidence that they will richly repay examination and study.

* Copies of it may possibly still be obtained from the printers, the University Press of Cambridge, Massachusetts.

DECLARATION OF PRINCIPLES PROMULGATED AT CINCINNATI, OHIO, 1870

1. As Adopted by the Congress

I. Crime is an intentional violation of duties imposed by law, which inflicts an injury upon others. Criminals are persons convicted of crime by competent courts. Punishment is suffering inflicted on the criminal for the wrongdoing done by him, with a special view to secure his reformation.

II. The treatment of criminals by society is for the protection of society. But since such treatment is directed to the criminal rather than to the crime, its great object should be his moral regeneration. Hence the supreme aim of prison discipline is the reformation of criminals, not the infliction of vindictive suffering.

III. The progressive classification of prisoners, based on character and worked on some well-adjusted mark system, should be established in all prisons above the common jail.

IV. Since hope is a more potent agent than fear, it should be made an ever-present force in the minds of prisoners, by a well-devised and skilfully applied system of rewards for good conduct, industry and attention to learning. Rewards, more than punishments, are essential to every good prison system.

V. The prisoner's destiny should be placed, measurably, in his own hands; he must be put into circumstances where he will be able, through his own exertions, to continually better his own condition. A regulated self-interest must be brought into play, and made constantly operative.

VI. The two master forces opposed to the reform of the prison systems of our several states are political appointments and a consequent instability of administration. Until both are eliminated, the needed reforms are impossible.

VII. Special training, as well as high qualities of head and heart, is required to make a good prison or reformatory officer. Then only will the administration of public punishment become scientific, uniform and successful, when it is raised to the dignity of a profession, and men are specially trained for it, as they are for other pursuits.

VIII. Peremptory sentences ought to be replaced by those of indeterminate length. Sentences limited only by satisfactory proof of reformation should be substituted for those measured by mere lapse of time.

IX. Of all reformatory agencies, religion is first in importance, because most potent in its action upon the human heart and life.

X. Education is a vital force in the reformation of fallen men and women. Its tendency is to quicken the intellect, inspire self-respect, excite to higher aims, and afford a healthful substitute for low and vicious amusements. Education is, therefore, a matter of primary importance in prisons, and should be carried to the utmost extent consistent with the other purposes of such institutions.

XI. In order to the reformation of imprisoned criminals, there must be not only a sincere desire and intention to that end, but a serious conviction, in the minds of the prison officers, that they are capable of being reformed, since no man can heartily maintain a discipline at war with his inward beliefs; no man can earnestly strive to accomplish what in his heart he despairs of accomplishing.

XII. A system of prison discipline, to be truly reformatory, must gain the will of the convict. He is to be amended; but how is this possible with his mind in a state of hostility? No system can hope to succeed which does not secure this harmony of wills, so that the prisoner shall choose for himself what his officer chooses for him. But, to this end, the officer must really choose the good of the prisoner, and the prisoner must remain in his choice long enough for virtue to become a habit. This consent of wills is an essential condition of reformation.

XIII. The interest of society and the interest of the convicted criminal are really identical, and they should be made practically so. At present there is a combat between crime and laws. Each sets the other at defiance, and, as a rule, there is little kindly feeling, and few friendly acts, on either side. It would be otherwise if criminals, on conviction, instead of being cast off were rather made the objects of a generous parental care; that is, if they were trained to virtue and not merely sentenced to suffering.

XIV. The prisoner's self-respect should be cultivated to the utmost, and every effort made to give back to him his manhood. There is no greater mistake in the whole compass of penal discipline than its studied imposition of degradation as a part of punishment.

Such imposition destroys every better impulse and aspiration. It crushes the weak, irritates the strong, and indisposes all to submission and reform. It is trampling where we ought to raise, and is therefore as unchristian in principle as it is unwise in policy.

XV. In prison administration, moral forces should be relied upon, with as little admixture of physical force as possible, and organized persuasion be made to take the place of coercive restraint, the object being to make upright and industrious freemen rather than orderly and obedient prisoners; moral training alone will make good citizens. To the latter of these ends, the living soul must be won; to the former, only the inert and obedient body.

XVI. Industrial training should have both a higher development and a greater breadth than has heretofore been, or is now, commonly given to it in our prisons. Work is no less an auxiliary to virtue than it is a means of support. Steady, active, honorable labor is the basis of all reformatory discipline. It not only aids reformation, but is essential to it. It was a maxim with Howard, "make men diligent and they will be honest"—a maxim which this congress regards as eminently sound and practical.

XVII. While industrial labor in prisons is of the highest importance and utility to the convict, and by no means injurious to the laborer outside, we regard the contract system of prison labor, as now commonly practiced in our country, as prejudicial alike to discipline, finance and the reformation of the prisoner, and sometimes injurious to the interest of the free laborer.

XVIII. The most valuable parts of the Irish prison system— the more strictly penal state of separate imprisonment, the reformatory stage of progressive classification, and the probationary stage of natural training—are believed to be as applicable to one country as another—to the United States as to Ireland.

XIX. Prisons, as well as prisoners, should be classified or graded so that there shall be prisons for the untried, for the incorrigible and for other degrees of depraved character, as well as separate establishments for women and for criminals of the younger class.

XX. It is the judgment of the congress, that repeated short sentences for minor criminals are worse than useless; that, in fact, they rather stimulate than repress transgression. Reformation is a work of time; and a benevolent regard to the good of the criminal himself, as well as to the protection of society, requires that his sentence be long enough for reformatory processes to take effect.

XXI. Preventive institutions, such as truant homes, industrial schools, etc., for the reception and treatment of children not yet criminal, but in danger of becoming so, constitute the true field of promise in which to labor for the repression of crime.

XXII. More systematic and comprehensive methods should be adopted to save discharged prisoners, by providing them with work and encouraging them to redeem their character and regain their lost position in society. The state has not discharged its whole duty to the criminal when it has punished him, nor even when it has reformed him. Having raised him up, it has the further duty to aid in holding him up. And to this end it is desirable that state societies be formed, which shall co-operate with each other in this work.

XXIII. The successful prosecution of crime requires the combined action of capital and labor, just as other crafts do. There are two well defined classes engaged in criminal operations, who may be called the capitalists and the operatives. It is worthy of inquiry, whether a more effective warfare may not be carried on against crime by striking at the capitalists as a class, than at the operatives one by one. Certainly, this double warfare should be vigorously pushed, since from it the best results, as regards repressive justice, may be reasonably hoped for.

XXIV. Since personal liberty is the rightful inheritance of every human being, it is the sentiment of this congress that the state which has deprived an innocent citizen of this right, and subjected him to penal restraint, should, on unquestionable proof of its mistake, make reasonable indemnification for such wrongful imprisonment.

XXV. Criminal lunacy is a question of vital interest to society; and facts show that our laws regarding insanity, in its relation to crime, need revision, in order to bring them to a more complete conformity to the demands of reason, justice and humanity; so that, when insanity is pleaded in bar of conviction, the investigation may be conducted with greater knowledge, dignity and fairness; criminal responsibility be more satisfactorily determined; the punishment of the sane criminal be made more sure, and the restraint of the insane be rendered at once more certain and more humane.

XXVI. While this congress would not shield the convicted criminal from the just responsibility of his misdeeds, it arraigns society itself as in no slight degree accountable for the invasion of its rights and the warfare upon its interests, practiced by the criminal classes. Does society take all the steps which it easily might to change, or at least to improve, the circumstances in our social state that lead to crime; or, when crime has been committed, to cure the proclivity to it generated by these circumstances? It cannot be pretended. Let society, then, lay the case earnestly to its conscience, and strive to mend in both particulars. Offenses, we are told by a high authority, must come; but a special woe is pronounced against those through whom they come. Let us take heed that that woe fall not upon our head.

XXVII. The exercise of executive clemency in the pardon of criminals is a practical question of grave importance and of great delicacy and difficulty. It is believed that the annual average of executive pardons from the prisons of the whole country reaches ten per cent of their population. The effect of the too free use of the pardoning power is to detract from the *certainty* of punishment for crimes, and to divert the mind of prisoners from the means supplied for their improvement. Pardons should issue for one or more of the following reasons; viz., to release the innocent, to correct mistakes made in imposing the sentence, to relieve such suffering from ill-health as requires release from imprisonment, and to facilitate or reward the real reformation of the prisoner. The exercise of this power should be by the executive, and should be guarded by careful examination as to the character of the prisoner and his conduct in prison. Furthermore, it is the opinion of this congress that governors of states should give to their respective legislatures the reasons, in each case, for their exercise of the pardoning power.

XXVIII. The proper duration of imprisonment for a violation of the laws of society is one of the most perplexing questions in criminal jurisprudence. The present extraordinary inequality of sentences for the same or similar crimes is a source of constant irritation among prisoners, and the discipline of our prisons suffers in consequence. The evil is one for which some remedy should be devised.

XXIX. Prison statistics, gathered from a wide field and skilfully digested, are essential to an exhibition of the true character and working of our prison systems. The collection, collation and reduction to tabulated forms of such statistics can best be effected through a national prison discipline society, with competent working committees in every state, or by the establishment of a national prison bureau, similar to the recently instituted national bureau of education.

XXX. Prison architecture is a matter of grave importance.

43

Prisons of every class should be substantial structures, affording gratification by their design and material to a pure taste, but not costly or highly ornate. We are of the opinion that those of moderate size are best, as regards both industrial and reformatory ends.

XXXI. The construction, organization and management of all prisons should be by the state, and they should form a graduated series of reformatory establishments, being arranged with a view to the industrial employment, intellectual education and moral training of the inmates.

XXXII. As a general rule, the maintenance of penal institutions, above the county jail, should be from the earnings of their inmates, and without cost to the state; nevertheless, the true standard of merit in their management is the rapidity and thoroughness of reformatory effect accomplished thereby.

XXXIII. A right application of the principles of sanitary science in the construction and arrangements of prisons is a point of vital importance. The apparatus for heating and ventilation should be the best that is known; sunlight, air and water should be afforded according to the abundance with which nature has provided them; the rations and clothing should be plain but wholesome, comfortable, and in sufficient but not extravagant quantity; the bedsteads, bed and bedding, including sheets and pillow cases, not costly but decent, and kept clean, well aired and free from vermin; the hospital accommodations, medical stores and surgical instruments should be all that humanity requires and science can supply; and all needed means for personal cleanliness should be without stint.

XXXIV. The principle of the responsibility of parents for the full or partial support of their criminal children in reformatory institutions has been extensively applied in Europe, and its practical working has been attended with the best results. It is worthy of inquiry whether this principle may not be advantageously introduced into the management of our American reformatory institutions.

XXXV. It is our conviction that one of the most effective agencies in the repression of crime would be the enactment of laws by which the education of all the children of the state should be made obligatory. Better to force education upon the people than to force them into prison to suffer for crimes, of which the neglect of education and consequent ignorance have been the occasion, if not the cause.

XXXVI. As a principle that crowns all, and is essential to all, it is our conviction that no prison system can be perfect, or even successful to the most desirable degree, without some central authority to sit at the helm, guiding, controlling, unifying and vitalizing the whole. We ardently hope to see all the departments of our preventive, reformatory and penal institutions in each state moulded into one harmonious and effective system; its parts mutually answering to and supporting each other; and the whole animated by the same spirit, aiming at the same objects, and subject to the same control; yet without loss of the advantages of voluntary aid and effort, wherever they are attainable.

XXXVII. This congress is of the opinion that, both in the official administration of such a system and in the voluntary co-operation of citizens therein, the agency of women may be employed with excellent effect.

2. As Originally Submitted by Dr. Wines

[In the published volume of Transactions, Dr. Wines says: "The foregoing Declaration of Principles is, in the main, a condensation of a paper, prepared and printed by the committee of arrangements in advance of the meeting, and distributed for examination to all persons invited to attend the same. The committee of arrangements did not expect that their paper would be adopted by the congress in a form so full as that in which it had originally appeared; and, indeed, they themselves prepared the condensed form for the business committee of the congress. As most of the articles in the original paper contain, severally, not only the statement of a principle, but also a short, incisive, pithy argument in support of it, the publishing committee have deemed it best to give the said paper a place in these transactions, and thus secure for it a more permanent form than it had as published in the 'programme of proceedings.'"]

I. Crime is an intentional violation of duties imposed by law, which inflicts an injury upon others. Criminals are persons convicted of crime by competent courts, and who are committed to custody. Punishment is suffering, moral or physical, inflicted on the criminal, for the wrong done by him, and especially with a view to prevent his relapse by reformation. Crime is thus a sort of moral disease, of which punishment is the remedy. The efficacy of the remedy is a question of social therapeutics, a question of the fitness and measure of the dose.

II. The treatment of criminals by society is for the protection of society. Since, however, punishment is directed, not to the crime but to the criminal, it is clear that it will not be able to guarantee the public security and re-establish the social harmony disturbed by the infraction, except by re-establishing moral harmony in the soul of the criminal himself, and by effecting, as far as possible, his regeneration—his new birth to respect for the laws.   Hence,

III. The supreme aim of prison discipline is the reformation of criminals, not the infliction of vindictive suffering.   In the prison laws of many of our states, there is a distinct recognition of this principle; and it is held by the wisest and most enlightened students of penitentiary science.   That the majority of imprisoned criminals are susceptible to reformatory influences is the opinion of the most competent prison officers, and is attested by the experience of Mrs. Fry at Newgate, Captain Maconochie at Norfolk Island, Colonel Montesinos at Valencia, Von Obermaier at Munich, Sir Walter Crofton in Ireland, and Count Sollohub at Moscow.   But neither in the United States nor in Europe, as a general thing, has the problem of reforming criminals yet been solved.   While a few are reformed, the mass still leave the penitentiary as hardened and dangerous as when they entered; in many cases, more so.   It is evident, therefore, that our aims and our methods need to be changed, so that practice shall conform to theory, and the process of public punishment be made, in fact as well as pretence, a process of reformation.

IV. The progressive classification of prisoners, based on merit, and not on any mere arbitrary principle, as age, crime, etc., should be established in all prisons above the common jail.   Such a system should include at least three stages; viz., 1. A penal stage, with separate imprisonment, longer or shorter according to conduct. 2. A reformatory stage, worked on some mark system, where the prisoners are advanced from class to class, as they earn such promotion gaining, at each successive step, increased comfort and privilege. 3. A probationary stage, into which are admitted only such as are judged to be reformed, and where the object is to test their moral soundness— the reality of their reformation.   The prisoner must be tried before he can be trusted.   It is the want of a guaranty of his reformation that builds a wall of granite between the discharged convict and honest bread.   This trial stage is an essential part of a reformatory prison system, since it furnishes to society the only guaranty it can have for the trustworthiness of the liberated prisoner; and such guaranty is the sole condition on which the various avenues of honest toil will be freely open to his entrance.

V. Since hope is a more potent agent than fear, it should be

46

made an ever present force in the minds of the prisoners, by a well devised and skilfully applied system of rewards for good conduct, industry, and attention to learning. Such reward should consist of: 1. A diminution of sentence. 2. A participation by prisoners in their earnings. 3. A gradual withdrawal of prison restraints. 4. Constantly increasing privileges, as they shall be earned by good conduct. Rewards, more than punishments, are essential to every good prison system.

VI. The prisoner's destiny, during his incarceration, should be placed measurably in his own hands; he must be put into circumstances where he will be able, through his own exertions, to continually better his condition. A regulated self-interest must be brought into play. In the prison, as in free society, there must be the stimulus of some personal advantage accruing from the prisoner's efforts. Giving prisoners an interest in their industry and good conduct tends to give them beneficial thoughts and habits, and what no severity of punishment or constancy in inflicting it will enforce, a moderate personal interest will readily obtain.

VII. The two master forces opposed to the reform of the prison systems of our several states are political appointments and instability of administration, which stand to each other in the relation of cause and effect. At present, there is scarcely a prison in the country in whose administration politics is not felt as a disturbing—in that of the great majority it enters as the controlling—power. To the needed reform, it is absolutely essential that political control be eliminated from our prison administration, and that greater stability be impressed thereupon. We acknowledge the importance and utility of party politics. In its appropriate sphere, it has a just and noble function. But there are precious interests, in reference to which the only proper rule, as far as politics is concerned, is: "Touch not, handle not." Religion is one of these. Education is another. And, surely, the penal institutions of a state constitute a third, since they combine, in a high degree, the characteristics of both, being at once, when properly conducted, educational and religious. Of all true and permanent reformation (and this is the end of prison discipline), the leading, vitalizing and controlling elements are education and religion—the discipline of the mind and heart. The chief value of any system of prison discipline consists in the intelligence and fidelity with which its administration favors and fosters the implantation and growth of virtuous principles in the prisoners. Prison administrators ought, therefore, first, to be selected with the greatest

47

care, and then retained during good behavior; which can never be done so long as changes in the official staff are made merely because one political party has gone down and another has gone up in an election.

VIII. The task of changing bad men and women into good ones is not to be confided to the first comers. It is a serious charge, demanding thorough preparation, entire self-devotion, a calm and cautious judgment, great firmness of purpose and steadiness of action, large experience, a true sympathy, and morality above suspicion. Prison officers, therefore, need a special education for their work; special training schools should be instituted for them; and prison administration should be raised to the dignity of a profession. Prison officers should be organized in a gradation of rank and emolument, so that persons entering the prison service in early life, and forming a class or profession by themselves, may be thoroughly trained in all their duties, serving successively as guards, keepers, deputy wardens, wardens of small prisons, and then, according to their ascertained merits, tested chiefly by the small proportion of reconvictions under them, as wardens of larger prisons. Thus alone can the details of prison discipline be gradually perfected and uniformity in its application attained. For only when the administration of public punishment is made a profession will it become scientific, uniform, successful.

IX. Peremptory sentences ought to be replaced by those of indeterminate duration; sentences limited only by satisfactory proof of reformation should be substituted for those measured by mere lapse of time. The abstract justness of this principle is obvious; the difficulty lies in its practical application. But this difficulty will vanish when the administration of our prisons is made permanent and placed in competent hands. With men of ability and experience at the head of our penal establishments, holding their offices during good behavior, we believe that it will be little, if at all, more difficult to judge correctly as to the moral cure of a criminal, than it is of the mental cure of a lunatic.

X. Of all reformatory agencies, religion is first in importance, because most potent in its action upon the human life and heart. We have a profound conviction of the inefficacy of all measures of reformation, except such as are based on religion, pervaded by its spirit, and vivified by its power. In vain are all devices of repression and coercion, if the heart and conscience, which are beyond all power of external restraint, are left untouched. Religion is the only power that is able to resist the irritation that saps the moral forces of these men of strong impulses, whose neglect of its teachings has been the occasion of their being immured within prison walls.

XI. Education is one of the vital forces in the reformation of fallen men and women, who have generally sinned through some form of ignorance, conjoined with vice. Its tendency is to quicken the intellect, expel old thoughts, give new ideas, supply material for meditation, inspire self-respect, support pride of character, excite to higher aims, open fresh fields of exertion, minister to social and personal improvement, and afford a healthful substitute for low and vicious amusements. Education is, therefore, a matter of primary importance in prisons, and should be carried to the utmost extent, consistent with the other purposes of such institutions. Schools and familiar lectures on common things, with illustrations by maps, globes, drawings, etc., should be instituted; or rather, a prison should be one great school, in which almost everything is made subservient to instruction in some form—moral, intellectual, industrial.

XII. No prison can be made a school of reform until there is, on the part of the officers, a hearty desire and intention to accomplish this object. At present there is no prevalent aim to this effect, and, consequently, no general results in this direction. Such a purpose, commonly entertained by prison officers, would instantly revolutionize prison administration, by changing its whole spirit, and fit reformatory processes will follow this change as naturally as the harvest follows the sowing. It is not so much any specific apparatus that is needed, as it is the introduction of a really benevolent spirit into our prison management. Once let it become the heartfelt *desire* and *intention* of prison officers to reform the criminals under their care, and they will speedily become inventive of the specific methods adapted to their work.

XIII. In order to the reformation of imprisoned criminals, there must be a serious conviction, in the minds of prison officers, that they are capable of being reformed, since no man can heartily maintain a discipline at war with his inward beliefs; no man can earnestly strive to accomplish what, in his heart, he despairs of accomplishing. Doubt is the prelude of failure; confidence a guaranty of success. Nothing so weakens moral forces as unbelief; nothing imparts to them such vigor as faith. "Be it unto thee according to thy faith," is not a mere dictum in theology; it is the statement, as well, of a fundamental principle of success in all human enterprises, especially when our work lies within the realm of mind and morals.

XIV. A system of prison discipline, to be truly reformatory, must gain the will of the convict. He is to be amended; but how is this possible with his mind in a state of hostility? No system can hope to succeed which does not secure this harmony of wills, so that the prisoner shall choose for himself what his officer chooses for him. But to this end the officer must really choose the good of the prisoner, and the prisoner must remain in his choice long enough for virtue to become a habit. This consent of wills is an essential condition of reformation, for a bad man never can be made good against his will. But such a harmony of wills is, happily, neither an impossibility nor an illusion. In the Irish system it has become a reality as conspicuous as it is pleasing. It was no less so in the prisons of Valencia and Munich, under Montesinos and Obermaier. Count Sollohub has secured it in his house of correction at Moscow. And nowhere can reformation become the rule instead of the exception, where this choice of the same things by prison keepers and prison inmates has not been attained.

XV. The interest of society and the interest of the convicted criminal are really identical, and they should be made practically so. At present there is a combat between crime and law in our whole country. Each sets the other at defiance, and, as a rule, there is little kindly feeling, and few friendly acts, on either side. The criminal seeks to be as evil as he can without incurring punishment, and the law is, for the most part, content with vindicating, or in plainer terms, revenging itself, with indiscriminate severity, on as many as it can detect. It would be otherwise if criminals on conviction, instead of being cast off, were rather made objects of a generous parental care; that is, if they were trained to virtue, and not merely sentenced to suffering. The hearts most proof against the denunciations of vengeance are precisely those most accessible to demonstrations of real interest; and the kindness thus displayed would be "twice blessed"—blessed to those who show and those who receive it. It would be a bond of sympathy and union between them. A happy reconciliation would have taken place between interests now too commonly regarded as antagonistic; and the prison would be made, without in the least impairing its discipline, an effective school of reform; for the conviction would have a solid basis to rest upon, that society is best served by saving, not sacrificing, its criminal members.

XVI. When a man is convicted of a felony or misdemeanor and shut up in prison, he cannot but feel the disgrace of his crime and sentence, and a degree of degradation consequent thereupon. This is a part of his punishment, ordained by heaven itself. Beyond this, no degradation, no disgrace, should be inflicted on the prisoner. His self-respect should be cultivated to the utmost, and every effort made to give back to him his manhood. A degraded dress, stripes, all disciplinary punishments that inflict unnecessary pain or humiliation should be abolished, as of evil influence. Instead the penalty for prison offenses should be the forfeiture of some privilege or of a part of the progress already made towards liberation, with or without a period of strict imprisonment. There is no greater mistake in the whole compass of penal discipline, than its imposition of degradation as a part of punishment. Such imposition destroys every better impulse and aspiration. It crushes the weak, irritates the strong, and indisposes all to submission and reform. It is trampling where we ought to raise, and is therefore as unchristian in principle as it is unwise in policy. On the other hand, no imposition would be so improving, none so favorable to the cultivation of the prisoner's self-respect, self-command, and recovery of manhood, as the making of every deviation from the line of right bear on present privilege or ultimate release. Such punishment would be as the drop of water that wears away the granite rock, and, without needless pain or wanton cruelty, would speedily subdue even the most refractory.

XVII. In prison administration, moral forces should be relied upon with as little admixture of physical force as possible; organized persuasion be made to take the place of coercive restraint; the object being to make upright and industrious *freemen*, rather than orderly and obedient *prisoners*. Brute force may make good prisoners, moral training alone will make good citizens; to the latter of these ends, the living soul must be won; to the former, only the inert and obedient body. Yet unsuitable indulgence is as pernicious as unsuitable severity. A struggle by the convict against opposing forces, whether in the form of inward propensity or outward temptation, is the true idea of prison discipline. A man at the bottom of a well may be lifted up by others, or make his own way to the top against intervening obstacles. The latter method affords the model for a true prison treatment. Mere lapse of time should never give his freedom to an imprisoned criminal; on the contrary he should be required to *earn* it by well directed efforts, resulting in well assured reform. It should be no holiday work for a prisoner to win his discharge. As a rule reformation may be attained only through a stern and severe training. It is in a benevolent adversity, whether in the freedom of ordinary life or the servitude of the prison, that all the manly virtues are born and nurtured. It is easy enough for a bad man to put up with a little more degradation, a little more contumely, a few more harsh restrictions; but to set his shoulder to the wheel, to command his temper, his appetites, his self-indulgent propensities, to struggle steadily out of his position—and all *voluntarily*, all from an *inward* impulse, stimulated by a moral necessity—this is a harder task, a far heavier imposition. And yet it is just this training that a right prison discipline must exact, and exact it until it has wrought its normal result in the reformation of the criminal, as the essential and sole condition of his restoration to freedom.

XVIII. Industrial training should have both a higher development and a greater breadth than has heretofore been, or is now, commonly the case in our prisons. Work is no less an auxiliary to virtue than it is a means of support. Steady, active, honorable labor is the basis of all reformatory discipline. It not only aids reformation, but is essential to it. It was a maxim with Howard, "Make men diligent and they will be honest." Eighty per cent of our imprisoned criminals never learned a trade—a plain indication of the sort of industrial training they need while in prison. In the central prisons of France, sixty-two distinct trades are taught. Montesinos introduced no less than forty-three in his one prison at Valencia, and gave to each convict the liberty of choosing which he would learn. Count Sollohub does the same now in his house of correction at Moscow. To teach a convict a trade is to place him out of the reach of want; it is to make him master of the great art of self-help. And unless he acquire, during his imprisonment, both the knowledge of some handicraft and the habit of work, that is, the power as well as the will to live honestly, he will in nine cases out of ten, sooner or later, give over the struggle, and return to criminal courses.

XIX. The doctrine has been proclaimed that "none of the skilled mechanic arts are to be introduced among convicts;" and a loud clamor has been raised in this and other countries, to which governments have sometimes weakly yielded, against the alleged competition of prison labor with free labor. We denounce the doctrine as inhuman, because it denies a right of humanity, not forfeited or alienated even by crime; and the clamor as baseless and unreasonable on the following grounds: 1. The products of prison labor, thrown into the general market, are not sufficient to interfere appreciably with those of mechanical and manufacturing labor outside.   2. It is contrary to a sound political economy to suppose that injury to the general interests of society can arise from the circumstance of a number of people being employed in making useful articles for which there is a demand in the community.   3. Whatever might be gained by individuals through a cessation of prison labor, would be lost to society at large in the cost of maintaining the prisoners.   4. Society is benefited by the production of the greatest possible amount of values, so that if prisoners are to cease working, society must be content to be poor by the amount of profit that would accrue from their work.   5. If the labor of men *in* prison is mischievous, their labor *out* of prison must be equally so; whence it follows by parity of reasoning, that society should be benefited by a cessation of labor on the part of people who live in a particular street, or whose names begin with a certain letter of the alphabet; and criminals instead of being reproached for their idleness ought to be applauded as martyrs to the public good, and as necessary though willing sacrifices on the altar of indolence.   6. If our imprisoned criminals had remained honest men the produce of their industry would be in competition with that of the complainants, the same as it is now.   Are we, then, to desire the commission of crime, that so much labor may be taken out of the labor market?   If the labor of prisoners is injurious to society, an equal amount of free labor must be injurious to the same extent.   Surely the same principle applies in both cases.   If not, where lies the difference?   It would, we think, puzzle any chopper of logic to show that the state is at once *benefited* by the labor of all her free citizens and injured by that of the small fraction who have been convicted of crime.   Can anything further be necessary to show the utter absurdity, and, consequently, the absolute futility, of the position taken by the complainants against prison labor?   7. Criminals ought surely to be made to earn their own support while undergoing their sentences, that society may be relieved, to that extent at least, of the burdens imposed upon it by their crimes.   8. Work is the basis of all reformatory prison discipline; so that if the reformation of criminals is important—a point conceded by all—it is no less important that they be trained while in prison to the practice and love of labor.

XX. While industrial labor in prisons, in whatever aspect viewed, is of the highest importance and utility, we regard the contract system of prison labor as prejudicial alike to discipline, finance and reformation. The directors of the Illinois penitentiary declare that more trouble to the discipline arises from the hundred men let to contractors in that prison, than from the thousand men worked by the state. A feature of prison management of which this can be said with truth—and we do not doubt the truth of the averment—cannot stand the scrutiny now everywhere directed to it. Ultimately, it must fall; and the sooner it falls, the better.

XXI. All the most valuable parts of the Irish or Crofton prison system—the initial punitive stage of separate imprisonment, the reformatory stage of progressive classification, and the probationary stage of moral imprisonment and natural training—are believed to be as applicable to one country as to another. Whether the stage of conditional liberty, or ticket-of-leave, can be introduced into our prison systems, is matter of grave doubt with many—doubt arising from the vast reach of our territory and the multiplication of separate jurisdictions therein. We incline to the belief that Yankee ingenuity is competent to devise· some method whereby this principle of the system, as well as the others, may receive practical application among us.

XXII. Prisons as well as prisoners, should be classified or graded, so that there shall be prisons for the untried; prisons for young criminals; prisons for women; prisons for misdemeanants; prisons for male felons; and prisons for the incorrigible. This idea has taken root widely and deeply in the public mind. We may well exchange congratulations on a fact so auspicious; and especially on the fact that acts for the creation of prisons for the younger class of criminals convicted of state prison offenses have been passed in Kentucky, Illinois and New York, into which will be introduced a really reformatory discipline; also, that acts creating separate prisons for women have been adopted by the legislatures of Indiana and Massachusetts. A pressing necessity at the present moment is for district prisons or houses of correction under state management, to which misdemeanants may be sentenced, and where after at the utmost one or two short imprisonments they may be sent for terms sufficiently long for reformatory processes to take effect upon them; or, better still, under sentences running until satisfactory proof of reformation shall have been given.

XXIII. It is believed that repeated short sentences are worse than useless; that, in fact, they rather stimulate than repress transgressions in the case of habitual drunkards, prostitutes, vagrants and petty transgressors of every name. The object here is less to punish than to save. Hence, the objection to long sentences, drawn from the disproportion between the sentence and the offense, is to no purpose. This is not the question. A lunatic who has committed no offense, but is simply afflicted with a malady that makes him dangerous, is restrained of his liberty until he is cured. Why should not the habitual violator of law, even though each separate offense may be trivial in itself, be treated in the same way? The principle of the treatment is the same in both cases—a benevolent regard to the good of the individual and the protection of society.

XXIV. Greater use should be made of the social principle in prison discipline than is now, or heretofore has been, common in our penitentiary establishments. The highest authorities concur in this judgment. It was a fundamental maxim with Captain Maconochie, who, of all men, went deepest into the philosophy of public punishment, that the criminal must be prepared for society in society. His words are: "Man is a social being; his duties are social; and only in society, as I think, can he be adequately trained for it." Mr. Frederick Hill, a gentleman of large experience as a prison inspector, first in Scotland and afterward in England, says: "When prisoners are brought together, they should really associate as human beings, and not be doomed to eternal dumbness, with their heads and eyes fixed like statues in one direction. All attempts to enforce such a system, and to carry on such a warfare with nature, must be productive of endless deception, and give rise to much irritating punishment." Count Sollohub, of Moscow, an able administrator and profound thinker, holds this language: "The isolation of man, the obligation imposed on him of perpetual silence, belongs to the principles against which the sentiments of the human race revolt. Man has no right to contravene the divine will. It is on this idea that the new Russian penitentiaries have been established. They do not recognize the right to impose perpetual silence; but they seek to prevent conversation becoming hurtful." The social principles of humanity are the great springs of improvement in free society; there is no reason to think that, when duly regulated and fairly applied, they will prove otherwise within the precincts of a prison.

XXV. Preventive institutions, such as public nurseries, truant homes, industrial schools, etc., for the reception and treatment of children not yet criminal, but in danger of becoming so, constitute the true field of promise in which to labor for the repression of crime. Here the brood may be killed in the egg, the stream cut off in the fountain; and whatever the cost of such agencies may be, it will be far less than the spoliations resulting from neglect and the expenses involved in arrests, trials and imprisonments.

XXVI. More systematic and comprehensive methods should be adopted to save discharged prisoners, by providing them with work, and encouraging them to redeem their character and regain their lost position in society. The state has not discharged its whole duty to the criminal when it has punished him, nor even when it has reformed him. Having raised him up, it has the further duty to aid in holding him up. In vain shall we have given the convict an improved mind and heart, in vain shall we have imparted to him the capacity for industrial labor and the desire to advance himself by worthy means, if, on his discharge, he finds the world in arms against him, with none to trust him, none to meet him kindly, none to give him the opportunity of earning honest bread.

XXVII. The successful prosecution of crime requires the combined action of capital and labor, just as other crafts do. There are two well defined classes engaged in criminal operations—the capitalists who furnish the means and the operatives who work the machinery. There are four classes of criminal capitalists—the owners of houses affording domiciles and places of entertainment to the depredators, the buyers of stolen goods, the pawnbrokers who lend money on such property, and the makers of burglarious and other criminal instruments. The criminal capitalists, being comparatively few, and much more sensitive to the terrors of the law, present the most vital and vulnerable point of the organization. It is worthy of inquiry whether society has not made a mistake in its warfare upon crime. The law now strikes at the many operative plunderers, one by one; would it not be wiser to strike at the few capitalists, as a class? Let it direct its blows against the connection between criminal capital and criminal labor, nor forbear its assaults until it has wholly broken and dissolved that union. We may rest assured that when this baleful organization shall be pierced in a vital part, it will perish; that when the corner stone of the leprous fabric shall be removed, the building will tumble into ruins.

XXVIII. Since personal liberty is a right as respectable as the right of property, it is plainly the duty of society to indemnify the citizen who has been unjustly imprisoned, as it indemnifies the citizen from whom it has taken his field or his house for some public use.

XXIX. Criminal lunacy is a question in which the whole community has a vital interest; and facts show that our laws regarding insanity, in its relation to crime, need revision in order to bring them to a conformity to the demands of reason, justice and humanity. To this end a commission should be formed of the ablest mental pathologists and criminal jurists, who should be charged with the duty of investigating this whole question, and of suggesting such provisions as would be suitable for enactment into law; so that when insanity is pleaded in bar of conviction, the investigation may be conducted with greater knowledge, dignity and fairness, criminal responsibility be more satisfactorily determined, the punishment of the sane criminal be made more sure, and the restraint of the insane be rendered at once more certain and more humane.

XXX. While this congress would not shield the convicted criminal from the just responsibility of his misdeeds, it arraigns society itself as in no slight degree accountable for the invasion of its rights and the warfare upon its interests, practiced by the criminal classes. In attempting to weigh the ill desert of criminals, it is too common to ignore the degree in which their follies and foibles, leading to crime, are the natural, almost indeed the inevitable result, either of the circumstances in which they were born, or of the indifference, the neglect, even the positive injustice of their more favored brethren; insomuch that what we are compelled by duty to society to punish as criminality, is, in truth, misfortune, not less than fault. Surely, then, the whole guilt, incurred by their offenses, is not theirs; but no inconsiderable part of it rests on the shoulders of society. Does society take all the steps it easily might, to change, or at least to improve, the circumstances in our social state that thus lead to crime? or, when it has been committed, to cure the proclivity to it generated by these circumstances? It cannot be pretended. Let society then lay the case earnestly to its conscience, and strive to mend in both particulars. Offenses must come, but a special woe is denounced against those through whom they come. Let us take heed that that woe fall not upon our head.

XXXI. The exercise of executive clemency, in the pardon of criminals, viewed as a practical question, is one of grave importance, and, at the same time, of great delicacy and difficulty. Of the fifteen thousand criminals confined in the state prisons of the United States, fifteen hundred, that is, ten per cent, not counting those released under commutation laws, were pardoned during the last year; and this proportion was rather below than above that furnished by the statistics of former years. In some states, the average proportion of pardons has reached the extraordinary figure of thirty to forty per cent; and even in Massachusetts, the annual average, during the entire history of her state prison, has been twenty per cent. The effect of this free use of the pardoning power is, in one word, to demoralize the prison populations of the land. The hopes of all are thus more or less excited; their minds are unsettled; they never become reconciled to their lot; the discipline of the prison is disturbed; the labor of the prisoners has less heart and, of course, less profit in it; and their reformation is impeded, if not defeated, by having their thoughts directed to another and inferior end. The prerogative of pardon is accompanied by a solemn responsibility. The executive head of the state, as a general rule, should not use it, except to prevent the infliction of a wrong on an innocent person. Neither official patronage, nor sympathy, nor generosity, affords a lawful occasion or a valid justification for its use. All exercise of clemency on such grounds must be partial, and therefore unjust; and, under it, what may be a kindness to one will be an injury to others. The logical issue of this reasoning is, that the prerogative of pardon should be exercised on some principle, and agreeably to some fixed rule. This power cannot rightfully be used on the ground that the convict's continuance in prison is a misfortune and a loss to himself and his family; or on the ground that his friends think he was unjustly convicted; or on the ground that his neighbors are anxious for his release, and express that anxiety in long and earnest petitions; or even on the ground that the prosecuting attorney who tried the case and the judge who pronounced the sentence recommend it. In what cases then, and for what reasons, may a pardon be properly granted? We answer: 1. In all cases where it can be made to appear that, since the conviction of the prisoner, such facts have come to light as would, if produced upon his trial and taken in connection with the proof on which he was convicted, have established his innocence. 2. In all cases where it can be made to appear that such newly discovered proof, if given upon the trial, would have so far mitigated the offense charged, as to entitle the criminal to a lighter sentence than the one imposed upon him. In the former of these classes of cases, it would be not only the right but the imperative duty of the executive to grant an instant discharge to the prisoner, not as an act of grace, but as the correction of a grievous wrong; and it would be the duty of society to indemnify the sufferer for the wrong done him. In the latter class, it would be equally the duty of the executive to remit such portion of the sentence as justice might seem to demand. But the new proof had need consist of well-established facts, subject to the same rules of evidence as though offered upon the trial. Not supposition, or hearsay, or sympathy, or impressions, or surmises, or entreaties, but *facts*, clear and indubitable, can be accepted as the legitimate ground for executive interposition. There may be other isolated and extraordinary cases, in which clemency may be properly extended to imprisoned criminals; but these would have to be decided upon their special claims and merits; and generally, no doubt, there would be some recognized principle that would control the decision.

XXXII. The proper duration of imprisonment for a violation of the laws of society is one of the most perplexing questions in criminal jurisprudence. The law fixes a minimum and maximum for the period of incarceration, leaving a broad interval between the two extremes, so that a wide discretion is left to the courts in determining the length of each individual sentence. We offer a few instances of the manner in which this discretion is used: one man was sentenced to the Maryland penitentiary for ten years for stealing a piece of calico worth only ten dollars; another was sentenced for the same term for perpetrating an atrocious homicide. Two brothers in Maine were convicted of larceny, under circumstances of about equal aggravation. They were both sentenced to the state prison, but by different judges—one for one year, the other for six. Three men in Wisconsin were convicted of forgery. The first forged a check for $3,000—his third offense—and was sentenced to state prison for four years. The second forged a note for $11—his first offense—and was sentenced for four years. The third forged a check for several thousand dollars, and was sentenced for but one year! In Massachusetts one man passed three counterfeit five-dollar bank notes, and was sentenced to state prison for fifteen years; another passed four twenty-dollar notes, and was sentenced for only four years. One man, for having in his possession ten counterfeit bank bills, was sentenced for one year; another who had committed the same offense, for twelve years. Surely such inequalities—and they are occurring every day—are beyond all bounds of reason. They engender great dissatisfaction among prisoners, and the discipline suffers in consequence. No logic can possibly convince a man that it is just that he should suffer the same penalty for stealing a piece of calico that is inflicted on another for a homicide; or that he should have four years' imprisonment for forging a note of hand for eleven dollars, while another gets but one for forging a check for thousands; or that for passing fifteen dollars in bad money he should serve a term of fifteen years in state prison, while his neighbor is let off with but four years for passing eighty. Obviously, this is an evil to which some remedy ought to be applied. What that remedy shall be—whether judicial discretion shall be confined within narrower limits, whether the single judge who tries shall simply send the convict to prison, leaving the term of imprisonment to be fixed by the full bench, or whether some other measure shall be deemed more fit and effective—we leave to the determination of statesmen, content to have indicated our belief that there is a wrong here that needs to be righted.

XXXIII. The science of statistics, especially as relating to crime and criminal administration, is too little appreciated, and therefore too much neglected, in the United States. The laws of social phenomena can be ascertained only by the accumulation, classification and analysis of facts. Returns of such facts, carefully gathered and skilfully digested, can alone show the true character and working of any system of prison discipline. But the local and the special are here to little purpose; it is the general only, that has value; that is, returns so numerous and drawn from so wide a field as to give real significance to the results. The problem is, how to gather, collate and reduce to tabulated forms, upon some uniform system, the facts which we want. In a country so vast as ours, with distinct penal jurisdiction in every state, and the general government powerless as regards legislation in this department, it is evident that such a result can be effected, if effected at all, only by moral power; and such power, as it seems to us, can be effected in only one or other of two ways, either first, by the institution of a national prison discipline society, with competent working committee in each state; or, secondly, through the establishment, by the general government of a national prison bureau, charged with the duty of devising and promulgating the best forms for prison registers; the best system of recording criminal proceedings; the best modes of tabulating penal statistics; and the best means of securing the preparation of comprehensive, scientific and accurate prison returns. The model for such a bureau we have in the recently instituted national bureau of education. Doubtless it would cost its annual thousands; but indirectly it would save the nation its annual ten thousands. Let it be remembered that crime is the foe against which we war, a mischief great and multiform; and it is to lead the battle and suggest the best methods of assault that this bureau is needed. The conflict must be bold, skilful, sleepless, and with weapons of love rather than vengeance. So assailed, the evil will yield, slowly no doubt, but surely, to the attack.

XXXIV. In previous propositions, we have declared our judgment as to the value of education in prisons and the importance of cultivating the manhood and self-respect of the convict; we now add the declaration of our belief, that both these ends would be materially served by the establishment, under competent editorial guidance, of a weekly newspaper designed for, and adapted to, the wants of imprisoned criminals. Any man, removed for years from active participation in the affairs of life, must have some facility of this sort to enable him to keep pace with passing events. In the nature of things, it must be difficult, if not impossible, for a person, after the seclusion of a long imprisonment, to succeed in the competitions of life; and it seems a duty of society to fortify his purposes and chances of amendment by affording him, during his incarceration, such a knowledge of the world and its doings as may be requisite to success. No better means to this end occurs to us than the general diffusion among prisoners of a newspaper of the character here suggested.

XXXV. Prison architecture is a matter of grave importance. It is impossible, in a brief statement such as is alone suited to the purposes of this paper, to express fully our views on this question. Mere hints, few and brief, are all that can be attempted. Prisons of every class should be substantial structures, affording gratification by their design and material to a pure taste, but not costly or highly ornate. The chief points to be aimed at in prison construction are security, perfect ventilation, an unfailing supply of pure water, the best facilities for industrial labor, convenience of markets, ease of supervision, adaptation to reformatory aims, and a rigid economy. Costly materials and elaborate adornments are not essential to any of these ends, and are subversive of the last. It was a saying of Jeremy Bentham, that "a prison should be so arranged that its chief officer can see all, know all, and care for all." We subscribe to the sentiment. The proper size of prisons is a point of much practical interest. Prisons containing too many inmates interfere with the principle of individualization, that is, with the study of the character of each individual prisoner, and the adaptation of the discipline, as far as practicable, to his personal peculiarities. It is obvious that the application of this principle is possible only in prisons of a moderate size. In our judgment, three hundred inmates are enough to form the population of a single prison; and in no case would we have the number exceed five or six hundred.

XXXVI. The organization and construction of prisons should

be by the state, and they should form a graduated series of reformatory establishments, with facilities for further classifying the inmates of each; they should be constructed with a view to the industrial employment, intellectual education and moral training of the criminals.

XXXVII. As a general rule, the maintenance of all penal institutions, above the county jail, should be from the earnings of their inmates, and without cost to the state. Yet the true standard of merit in their management should be the rapidity and thoroughness of reformatory effect, which is to be sought through the healing and harmonious development of the body, the mind, and the moral nature; and prisoners should be restored to society only at such times and on such conditions as shall give good hope of future rectitude.

XXXVIII. A right application of the principles of sanitary science in the construction and arrangements of prisons is another point of vital importance. The apparatus for heating and ventilating should be the best that is known; sunlight, air and water should be afforded according to the abundance with which nature has provided them; the rations and clothing should be plain, but wholesome, comfortable, and in sufficient but not extravagant quantity; the bedsteads, beds and bedding, including sheets and pillow-cases, not costly but decent, and kept clean, well aired and free from vermin; the hospital accommodations, medical stores and surgical instruments should be all that humanity requires and science can supply; and all needed means for personal cleanliness should be without stint.

XXXIX. The principle of the pecuniary responsibility of parents for the full or partial support of criminal children in reformatory institutions has been extensively applied in Europe, and, wherever tried, has been found to work well in practice. No principle could be more just or reasonable. The expense of such maintenance must fall on somebody; and on whom can it fall more fitly than the child's parent, whose neglect or vices have probably been the occasion of its lapse into crime? Two advantages would be likely to result from the enforcement of this principle: first, it would relieve the public in part, of the burden of supporting its neglected and criminal children; but, second, and chiefly, the fear of compelled contribution for the support of their children in a reform school would be a strong motive with parents, in the absence of higher ones, to a greater care of their education and conduct, that so the burden entailed by their criminal practices might be avoided.

XL. It is our intimate conviction, that one of the most effective agencies in the repression of crime would be the enactment of laws, by which the education of all the children of the state should be made obligatory. Better to force education upon the people than to force them into prison to expiate crimes, of which the neglect of education and consequent ignorance have been the occasion, if not the cause.

XLI. As a principle that crowns all and is essential to all, it is our conviction that no prison system can be perfect, or successful to the most desirable extent, without some central and supreme authority to sit at the helm, guiding, controlling, unifying, vitalizing the whole. No wiser words were uttered by the committee of 1850 on prison discipline, in the British parliament, than their declaration that "it is desirable that the legislature should intrust increased power to some central authority." Without such an authority, ready at all times for deliberation and action, there can be no consistent and homogeneous system of administration, no well-directed experiments, no careful deductions, no establishment of broad principles of prison discipline, nor any skilfully devised plans for carrying such principles into effect. But under a central board or bureau, improvements of every kind could be readily introduced, and that, too, in the safest manner, by first trying the plan proposed on a small scale and under the best circumstances for insuring trustworthy results, and then, if successful, gradually, under the guidance of experience, extending the sphere of its operations. We ardently hope to see all the departments of our preventive, reformatory and penal institutions in each state moulded into one harmonious and effective system; its parts mutually answering to and supporting each other; and the whole animated by the same spirit, aiming at the same objects, and subject to the same control, yet without the loss of the advantages of voluntary aid and effort, wherever they are attainable.

II

E. C. WINES AND PRISON REFORM

A MEMOIR by F. B. SANBORN*

THE history of great reforms is the story of many laborers toiling, either in association or widely separated, towards the same chief end. But it is also, in most instances, the personal biography of some one man or woman, to whose devotion and perseverance, for a series of years, the labor of the many was indebted for wise direction, wide advertisement, and practical application at the right place and time. Such a person, in our special task,—the reformation of prison discipline, and the final establishment of prison science,—was the late Dr. Enoch Cobb Wines; and it is a labor of love that one of his early associates now attempts in this essay.

I had never heard of Dr. Wines, except as the author of a few books, when in October, 1863, Governor Andrew of Massachusetts, distinguished as a philanthropist, made me the first secretary of the first Board of State Charities in the United States. Among the many duties of the secretary was the inspection and supervision of some thirty prisons, large and small, in that old Commonwealth, managed, as they were, under an antique and heterogeneous system of laws and customs that had been forming ever since the Pilgrim Fathers landed on Plymouth Rock in 1620. The new secretary of a new board could not for nearly a year devote himself to the examination of this system, so pressing was the need to reorganize establishments for the poor and the insane. But during 1864 I visited all our prisons, and some in other states, and investigated what was then a new system, the Irish convict law and practice. Upon this, and upon the defects of our own prisons, I reported in February, 1865, to the Massachusetts legislature. I also presented the results of the inquiry into European prison systems in the *North American Review* for January, 1866. My report and article fell into the hands of Dr. Wines and Professor Dwight, then investigating the whole prison system of the United

* For years an associate of Dr. Wines in prison reform work.

F. B. Sanborn

States, and I was able officially to promote their inquiry in Massachusetts. A similarity of aims and enthusiasm soon brought us together, the elder and the younger, in prosecuting the task Dr. Wines had undertaken.

We traveled together, visited prisons and addressed audiences in company, and he spent at my house in Concord one or two of those last days of his ever active life which were consecrated to the publication of his last monumental book at Cambridge, where he died, December 10, 1879. He was not quite seventy-four at his death, being born at Hanover, New Jersey, February 17, 1806. His prison work was not taken up till he was past fifty-five, and I joined him in it at three-and-thirty. As Wordsworth sings of an early companion:

> We talked with open heart, and tongue
> Affectionate and true;
> A pair of friends, though I was young,
> And Matthew seventy-two.

I am indebted to Dr. Frederick Howard Wines for recollections of earlier years of his father's life, and an estimate of his admirable qualities, which few are so competent to give. He writes:

"My father possessed one of the rarest types of mind. He seemed not to need the slow process of logical thought in order to arrive at conclusions; nor yet did he reach them by intuition. He rather appeared to grasp them. I often thought his mind resembled a clear pool, into which a truth once cast was instantly enveloped on all sides at once. He felt it, felt the whole of it, and accepted it for what it was. Neither a wit nor a scientist, his mind flowed more freely in the channels of metaphysics and philosophy. Yet he never lost his bearings in a tangle of speculation, and he never cut the thread which binds speculative thought to the real and practical. In his last days he told me, with a face made radiant by inward light, 'I have been greatly blessed; I have never had a religious doubt.' I looked at him with amazement; for the moment my faith was almost shaken in his intellectuality. Most men, as Browning has said, lead 'a life of doubt diversified by faith,' or else 'a life of faith diversified by doubt.' Dr. Wines was an exceptional man in this regard, as in many others.

"The foundation for his work in life was a robust physical constitution, invigorated by his environment and early occupation. His father was a farmer, at first in New Jersey and afterward in Vermont, on the shore of Lake Champlain. We know how simple and how stern was life on a New England farm one hundred years ago. The first care of a Puritan parent was to instil a firm religious sentiment and strict principles of moral integrity; to teach his children to make Duty their watchword, and to dread the enervating influence of self-indulgence upon character. My father was subjected to no temptation such as overpowers and destroys many another. He passed through the experience called 'conversion'; united with the Church, and doubtless said to himself, 'I have made up my mind to do right.' He never changed it. Like Paul of old, he fought the fight and kept the faith.

"Such a nature could not be held within the narrow confines of a remote country farm. As he approached manhood he determined to go to college. Middlebury was near his home, and he went there. His father, though not a poor man, could not afford to furnish the means required for a liberal education; so the boy earned the money and paid his own way. He prepared himself; and, to show his readiness, I may mention that, finding in his Latin grammar larger and smaller type, he mastered in a single week the paragraphs of chief importance, printed in the larger type. One night in college he worked late over a mathematical problem which he could not then solve. Exhausted, he jumped into bed, and blew out his candle on the small table where he left paper and pencil for the morning. Imagine his surprise then to find the problem solved in his own handwriting! He had done the task in the dark, without any knowledge or remembrance of the fact. Such was the determination with which he attacked any problem before him.

"His original purpose was to prepare for the Christian ministry; whether influenced by the remarkable power and popular esteem of clergymen at that period, I cannot say. Perhaps his mother wished to see him in the pulpit; but my belief is that the impulse came from himself. He had a passion for saving men. Yet he began his career as a schoolmaster, and for some years he conducted a private classical school for boys in Washington on Pennsylvania Avenue, directly opposite the park enclosing the Capitol. There he met, courted and married my mother.

"From Washington he entered the navy, as a teacher of midshipmen, long before the Naval Academy at Annapolis was founded; and he went with his pupils on a voyage to the Mediterranean in the frigate Constellation, now employed as a training-ship. In this relation he served two years and a half, during which he kept a journal, and soon after published two volumes describing his experiences, which were soon reprinted in London.* His account of the American navy therein was transferred bodily to the early editions of Chambers' Cyclopedia. The difficulties encountered in his work afloat impressed him with the need of a national naval academy, for the establishment of which he was an enthusiastic advocate.

"Later he became proprietor and principal of the Edgehill school for boys at Princeton, a preparatory school for the college. There he interested himself in a state normal school for teachers,—another forward movement in which he took a prominent part. There he wrote two books on popular education, among the first on that topic printed in the United States. He was invited to Philadelphia from Princeton as one of the four original professors selected to open the new city high school, since so eminent, and one of the first of its class organized in this country. He remained in this position until after 1840, and during his residence in Philadelphia wrote often for the *United States Gazette*, a newspaper edited by his friend Joseph R. Chandler,—among other things, some letters from New England, which he soon collected into a small volume containing his early impressions of Boston and Harvard College. A more important work was unique at the time of its publication in 1839,—A Peep at China in Mr. Dunn's Chinese Collection. This was a collection of articles belonging to Nathan Dunn of Philadelphia,—said at the time to be the largest or richest Chinese collection in Western lands; larger than even that at the Hague. The collections then existing at Salem in Massachusetts, and in the rooms of the London East India Company, though rich in East Indian curios, were not equally so in objects illustrative of Chinese life, in which Dr. Wines took a great interest even then. The international and philanthropic bent of his mind is shown in a sentence of his preface to this considerable brochure: 'By some, the following pages may be regarded as an "Apology for the Chinese"; but it is no more an apology than truth and justice demand.' "

It may be remembered that in his last volume, published after his death, Dr. Wines opens with an account of ancient prisons, and gives an early date to the Chinese convict system, then nearly 4000 years old. A curious anecdote, told in this connection, suggests to Dr. Wines that the cellular system originated in China. A king being given over to vice, his premier, Y-in, declared, "No communication

*Their full title was, Two Years and a Half in the Navy; or Journal of a Cruise in the Mediterranean and Levant, on Board of the U. S. Frigate Constellation in the years 1829, 1830, and 1831. Carey and Lea, Chestnut Street, Philadelphia.

must be allowed him with evil companions. I will cause to be built a palace in Tong; there, near the ashes of his royal sire, I will give him instructions, to the end that he may no longer pursue a vicious life."

Accordingly the king lived in his new palace according to the Eastern Penitentiary plan, and at length, says Dr. Wines, "entered into the true path of virtue." This first case of cellular imprisonment, he adds, "is the only case on record in all antiquity of a reformed prisoner." Although in Philadelphia for several years, and no doubt occasionally at the Eastern Penitentiary, Dr. Wines seems to have been more familiar with the Chinese Collection than with the then famous and much disputed prison, which European experts were inspecting and imitating across the Atlantic.

At Princeton, before going to live in Philadelphia, Dr. Wines edited for a time a Monthly Advocate of Education, but it may not have been till 1847 that he publicly advocated a state normal school for New Jersey. In that year, as one of a Convention of the Friends of Education in Burlington County, he reported for a committee an argument for such a school, and a form of petition to the New Jersey legislature requesting its establishment. Letters appended to this report were written to Dr. Wines by Governors Seward of New York and Edward Everett of Massachusetts, Gen. Dix and Bishop Alonzo Potter of New York, Horace Mann, then active with Dr. S. G. Howe in reforming the schools of Boston, and J. R. Chandler of Philadelphia. This list of his correspondents shows how active he was at that date in interesting men of great public influence in the measures he was advocating. He was then (1847) at the head of the Oaklands school at Burlington, New Jersey, of which he took charge in 1844, having left Philadelphia some time before. In 1848-49 the slavery question attracted his attention and claimed his ready pen; for he issued in 1849 a pamphlet of 44 pages, Thoughts on Slavery, with a motto from Paradise Lost, ending

But man over man
He made not lord; such title to himself
Reserving, human left from human free.

It closed with this prophetic declaration:

"The vote by which involuntary servitude has been excluded forever from the Oregon Territory is the pledge of similar triumphs when the same contest shall be renewed on the soil of New Mexico and California. If the friends of human freedom be but true to their cause and themselves, we shall be spared the humiliation of adding to the crime of national plunder the deeper, darker stain of filling regions now happily exempt from such evils, with the clank, the tears and the blight of slavery. Spirit of Wilberforce, of Clarkson and of Channing, breathe upon our hearts, and arm us for the conflict."*

In this sentiment Dr. Wines was then in accord with the Adamses, Webster, Everett and the Whig party generally, to which he had belonged, although some of them afterward changed their attitude, as Dr. Wines did not. Seldom, however, did he take part in political debates, being more deeply interested in questions of education and religion. A signal instance of the latter was an exposition of his long-considered view of Mosaic legislation, concerning which his son says:

"While in Philadelphia about 1840, he had been asked by a Hebrew Association to give a public address on Moses the Hebrew Lawgiver, which was so well received that in after years he expanded it into a volume, for which he long made elaborate studies. His results were embodied in a series of lectures, which he read at a number of places in New England. In these he took for his main thesis the proposition that the codes of Christendom are founded in principle on the misunderstood and much maligned Mosaic Law. Proceeding from this, he wrote out the first volume of what he hoped might be a work of interest and value, afterwards published at New York by the Putnams, under the title, A Commentary on the Laws

---

* These were the views of Dr. Wines before the general emancipation, and it may be well to place on record some later views, written in correction of remarks made by his intimate friend, Richard Vaux of Philadelphia, at the Prison Congress of New York, in June, 1876. Dr. Wines added a long note (pp. 456-7) to the address of Mr. Vaux on Prison Discipline, in which he said:

"One word as to race. My friend says, 'The Negro is by *nature* debased and degraded.' I would substitute *slavery* for *nature* in his proposition. His corollary is, 'Apply a different prison discipline to him from what you do to the white man,'—the effect of which would be to widen the chasm between the two races. I say: Diminish the chasm as fast as possible, and in the end close it up by education, religion, and all civilizing, elevating, refining influences; and let all positions, dignities, trusts, responsibilities be open to the Negro as to the white man, whenever he shows himself capable and worthy."

In his own paper, read at the same Congress (p. 408), Dr. Wines said of Moses and his code: "As to slavery, it never had a more hearty hater than Moses; but he did not uproot it by one mighty wrench, for that would have been to do violence to what was then the common sentiment and common practice of the race. But he put in motion a train of influences which were intended to destroy it, and in the end did destroy it among the Jews; and that, not as it has been destroyed among us, but gently, peacefully, without tumult or commotion; above all, without the shedding of fraternal blood."

of the Ancient Hebrews.* This was intended by him to be merely preliminary to a second volume, wherein he designed to reduce the prescriptions and sanctions of the Mosaic Code to the form of a modern law-book; analysing, classifying and restating them in language 'understandable by the people!' With his materials already collected he would have carried out this plan, had he lived longer. When he died, the *Jewish Messenger*, an organ of the Hebrews, observed that, while no man who knew him could doubt that he was a Christian, yet the Jews had never a better friend than they had now lost in Dr. Wines.†

"At long and at last he entered the Christian ministry, a little after 1850; at first to supply a Congregational pulpit in Cornwall, Vermont, and soon after as a Presbyterian pastor in East Hampton on Long Island, where Dr. Lyman Beecher had preceded him, many years before. (It was the parish where, as Mrs. Stowe relates in her father's Life, Dr. Beecher once remarked that the pastor was expected to take part of his pay in whales,—since by an old usage he was entitled to a fair share in any stranded whales within the parish bounds.)

The salary of Dr. Wines was but $600 in money, with the use of a parsonage; and it will illustrate a feature of his character to mention that he at once set aside one-tenth of this small stipend for his benevolences, and lived, with his wife and four children, on $540. From East Hampton he went in the summer of 1853 to be professor of Latin and Greek in Washington College, at Washington in Pennsylvania, at which I graduated in 1857, and where my friend, the late John Milligan, graduated later."

After six years at Washington College, Dr. Wines was invited by friends in St. Louis who wished to found another university there, to be its first president. The occasion of this invitation was the

---

* A commentary on the Laws of the Ancient Hebrews was published at New York in 1853, more than twenty years after his first two volumes came out in Philadelphia in 1832.

† In this connection I may quote what Dr. F. H. Wines writes:
"It might have been supposed that Mr. Vaux and my father could have little in common. They were of different professions, divergent politics, different shades of religious thought, with widely variant social experiences and circles of acquaintance; and they held divergent theories of prison management. Yet Mr. Vaux said to me, and repeated it warmly, 'There is nothing I would not do for Dr. Wines.' When I remarked that his children sometimes wished he were more a man of the world, Mr. Vaux threw up his hands and exclaimed, 'My God! it would have spoiled him!' I may add that he agreed in my father's lofty estimate of Moses and of Paul, whom Mr. Vaux once characterized as the two greatest men known to serious students of the history of civilization."

previous establishment of Washington University at St. Louis, under the administration of its first chancellor, Joseph Gibson Hoyt, my former teacher at Exeter, New Hampshire. He was a graduate of Yale in 1840, and had long been connected with a Congregational church in New Hampshire; but as some of the founders of Dr. Hoyt's university, particularly the Smiths of St. Louis (originally from New Hampshire), were Unitarians, a group of wealthy and prominent Calvinists desired collegiate instruction in their city under influences of which Dr. Wines was a representative. He therefore opened a preparatory school at St. Louis; but the political agitation of 1860, followed by the Civil War, so injured and temporarily destroyed the ancient business of the city, that the proposed university never materialized, and Dr. Wines finally gave up the business of instruction, in which he had been for more than thirty years engaged. Of his character and influence in this part of his life his son says:

, "Few men can have ever felt for a father deeper reverence or a warmer affection than I for him. It never occurred to me that it would be possible to disobey him. If he had told me to hold my hand in the fire, I thought I should have no choice but to do it. It never entered my mind that he had been or could be guilty of a wrong act; for he had the courage of a man and the purity of a woman. The influence that he had over me, I noticed that he had over other boys and men. He long had the habit to rise early,—before daylight in winter,—and spend the first morning hour in meditation and the exercises of private devotion. To this practice he doubtless owed much of the power over others which he exerted, and which had this hidden source. In teaching he discarded corporal punishment, as something for which he had no use and felt no need. He could govern a boy without it. His authority inspired affection also."

At this point in his career, and before considering Dr. Wines in his prison work at New York, to which he removed in 1862, and from which center his influence was to radiate in all directions, I will pause awhile to point out what was his preparation for essentially a new task, in which he succeeded beyond all reasonable expectation, far beyond what any other American at that time could have done. Like his friend of later years, Dr. Howe, who had preceded him by thirty years in his practical experience of prison life, and by nearly twenty years in his grasp of the essential principles of prison science, Dr. Wines was (as ancient Lloyd so well describes Sir

Anthony Brown of the Tudor reigns) "the best compound in the world, a learned, an honest and a traveled man; a good nature, a large soul and a settled mind." He was less than five years younger than Howe, and outlived him by less than four years; so that their lives covered much the same period, and almost exactly the same space of time. Their travels began at about the same age (three-and-twenty), and were directed to the same regions in Europe, the countries bordering the Mediterranean. Dr. Howe had more experience with the British navy, Dr. Wines with the American; and both in their narrations described with enthusiasm the same ancient lands, Greece and Italy, with their islands and shores. Both happened to be once in Greece at the same time, near the close of the short administration of Count Capodistrias, first and only president of emancipated Hellas. Capodistrias granted to Howe the thousand or two acres at Hexamilia, near Corinth, where Howe established his unique colony of homeless Greek refugees in 1830, and governed them with the aid of his eccentric friend, the Scotch David Urquhart. Dr. Wines, in his hurried visit to Corinth from Nauplia, rode near this colony, but does not seem to have known of its existence; indeed, it was known to few but its beneficiaries, who welcomed Howe back there in 1844, when he revisited Greece after a long absence. In his second volume of 1832, Dr. Wines thus speaks of Capodistrias, who was assassinated by the sons of old Mavromichali, the ancestor of the late Greek premier:

"May, 1830. Nauplia. The President, the Governor of the city, and most of the officers of the government visited our ship while she lay at Napoli. Capodistrias then gave a splendid entertainment at his palace, at which, however, I had not the honor of being present. When we were again at Napoli in July I called on him, in company with the Captain and the Purser of our frigate. He was a man of the most captivating manners, and of easy conversation. I judged him to be about 65 years of age.*

"He was rather above the ordinary stature, with a high forehead, grey hair, large dark greyish eyes, long features, an intelligent but care-worn expression of countenance, and a form perfectly symmetrical and graceful. His dress was as plain as the simplest re-

---

* He was in fact but little above fifty; had been brought up at the court of Alexander of Russia, and there acquired the ease of manner noticed by his visitors. He was a patriot and a man of ability, but believed to favor a Russian party in Greece, and had involved himself in one of those feuds for which the Greek revolutionists were notorious, and which cost several of them their lives.

publican could have desired it, and his palace was of plain construction and plainly furnished. It is true that guards were stationed at the entrance,—a regal precaution,—but this was rendered necessary by the character of the people and the state of the country. His conversation, in Italian, was chiefly a detail of political news, in answer to inquiries made by Captain Wadsworth. No allusion was made to the state of Greece, or to his own administration. The country was verging to a revolution. One province was in actual revolt, and some others in not a much better state. The opposition numbered such men as Miaulis, Tombazi, Canaris (naval heroes), Mavrocordato, Conduriotti, General Church, and almost all the officers of the navy. The charges made against Capodistrias were principally these,—subserviency to Russia, abolition of freedom of the press, embezzlement of the public treasures, and the employment of bribes and menaces to corrupt and overawe the legislative and judicial authorities. In confirmation of the last charge, I was assured by an English lawyer resident at Argos that no decision could be obtained, in any court, in favor of a man known to be obnoxious to the President. Whether all these charges were true, I cannot know; but I do know that they were generally believed by the Greek people. It would be unjust to deny that Capodistrias did much to promote civilization; that his efforts were unwearied to facilitate intercourse between different parts of the republic, by the suppression of piracy and robbery; that he gave to education the countenance and support of an enlightened and patriotic statesman; and finally that he introduced something like order and efficiency into public affairs. On the whole, his administration was partly good and partly bad; and had the Greeks been a better people, he would have been a better ruler."

The only hint that this early book gives of an interest by the author in prison affairs was his visit to the State Prison of Greece, then not far from the palace of Capodistrias, which, in turn, was near the church where he was assassinated by the young Mavromichalis, in October, 1831. Dr. Wines says:

"The public penitentiary of Greece is within the fortress of the Palamedi (the citadel of Nauplia). It is an immense building, with walls of prodigious thickness, and from 40 to 60 feet in height. About 40 prisoners were confined within its cells when we were there. A short time previous one poor fellow had attempted to escape by throwing himself from the top of the wall, to which, somehow or other, he had managed to climb. His body was dreadfully mangled by the fall, and he died in three days."

In his State of Prisons, issued in 1880, after the death of its author, Dr. Wines said of Greece half a century later:

"There are 17 detention prisons, in which, for want of room elsewhere, are also ordinarily confined those sentenced to imprisonment not exceeding a year. There are seven convict prisons. The average number of prisoners is 3600. The annual movement indicates a population of about 8000 during the year."

The enthusiasm of the naval schoolmaster was aroused, as with all travelers in Greece, by the glory of its sunlight and the beauty of its scenery. He said:

"I have beheld with rapture the prospects obtained from the Keep at Carisbrooke Castle, from the Rock of Gibraltar, from the Leaning Tower of Pisa, from the ridge of the crater of Vesuvius, and from the Acropolis at Sardis; but which of them can be compared to that enjoyed on the top of Acro-Corinthos? Here the view is without limits in every direction, and comprehends every description of scenery, from the most desolate sublimity to the softest beauty that adorns the enchanting vales of Greece. Facing the Gulf of Lepanto, the spectator will have before him the plain of Corinth, from four to five miles wide, and from ten to fifteen long; gay with numerous villages and diversified by extensive olive groves, green parterres and golden wheatfields. On his right the gigantic ranges of Cithaeron, Helicon and Parnassus, towering far into the clouds, stretch in apparently interminable outlines to the interior of Northern Greece. Turning his eye to the left, it will rest on the Peloponnesus, exhibiting mountains piled on mountains, with here and there a green valley. Then facing to the east, he will look down on the Saronic Gulf, its bosom gemmed with verdant islets; and far beyond he will discern the promontory of Sunium and the coast of Attica, among whose sacred hills shoots up the still more sacred Acropolis of the city of Minerva. . . . Never shall I forget the wild sublimity of these mountains, or the smiling loveliness of these valleys; never forget the balmy mildness of Grecian evenings, or the celestial purity of the climate. Never shall I forget the clear, deep blue of her waves, or the soft splendors of her moonlight nights; above all, never forget a sunset I once beheld while standing among the ruins of Athens. In the theatre of Herodes Atticus I was between the setting sun and Mount Hymettus, whose western side in its whole extent seemed enveloped in a robe of the softest, most brilliant purple. As the sun continued to sink, so that his rays ceased successively to strike on different parts of the mountain, the purple tints gradually retreated before a line of sombre hues; and it required little imagination to fancy that I beheld the dark Spirit of Barbarism chasing away the delicate and glorious splendors of Grecian genius."

As I quote, I recognize how faithful is the picture, often seen by me. With descriptions as glowing as this are mingled, in this early book, the soundest observations on men and things, and a perception and record of the graceful or the dismal traits of human nature. The three years therein registered gave him the opportunity for a study of mankind in various countries and under changing conditions; made him familiar with the languages and the manners of the older nations, and trained him in the politeness of the man of the world, whom no situation surprises. His education had given him a written style of learning and good taste; his habits of industry were fixed, and as restful as the leisure of other men; so that thirty years later, at the age of fifty-six, he was well prepared for the new task he then undertook. His son says:

"You are as familiar as I with the main facts of his subsequent career, for which, it soon appeared, his service in the navy, his European tour, and his whole life's discipline had trained him. Though without diplomatic experience, his habit of associating with men of education and influence in this country and abroad, stood him now in good stead. While stationed at the town of Port Mahon, he had become so familiar with Spanish that he said he sometimes dreamed in that tongue; and he had a serviceable knowledge of written French and Italian, without acquiring much readiness in speaking either." These languages were useful in his early prison inquiries, and vitally so when he took up the organization of an international prison congress, following out his rapid success in holding national prison congresses in the United States.

On the 24th of July, 1862, when Dr. Wines took his seat as secretary of the New York Prison Association, that semi-public organization had existed for some sixteen years. He held that place eight years and four months. In 1871, following the Cincinnati Congress, he was made secretary of the National Prison Association there organized; and in the same year was appointed by President Grant a special commissioner of the United States to secure the adhesion of the chief European governments to his project of holding an international congress in London. He succeeded in accomplishing the task assigned, and the first International Prison Congress met at

London in 1872, under the presidency of the Earl of Carnarvon. Thus in the ten years following his first prison appointment in New York, he had triumphantly accomplished what few persons acquainted with the obstacles to be surmounted, and with the indifference of the widely separated and often jealous communities in which he worked during these ten years, would in 1862–65 have looked upon as practicable.

THE NEW YORK PRISON ASSOCIATION

This had been founded by good men of wide experience and extensive theoretical knowledge, but without much power of bringing great results to pass. In its first seventeen years its total income had been less than $41,000, an average yearly revenue of only $2400. Before the new secretary had been a year in office, with the aid of his associates he had secured a yearly appropriation of $5500 from the public authorities of the city and state of New York. When he gave up his office at the close of 1870, the total income of the society had reached $14,000 a year; the aggregate receipts during his term of service being nearly $100,000, or more than twice the amount received during its first seventeen years.

The work carried on in the New York Prison Association, by means of this large increase of its funds, soon extended beyond the limits of that state, and made Dr. Wines known all over the United States. The inquiry into the general prison situation in the United States, in which Theodore W. Dwight was joined with Dr. Wines, was plainly a national work, and was utilized in each of the states where efforts were making to improve the local prisons. It made Mr. Brockway, then managing a prison in Detroit, known to Dr. Wines, and the two men thereafter worked together and accepted me as a volunteer colleague. We found the American Social Science Association, which a few of us had organized at Boston in October, 1865, a very useful auxiliary in bringing together the persons, then not very numerous, who had a serious interest in reforming prisons; and the organization of the Cincinnati Prison Congress in October, 1870, was partly the task of the New York Prison Association and partly of the Social Science Association, which had members in many states. When it came to organizing an international congress, however, the Prison Association hesitated and balked. Dr. Wines gives an account of his successful efforts in his last book.*

***

* The State of Prisons, p. 46. Quoted by Dr. F. H. Wines in the previous article.

This brief page hints at the result of five years' labor by Dr. Wines and his intimate friends; but what an incessant and widespread labor it was! The reforms urged by me on the Massachusetts legislature in 1865 had been favored and extended by the reports of the New York Prison Association, and especially by Dr. Wines and Professor Dwight, in the report already mentioned. But they had covered a much wider region in their inquiries, and summoned a far greater array of witnesses to the evils that were to be removed, and to the remedies that ought to be applied.

Massachusetts had anticipated New York in laying before the people of America the then recent theories of Captain Maconochie, which, reduced to practice, had demonstrated their soundness under the system of Captain Walter Crofton, and had been introduced with full authority in Ireland in 1854. But New York had anticipated both Massachusetts and Ireland in furnishing a youth of genius, fortified with common sense and business tact, who was building prisons, and showing how they ought to be administered, while Dr. Wines and I were talking about the principles involved. This powerful ally was Z. R. Brockway, originally of Connecticut, but who in his early manhood had migrated to New York. There, under a New Hampshire prison disciplinarian, Amos Pilsbury, he was learning at Albany the lessons upon which he so much improved afterward at Rochester, Detroit and Elmira. We made his personal acquaintance at Detroit in 1866–67, and from that time forward he became a most efficient member of the volunteers of Prison Reform.

But Mr. Brockway, like other prison administrators, was fixed to one spot, and had not the wide range of travel and correspondence that Dr. Wines enjoyed after having first created the occasion for it. The New York secretary traversed the whole North, and opened correspondence with all Europe and some regions of Asia, Africa and South America. By 1869 he was in communication with nearly every person known to be actively interested in prison reformation. Maconochie had died before either Dr. Wines or I took up this question,—October 25, 1860,—but his widow and the widow of Horace Mann (with whom Maconochie had corresponded) furnished us with his inspiring and convincing pamphlets, and with a manuscript which the late Dr. Edward Everett Hale afterwards printed in his short-lived Social Science magazine, *Old and New*. The doctrines of Maconochie were accepted or thought out by others; and it was readily seen that the two old and famous modes of prison management, the Auburn and the Philadelphia systems, were confessedly inadequate, often inapplicable, and needed to be combined and supplemented or superseded. This, in his tentative way, Mr. Brockway was doing at Detroit, as it had been done on a larger scale in Ireland by Sir Walter Crofton and his associates. To this fermenting and promising condition of the public mind, Dr. Wines and his New York Prison Association had largely contributed.

THE NATIONAL PRISON ASSOCIATION

But Dr. Wines, like his son since his time, was nothing if not national. To limit himself to a single state, even so important as New York, was out of the question. He therefore early joined the American Social Science Association, and put himself in communication with the British Social Science Association, upon whose model ours was fashioned, but which ours has outlived. Through these organizations, and the slowly increasing state boards, Dr. Wines agitated for an American Prison Congress, and before he left his New York field of action, it had been successfully held at Cincinnati, in the week beginning October 12, 1870. Twenty-five states and the Colombian republic in South America, and Canada in North America, were there represented.

As chairman of the committee of arrangements, of which Dr. Wines had been far the most efficient member, I had the honor of calling the Congress to order; and three of us, Mr. Brockway, Dr. Wines and myself, were the working force on the business committee of the sessions. To us as a sub-committee was referred the draft of a Declaration of Principles, prepared by Dr. Wines; and over this we spent many deliberative hours. As printed in the volume of Transactions, it makes six pages and a half, in thirty-seven separate sections; and, but for the abbreviating powers of his two colleagues, the draft of Dr. Wines would have run to eight or ten pages. His habit of stating all things methodically, whether they were matters generally known and accepted, or were still open to debate, was invaluable; but something must be conceded to the brevity of human life, and the dulness of mankind in general. When we urged this, and shortened the Doctor's periods, his good nature, and his faith in our friendship made him yield; but not without a pang.

I have had occasion to mention the persistence of Dr. Wines in all his good works, and shall need to recur to that trait; it was the perseverance of the saints, and not without some of the *naïveté* of that class. The affection of an author for his own work is one of those natural sentiments, like what the phrenologists used to call in

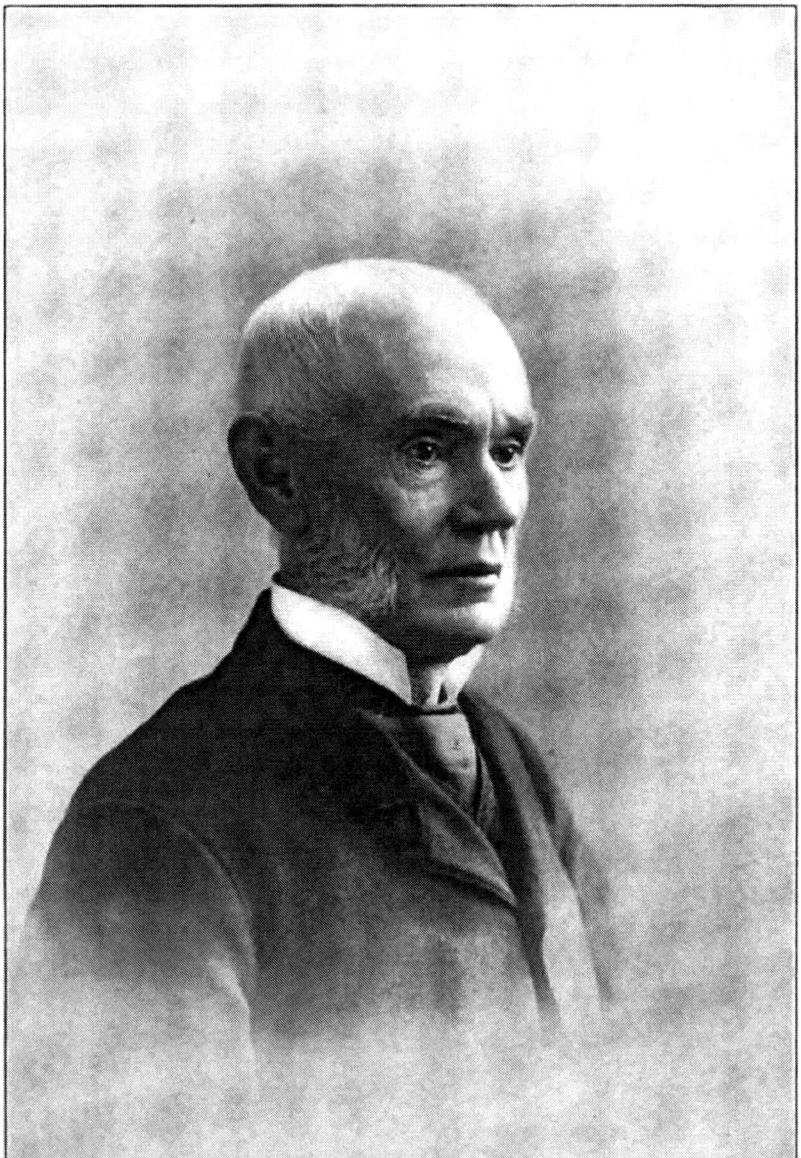

A. G. Byers

their sesquipedalian way, "philoprogenitiveness." It was manifested in this case by Dr. Wines in a pleasing manner. As editor of the Cincinnati volume of Transactions, of 650 pages (or, when combined with the report of the New York Prison Association, of nearly 850), he loyally printed there the abridged Declaration, but immediately followed it with his own original draft, prefaced thus:

"The foregoing DECLARATION OF PRINCIPLES is in the main a condensation of a paper prepared and printed by the committee of arrangements, in advance of the meeting, and distributed for examination to all persons invited to attend the same. The committee did not expect that their paper would be adopted by the Congress in a form so full as that in which it had originally appeared; and indeed, they themselves prepared the condensed form for the business committee of the Congress. As most of the articles in the original paper contain, severally, not only the statement of a principle, but also a short, incisive, pithy argument in support of it, the publishing committee have deemed it best to give the said paper a place in these Transactions, and thus secure for it a more permanent form than it had as published in the Programme of Proceedings."

Then follow seventeen solid pages of the draft,—the Declaration having occupied, as has been said, but six and a half. In the Transactions of the International Penitentiary Congress of London, two years later, the same draft reappeared, but now reduced from seventeen pages to eight, and entitled Propositions Submitted to the Congress by the American Delegation. In this abridgment the official Declaration is as much shortened as the original draft, and its thirty-seven sections, as well as the forty-one of the draft, are reduced to but twenty-five.

My own share in the work of the Cincinnati Congress, besides serving on its committees, was chiefly restricted to a brief paper answering the question, How Far is the Irish Prison System Applicable to American Prisons? It followed a longer paper by Sir Walter Crofton on the system as introduced by him in Ireland, and as administered by himself and others for fourteen years in its final form. In this paper he said, "It has been the means of securing the objects contemplated to their fullest extent, and has abundantly refuted the objections made to it."

It is safe to say that every advance in the improvement of prisons and the restoration of culprits to fairly honest lives in American society, since the Cincinnati Prison Congress adjourned, nearly forty years ago, has followed the lines laid down in its Declaration of Principles. Much has been done in this interval, and, alas! much

still remains to do; particularly in the matters of compulsory education, and a uniform system of prisons, duly classified and with the
best appliances for labor, school training and self-support. But
although he did not live to see all the good results which we see, Dr.
Wines knew before his unexpected death, that the good seed he had
so diligently sown was bearing abundant fruit. The National Association was organized, and the work of the New York Prison
Association went on vigorously; and between these two bodies, the
indeterminate sentence, and the Elmira Reformatory Prison were
both satisfactorily working before December, 1879. Mr. Brockway
took charge of the Elmira experiment in 1876, and it had become an
undoubted success long before he resigned its direction in 1900.

THE INTERNATIONAL CONGRESSES

In a certain sense, the Cincinnati Congress was international;
for the most eminent European prison reformers and criminal jurists
participated in its proceedings by papers and letters; but it led to an
actual assemblage of a more international character in 1872, and on
several after occasions. From the first, Dr. Wines had aimed at this
final result, and he was encouraged to persevere by the words of
sympathy that he early received from Europe. His son writes me:

"Dr. Wines entered into active correspondence with prison
officials and students of criminology in all the countries of Europe.
Among them was Count Sollohub, the head of the prison administration of Russia, who wrote him that the time was ripe for convening
an international congress; that, owing to political complications, no
European nation could then take the initiative, and America alone
could and should do it. He therefore urged my father to attempt this
great undertaking. Dr. Wines laid the matter before the directors
of the New York Prison Association, who thought it beyond their
province, and perhaps beyond the authorization of their state charter,
—as it may have been. He therefore decided to act independently;
secured supporters and a committee of arrangements, under the
signatures of a call for the National Congress at Cincinnati, where
the National Prison Association was born. There the first steps
were taken toward the organization of an International Prison Congress, which eventuated so happily for us and for the world.

'"Before starting for Europe on this errand, under the commission of the United States, he laid out his route in advance, and
settled the dates when he would endeavor to be at each point to be
visited. This schedule he adhered to, with as much tenacity as cir-

cumstances would allow. For instance, in Berlin, when he called to lay his mission before the great Bismarck, the German Chancellor, word was sent him that he could be received the next day or the day after. 'But tell the Count,' he said, 'that I leave Berlin tonight;' and Bismarck sent for him at once. In Italy, when he arrived, the Court was at the Italian summer capital, during the heat of summer. The king, at the conclusion of the interview granted to my father, said, 'Have you been in Rome?' 'No, your Majesty.' 'Not seen Rome? You must visit there before leaving Italy.' 'I should love to, your Majesty, but I have no time.' The King insisted, and the outcome was that Dr. Wines went to Rome as the guest of the government, accompanied by a gentleman of the Court, who engaged a magnificent suite of apartments for his entertainment, and acted for two days as his personal attendant and guide, showing him as much as he could in that brief time. Two days was all that Dr. Wines would spare for his personal gratification.

"Mr. Peterson of Christiania told me with much glee, in excellent English, spoken with a charming accent, that when he had shown Dr. Wines everything in and about the prison, and they had taken lunch together, he said, 'Now, Dr. Wines, where shall we go this afternoon? Shall we go to such a place, or such a place?' And your father said, 'What is there? Is there a pree-sone there?' And I laughed and said, 'No, there is no pree-sone there; but there is a fine park, and many beautiful ladies, and much to see and enjoy.' And your father said, 'I go nowhere where there is not a pree-sone.' The dear old gentleman added, with great emphasis, 'Mr. Wines, I loaf your fader.' My mother, who was present, and nearly seventy years old, said, 'Mr. Peterson, I hope you love me, too.' He put his hand on his heart and replied, 'Oh yes, Mrs. Wines, I love you, too; but Dr. Wines, he has the first place in my heart.'

"Dr. Wines had the wisdom of the heart; a higher, nobler attribute than mere intellectual acumen. The quality of his emotional nature (although he was neither impulsive nor sentimental) endeared him to those in sympathy with his aims. They felt that he saw 'the light that never was on sea or land.' They took delight in his simplicity, his sincerity, his *naïveté*, his directness, his heartiness and *bonhomie*. He attached them to himself, and could lead them wherever he went.

"As a critic, he had that prime requisite, the capacity to admire. His eye caught first the beauty in individual character and conduct; he was not blind to defect or deformity, but viewed it with the eye of charity. Yet he was stern and uncompromising in his attitude toward wrong; he loved the sinner, not his sin. His childlike faith in God was accompanied by faith in the essential manhood of every person created in the image of God. The rock on which rested every conviction he entertained regarding the prison question, in gross or in detail, was his unshakable belief in the salvability of man; in the possibilities hidden within the inner consciousness of the worst men; the essential oneness of human nature.

"I once asked him how he dared to set up his belief in the reformability of convicted felons, in opposition to the general opinion of prison keepers (who had better opportunities to study them than he had), that, as a class, they are beyond hope. With indignant earnestness, he exclaimed, 'They have not tried. How does any man know what he can do till he tries?' He had faith in the unseen possibilities, not of convicts only, but of wardens and guards,—and even of prison contractors, for whose inhuman greed and devious political and business methods he felt intense scorn."

In this generous spirit Dr. Wines had devoted himself to the improvement of the prison system of New York, and to the broader inquiries of which I have spoken, and which first attracted my attention and that of our friend Brockway. As the secretary of the newly formed National Prison Association, from 1870 onward, and as commissioner of the United States to visit Europe and arrange for an international congress, his labors were incessant, systematic, and very fruitful. As one of the first corporate members of the National Prison Association, of which Mr. Brockway and myself are almost the only survivors, and as one of its directors in 1876, I joined in a statement from which I may copy here the remarkable facts that we then made public. We said:

"It is known to the public of our own country and of Europe that the Reverend Dr. E. C. Wines has devoted the last fourteen years to the study of the problems of crime, its treatment and its diminution; for eight years as secretary of the Prison Association of New York, and for six years as secretary of the National Prison Association. The success of the last-named association is almost wholly due to his wise, persistent and unselfish efforts, in the face of great discouragements. Since the organization of the prison congress at Cincinnati in 1870, three similar congresses have been held in this country, at Baltimore, St. Louis and New York; and one international congress at London; while the work of preparation for a second international congress, at Stockholm in Sweden, is already well advanced.   These congresses have resulted in the mutual acquaintance, sympathy and support of men engaged in the prison work, who were before almost wholly isolated from each other; have enlarged the views and elevated the aims of prison officials throughout this country, and have attracted very general attention on the part of the public to the importance of the questions involved.   They have given an impetus truly wonderful to the movement in behalf of prison reform everywhere; and their published Transactions are a treasury of information for the student, the statesman and the philanthropist, upon all the points of this general subject.   The importance and value of these meetings have been recognized by our national and state governments, and by nearly all the governments of Europe, where the movement for prison reform has been put forward by many years.

"These results have involved Dr. Wines in the most arduous labors for their accomplishment.   As United States Penitentiary Commissioner, and as our secretary, he has crossed the Atlantic eight times, has negotiated, generally in person, with all the European governments, and repeatedly made long journeys in the United States.   He has traveled not less than 60,000 miles, has written 15,000 letters, prepared, edited and published five volumes of Transactions, and has a sixth now (1876) ready for the press.   In addition to all this he has been the only financial agent of the National Association for the raising of funds to sustain his work.   These collections, made at irregular intervals, amid other duties, have amounted during the past six years to about $20,000, or but $3500 a year for expenses of every description, and he has seldom received the yearly salary of $4000 originally pledged to him as secretary."

Notwithstanding this record of invaluable service, the year 1876 proved to be an unfortunate one for raising money and obtaining Congressional appropriations to carry on the national and international work.   The Stockholm Prison Congress was not absolutely settled on for place and date; and a senator from the Pacific coast, who for one reason or another opposed the appropriation, was able to defeat it.   Dr. Wines, writing late in July, 1876, said:

"As to the loss of our appropriation at Washington: Senator X. made a speech against it.   He reasoned skilfully upon the uncertainty of there being any congress, because there is to be none this year,—the time originally appointed.   He painted the United States Commissioner as wandering about Europe in search of a prison congress, and probably being obliged to return without finding it, after spending thousands of dollars in the search. This was his principal weapon, and there was nobody that knew how to turn it."

The election of General Hayes as president in the winter of 1876–77 placed in authority at Washington a sincere friend of Dr. Wines and of prison reform; and the needful appropriation was made in the first year of his presidency. After retiring to private life in 1881, and when the National Prison Association, which slumbered for a few years in consequence of the death of Dr. Wines, was revived in 1882, General Hayes became its president, and we had the honor and pleasure of meeting with him in that capacity for several years. This association is now active, but its finances are not yet on that secure basis which Dr. Wines suggested in 1876, and which, had he been a younger man, he would doubtless have established, in the manner suggested by him in a letter to Dr. F. H. Wines in the summer of 1876, on the subject of the appeal to the country for funds, of which an extract has here been given. Writing from Irvington, July 23, 1876, he said:

"I have delayed so long to answer your two letters, partly because I do not know what to say, and partly (perhaps chiefly) because, from the depressing influence of the weather and the circumstances, I seem to have lost all elasticity and spring of both mind and body. The proposed scheme can be really carried into effect, if at all, only, in my opinion, by personal effort; and probably the persons cannot be found in the different states who will or can give to it the necessary attention and effort. *My* hands are necessarily tied in an undertaking of this sort; and from your relation to me, you are scarcely more free to take an active part in it than I am. So, upon the whole, I suppose it must be given up.

"Of late I have been thinking of another plan, which, if it can be carried into effect, will be better, because it will give a permanent foundation to the work of the National Prison Association, and enable it to live and move forward in the coming years. It is, through the co-operation of the pastors and other leading citizens, to make a thorough canvass of New York for membership subscriptions of $5, with the distinct understanding that they are to be regarded as annual subscriptions, payable each year in the month of May, till formally withdrawn. This work, by using a carriage for the purpose, I think I might still undertake myself; and it seems to me that 1000 subscriptions of this sort, perhaps more, might readily be secured in the city of New York. With this as a basis, the same work might then be pushed in other large cities, as Boston, Philadelphia, etc. When the East shall have been pretty well secured for the work in this way, (that is, upon this moderate *individual* scale,) it might then be pushed in the West with better hope of success.

"If we could get throughout the country 4000 annual memberships, it would put the work on a solid and enduring basis; because it would not be difficult to make up with new subscriptions the annual losses occurring by death and withdrawals. Even 2000 such memberships would give the Association a living income.

"I have long been in favor of getting good, earnest working women upon our Board of Directors; *and that must be done.* Women are more sympathetic than men, and they have more leisure for such work. A score or two enlisted in the work of collecting funds would, I believe, accomplish much in this way. These, then, are my present thoughts.

"There is a special objection to undertaking the proposed scheme just now; it is that we are entering upon a presidential election, and the rich men of both parties will be called upon for large subscriptions to carry on the canvass."

This was an excellent plan, but the time was unfavorable. Besides the excitement of the general election, there were individual exigencies in 1876. Mr. Brockway was beginning his great work in Elmira, and had little time or thought for anything else. I was ending a two years' chairmanship of the State Board of Charities, declining a reappointment, in consequence of unsuitable conditions at the Tewksbury State Almshouse; and I was also pledged to promote the infant years of the National Conference of Charities and Correction, which had not become the wide-reaching organization it is now; while the Social Science Association also claimed my attention as secretary. Other friends of Dr. Wines were also occupied with other thoughts, and could only give him their sympathy and occasional aid. Consequently, his plan was never put in force, and his later years were rather hampered by pecuniary cares.

In this particular Dr. Wines had the usual fortune of men of generosity who render public service; but he was exempt from the calumny that is often the lot of such benefactors. He was, of course, subject to the misconstruction and impertinence that is unavoidable in these careers. Dr. Theodore Dwight, already mentioned, who was his companion in a tour of inspection of American prisons, under the authority of the New York Prison Association, and by order of the state of New York, in 1865–66, once mentioned an incident of their visit to a large prison of the middle West. The warden had thought it might be of advantage to his men, and certainly courteous to his distinguished guests, if he should assemble the whole body of prisoners in the chapel for an hour or two, to hear remarks by the visitors from New York. Dr. Wines was addressing the convicts as his friends, and had their close attention, when the prison contractor entered the room, and rudely interrupted the speaker, saying, "Doctor, are you aware that you are addressing these men *on my time?*" Earlier in his official service, and while Horatio Seymour, who had occasioned some censure by addressing rioters in New York City as "My friends," was governor of New York, Dr. Wines was once visiting Sing Sing prison in company with Governor Seymour. Hearing him address the convicts in his usual manner, as I have heard him in several prisons, the governor remarked with a smile, "Doctor, I believe you and I are the only persons in this state who consider convicts as our friends." It was not literally true, but the number was certainly small. On this point his son says:

"Such faith and such charity,—such a root and such a stem,— could not but culminate in the bright flower of Hope. Dr. Charlton T. Lewis has said that in the management of prisons, and in all our dealings with convicts, we have to choose between fear and hope as motives to action. Fear degrades and hope uplifts. The penal codes of the past were founded on fear; those of the future will be based on hope. The gradual supplanting of fear by hope is a barometric test of the advance of modern civilization. The soul of Dr. Wines was alive with hope; it shone in his countenance, it breathed in every word from his lips or his pen. He inspired hope in all who came under his influence; it radiated from his personality. Men lighted their candles afresh at his flame; their fainting strength renewed as they drank of his spirit.

"But for this serene and rational optimism the examples of other men's labors in the past, and the record of their achievements would not have so appealed to him; men like Montesinos and Obermaier, and Maconochie, like Clement XI and Vilain XIV and Beccaria and John Howard. He gloried in calling attention to them. They were in his thought harbingers of the dawn of a new day. But for this he would not have been so ready to accept the teachings of Whately and Marsangy, of Davenport Hill and Crofton,—pioneers of human thought, messengers proclaiming a new evangel. Nor would he otherwise have manifested such sympathy with our own Brockway, who sought to create a new era of hope for the condemned outcasts of the world, by the introduction of the indeterminate sen-

Ellen C Johnson

tence in the New York Code, and who demonstrated the practicability and the great value of this innovation in criminal law. A genius and a hero, Brockway stands alone among our prison officials, and the memory of what he achieved can never die. Yet, but for my father the Elmira prison would not have been, nor the Sherborn reformatory for women; while the juvenile court, the probation officer and the parole system for first offenders (children or adults) might have been delayed for a generation. Other men *might have* done what he did, but *he* did it; not alone, but with the aid of the few who stood by him while alive, and the many who have followed in his steps since his death. Count di Foresti, an Italian Councillor, has said of him, 'To Dr. Wines, more than to any other individual, is due the great reform which is the glory of the latter half of the nineteenth century.' "

Such is the verdict of filial regard and of disinterested friendship; and if impartial history shall modify it, there will still be enough glory due him in the field where he exhausted his strength without chilling his hope. In spite of discouragements, which by 1876 were the weightier because Dr. Wines had become threescore and ten, and was suffering from a serious lameness, he continued his efforts, and gave his last toil to the compilation of that volume which carries his name down as author of a book that nobody else could have written,—his State of Prisons and of Child-Saving Institutions in the Civilized World. This work, of more than 700 pages, he lived to complete, though not to see it through the press of his friend the Cambridge printer, John Wilson, at whose house he died, in December, 1879. It was a death unexpected, but for which his whole life had been a preparation.

THE AMERICAN REFORMATORY PRISON SYSTEM

By Z. R. BROCKWAY

THE American reformatory prison system is based on the principle of protection in place of punishment; on the principle of the indeterminate sentence instead of the usual time sentence; and on the purpose of rehabilitation of offenders rather than their restraint by intimidation. This theory works a change of attitude on the part of the state, a change of the relation of the offenders, and involves a different prison procedure. Together with punishments by imprisonment, every other form of punishment for crimes has, doubtless, to some extent, if vaguely, contained a purpose of protection, yet other aims subversive of protection have unduly influenced criminal legislation and the prison practice: a hateful temper bred of gross superstition attached to the punishments in defense of the gods and to gain their favor; punishment inflicted, assumptively, to equalize the world-balance of diffused morality; to the measuring out of pains in order to meet some notion of impossible justice; punishments to mend the fractured laws and vindicate the state; to intimidate offenders and the tempted and thus deter from crimes; and, by the sufferings of punishments, to induce a salutary reforming penitence. This hateful spirit, under the name retribution, but with somewhat softened severity, characterized the penitentiary system of the last century. But during the latter half of that century better biological and moral conceptions, largely due to the investigations and publications of Charles Darwin, enabled the enactment of more rational criminal laws. The New York law (1877) eliminates the punishment theory, and laws patterned after it, since enacted in other states, also exclude the punitive principle. Thus, in theory and gradually in fact the attitude of the state is becoming changed from its former vengefulness to that of dignified serenity, neither vindictive nor lovelorn, but firmly and nobly corrective.

It is not attempted, now, either accurately to estimate or, in any direct way, artfully to influence the unrelated inward moral state of the prisoners. It is not denied that idiosyncrasies influence the individual conduct and that these are subject to changes; nor is it doubted that every human impulse and action is, in some way, related to God and the universe of things. But, since the real relation is inscrutable to any but the individual himself within his own variant range of self-consciousness, that relation cannot be deciphered nor properly directed by the legislature, the courts, or by officers of the law. Of course the majority, at any time, may fix the bounds of allowable behavior with due regard to the social welfare, and may erect a standard of social-moral right and wrong; but the morality of motives cannot be so determined. Also this criterion of the social demand may itself be reversed or modified by change of time and place and immediate condition; and the very terms Good and Evil are always of capricious significance. "Evils as they are termed are goods to the unjust, and only evils to the just, and goods are truly good to the good but evil to the evil." The effect of conduct does not reliably reveal the real moral motive, for well-intentioned conduct may prove injurious and evil intentions may lead to benefits. Recently one of my former prisoners died after his twenty years of good service and behavior on the editorial staff of a leading metropolitan newspaper. When, as a prisoner, he was compelled to change his daily conduct he at once seized upon the educational advantages at hand to prepare for a notable criminal career. He never suffered any conscious revolution of motive, but gradually and imperceptibly his inward intention, rated evil, faded out. Then, like an aeronaut in an unballasted balloon, he floated unconsciously into the higher social and so higher moral altitude.

None can gainsay Plato's definition that, "he is good whose soul is good. . . . The virtuous principle is intellectual, not emotional or voluntary. . . . It is knowledge that determines the will." If to this we add Aristotle's criterion of virtue, that, "virtue is a habit accompanied with deliberate preference in the relative mean defined by reason as a prudent man defines," we may accept Lord Bacon's declaration that, "there is no man doeth wrong for the wrong's sake but to purchase for himself a pleasure or profit." In the depths of human action thus fathomed there seems to disappear any trace of intrinsic unrelated morality of conduct.

It is, therefore, a principle of the newer penology that the state shall not judge the heart's intentions, and shall not designedly trespass upon the mystical field of the soul's moral relations; but, instead, shall remain devoted to the rational regulation of the prisoner's conduct with sole regard to the public security.

Having thus relinquished pursuit of mystic morality because it is deemed impossible correctly to estimate intrinsic moral quality, the pursuit of administrative justice is for a similar reason also withdrawn. Justice Fry, who firmly held to the doctrine of just punishment for crimes, admitted that the doctrine takes root "in the endeavor to find a fitness of pain to sin which the world does not satisfactorily supply," and, in his dilemma, advocated that always the greatest conceivable injury of the various crimes should govern the amount of penalty. He would strike offenders hard enough to compensate the greatest possible evil, and so fully recompense the lesser wrong. This is a vain random reach for justice disregardful of involved severity.

Doubtless through all sentient being there exists an instinctive sense named or misnamed justice; but it has a movable interpretation according to the man and the circumstances: it is a chimera in whose name unfair may appear as fair and wrong take on the guise of right. "Divine equity gives to the greater more and to the inferior less (supposedly) in proportion to the nature of each." "Justice is always the distribution of natural equity among unequals," but what human intelligence is sufficient for these things? Our human equity and clemency, esteemed equitable, must infract the strict rule of justice.

Notwithstanding the world-wide similarity in terminology of crimes there is great dissimilarity of the penalties attached; and, within the discretionary margin of the laws, different magistrates and the same magistrate at different times fortuitously change the notion of desert and vary penalties. Casual circumstances and personal peculiarities and moods so affect the judgment of men as to preclude uniformity of rule or practice. And so different is the experience of imprisonment upon different prisoners—one's privation another's privilege—that uniformity itself would subvert the intended equality. The blindfold image of justice is most appropriate, for it not only typifies the intended impartiality but also the impossibility for a correct adjustment of the scales.

It is believed that the nearest possible approach to criminal justice is reached unsought—when it is left to nature; that "according to the natural order of things, the way of the transgressor *is* (already) hard"; and, that nature's truest requital for every phase of morbidity—whether of the body, the mind, or the social

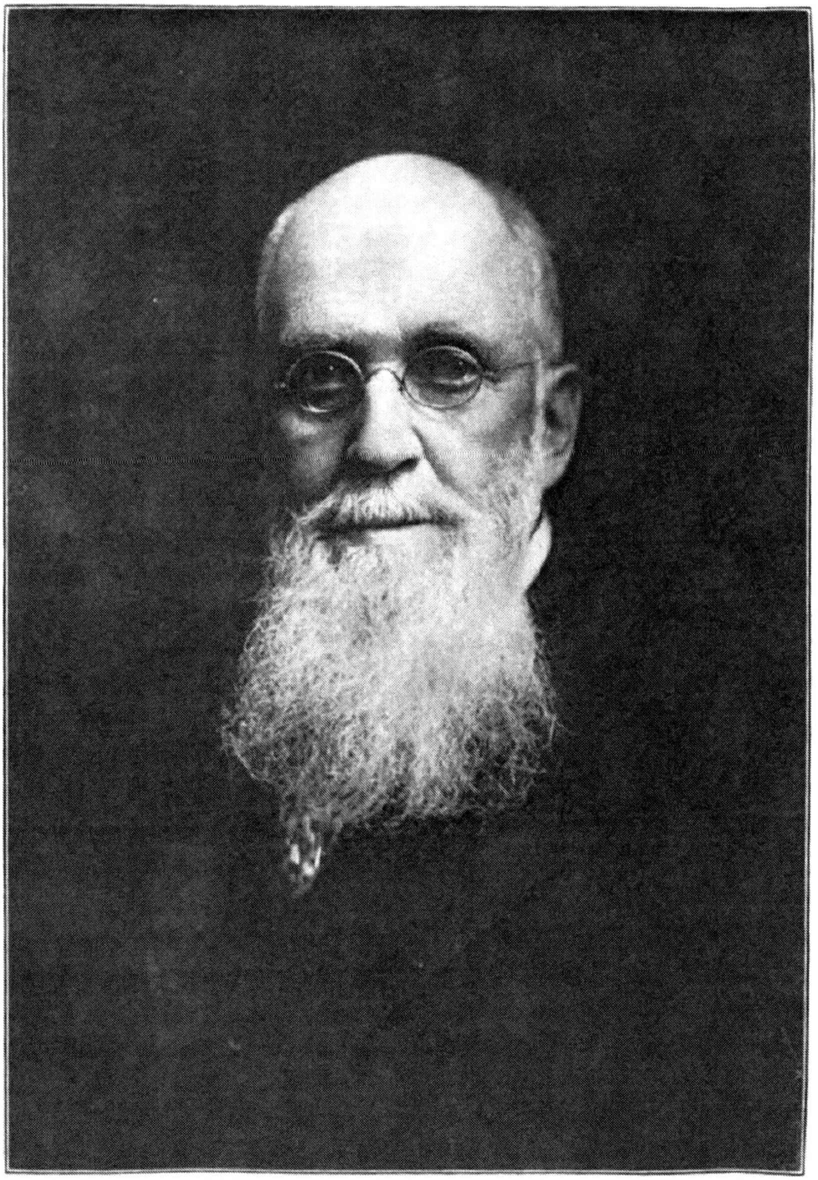

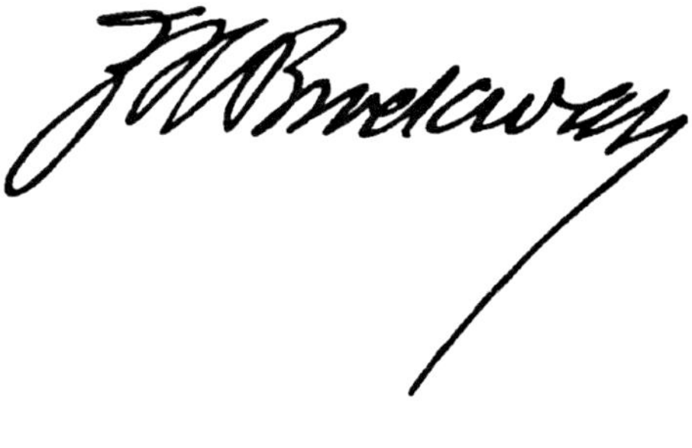

status—is found in the necessary accompanying pains of the process of recovery.

Little reliance is placed in the deterrent principle alone for restraint of crimes or regulation of the conduct and character of offenders. No doubt the experience of pain and pleasure possesses a certain educational value, teaching what is profitable and the reverse; but fear is at best but the beginning of wisdom and fear always evidences and usually effects a reduced and inconstant mental condition. Welfare and adversity, antithetically related, supplement each other, but there is a wide difference of the mood and degree of stability when the one or the other is pursued. Avoiding adversity is as voyaging among reefs and breakers in fear of wreck, while pursuit of welfare is like following the charted ocean path voyaging wide at sea. Strong and virtuous characters, well established, do not need and are rarely conscious of amenability to existing penal laws; weak characters easily get themselves enmeshed and stranded; the habitually wayward are unmindful and disregardful of legal penalties; and the small ratio of all the criminals included in the class of deliberate and professional offenders brave penalties and derive zest therefrom.

The bulk of prisoners consists of those who are weak, habitually wayward, and unreflective persons—who do not readily connect, in consciousness, a present infelicitous experience with its remoter cause and consequence. Certainty and celerity of detection and arrest or sudden confrontment with an immediate menacing force may call the halt; but such temporary deterrence cannot effect a permanent change of habitual tendency.

Among the many thousands of this inconsiderate class of prisoners that I have investigated, none is now recalled to memory who, antecedent to his crime, took serious account of the possible consequences. And a habitual criminal, a fair type of his class, on his discharge remarked: "I mean now to quit, *if I get on all right*, but not because I am afraid of prison. I am a man who is never afraid." Such men are no more hindered from crimes by the liability to be imprisoned, than railroad travelers are hindered from traveling because there are occasionally fatal railroad accidents. The professional class feels imprisonment to be accidental rather than naturally consequential. One, worrying over his imprisonment because of its interference with his customary associations and excitements, solemnly said: "This is a judgment on me for leaving my own line.

So long as I kept steadily at the sneak line I was prospered, but when I tackled burglary my bad luck began."

Ineffective too, for deterrence, is the supposed disgrace of a criminal conviction and committal to prison. The generality of prisoners do not feel any disgrace. A certain tone of respectability colors the prisoner's conception of crime, which is partly a product of his knowledge of current commercial irregularities, corrupt partisan politics, frauds committed in high places with avoidance of convictions, and jubilant newspaper notices of crimes and criminals. The very notoriety gained compensates and so shields the shallow character from any painful feeling of disgrace. His insensibility and *sangfroid* are further ministered to by the effect of long-delayed trials and the character of the trial; illuminated newspaper detailed accounts of the prisoner's personal appearance and bearing; the gladiatorial show of the legal combat of which the prisoner forms the central figure; the artifice and insincerity of the defense; the excusing and even extolling address of the defending counsel; these together with the chummy attention of jail and court servitors, jail visitors, and salvation seekers, excite the prisoner's self-importance—a new and gratifying consciousness perhaps—displacing the imaginary feeling of disgrace which the inexperienced onlooker himself seems to see. All this show has, too, an evil influence on the common observant crowd. Deterrence is also diminished or destroyed by the previous habitual associations of the average prisoner. In his accustomed haunts, arrests, police-court arraignment, station-house and jail confinement are jokingly mentioned and often considered an interesting personal distinction. Even a color of the heroic tinges the habitué who has actually "done time."

Increased severities either of statutory penalties or conditions of imprisonment cannot evoke and entail a salutary deterrent influence. The history of criminal punishments, the world over, shows that the most crimes accompanied the greatest severity and that they diminished as mitigation took place. Only transitory effects are produced by severities. The public sense as it becomes familiar rises, in due time, to the new conditions—automatically adjusts itself, thus neutralizing the intended effect. And mere severity of the prison régime reacts upon the prisoners with actual, if unconscious, brutalizing effect with diminishing consciousness of apparent discomfort. Beyond the possible temporary stimulation of alternative pain and pleasure experiences, deterrent measures are disused and the deterrent principle itself is disesteemed.

That phase of altruism which, in exercise, holds benevolence to others in subordination to self-interest, is dominantly present in our prison system. This altruistic sentiment exists in the protective purpose of the law which establishes it, pervades the administrative polity in all its details, and gains impulse with its sympathetic reward in individual reclamations achieved. But in its active agency the principle is a rational characteristic, not a mere sentimentalism. It is devoted to prompt enduring welfare rather than passing enjoyments. The paramount object always in view is a collective benefit sought and wrought through the well-being of individuals, and the individual welfare through a better adjustment to ordinary communal relations. In use and inculcation it is ego-altruism, for the personified state seeks her own advantage, and the prisoners pursue, whether voluntarily or compulsorily, their own advancement. The benefits are mutual—an increase of ultimate mutual abiding happiness. The principle of the New York law, as of the other laws patterned after it, notwithstanding their marring limitations, constitutes a radical change of spirit in criminal jurisprudence. A distinguished jurist has publicly declared that the change "is destined to change men's habits of thought concerning crime and the attitude of society toward criminals; to rewrite from end to end every penal code in Christendom; and to modify and ennoble the fundamental law of every state." It is a change from a plane where feeling sways, to the loftier realm and reign of wisdom. It is conceded that no human agency can operate quite free from emotional influence, but the emotions are always a dangerous element in law-making and governing. To this vitiating source are traced the undue severities of all time, and also the supersentimentality which now is, perhaps, the most serious menace of our prison system. The true course is a restrained and rational altruism—a brooding beneficence, impartial, and ever striving to promote the interdependent collective and individual welfare, subordinating, as needs be, transitory pleasure to the more permanent and the nobler good.

The attitude of the state to our prison system is thus shown to be: negative as to any punitive intention; negative as to administering exact justice for its own sake; negative as to the expectation of deterrence by intimidation; neutral as to regulating the mystical individual moral relations of prisoners; and a qualified attitude as to altruism. The state's affirmative attitude will subsequently casually appear.

This better attitude on the part of the organized state effects also a corresponding change of the relation of offenders toward the state. The change is real, though, for a time, it may not be prized by the prisoners or noticed by the administering authorities. Formerly, the fundamental relation was antagonistic—necessarily so, for under the definite-sentence plan the ever-present desire for release must be opposed by the prison government until expiration of the prescribed period of time. Now, under the new form of prison sentence, the desires of both parties are in accord—the prisoner wants to go and the government wishes the same; but only upon certain conditions. Here contradiction is likely to arise, but it soon of itself disappears, as regards the majority of prisoners, and the remainder of them, when they discern the peaceable fruits of the opposition, change to an accordance, which is often succeeded by a pleasing gratitude. While an outside observer might never note this changed relation by any change in the general appearance, it actually exists.

It is essentially the principle, "community of interest," which is the germinal basis of most of human concord. Its well-nigh magical effect is seen in states held in union under federal control; civil divisions of states bound in fealty to each other and the state government; communities made orderly; family integrity preserved; and it is seen in enduring common friendships of individuals. The inner shrine of community of interest is of course self-interest, but grown large enough to observe its outward dependence. Whenever self-interest is so wisely directed that self-indulgence is self-restrained in the interest of remoter better benefits; when individual consciousness enlarges to "colonial consciousness"; when the principle of interdependency dawns, then is born that mutuality which is indestructible and socially most desirable.

As to the "criminaloid" class distributed through communities, it is not expected that any striking demonstration or formal statistics shall soon reveal a decided change of attitude. But, with the certainty of cause and effect, improvement in tone and probity must occur in response to the new spirit of the criminal laws; the new purpose of the courts and court procedure; and to the renovated, more rational state-prison system; for to effect such changes necessitates a change in the general public sentiment, at once the final arbiter and most powerful molding social force.

AFFIRMATIVE PRINCIPLES

Under the indeterminate sentence it is intended, either by restraints or reformations, that prisoners once committed to our prisons shall then and thereafter be permanently withdrawn from the ranks of offenders. And the inherent evils of imprisonment are such that only genuine reformations can afford the intended protection.

To accomplish such protective reformations it is necessary, preliminarily, to fix upon the standard of reformatory requirement, to adopt the criterion, to organize and perfect the plan of procedure. The standard fixed is, simply, such habitual behavior, during actual and constructive custody, as fairly comports with the legitimate conduct of the orderly free social class to which the prisoner properly belongs in the community where he should and probably will dwell. The criterion of fitness for release is precisely the same performance subjected to tests while under prison tutelage by the merit and demerit marking system which, somewhat modified in strenuousness and with addition of its monetary valuations, is similar to the marking system of our National Military Academy; and tested, also, by proper supervision during a period of practical freedom while on parole. Both the standard and criterion must be somewhat pliant to meet the variant capacity of communities to absorb incongruous elements and because each prisoner must be fitted for his appropriate industrial and social niche.

It cannot too often be stated that prisoners are of inferior class and that our prison system is intended for treatment of defectives. Passing now, the somatic, psychic, and other anthropological data at hand in support of the above statement; premising that the defectiveness is of the bodily substance and form, in the mental capacity and its irregularity, and in emotional perversity, the aggregate of which in any large company of miscellaneous prisoners is always in excess of the defectiveness of the same number of free inhabitants; the inferiority of prisoners may, for the present convenience, be generalized under three divisions as follows:

1. Those who, in childhood and adolescence, are apparently normal, but closely scanned reveal peculiarities which, resulting in pernicious habits and crimes, develop later into some phase and degree of dementia.

2. Those clearly defective but with considerable normal mental power preserved. The mental defect is specific, in some one par-

ticular, such as the logical faculty. For instance, they are unable to master arithmetical examples which others of similar general intelligence easily grasp—they are deficient in judgment rather than depraved. At every trying crisis of life they are sure to "go wrong."

3. Those possessed of all the usual faculties except the regulative one, which is out of gear—not absent but disconnected and unavailable.

At the Elmira Reformatory when such inquiries were most searchingly made, it was discovered that out of the total inferior mass, numbering fifteen hundred men, five hundred were so very defective that they were temporarily withdrawn from the regular reformatory routine and were subjected to special renovating and stimulating treatment in order to bring them up to the standard of regular training.

Viewed *en masse*, prisoners are characterless; they lack positiveness, are without an inward dominant purpose. They are unduly influenced by instant, trivial circumstances, or by hidden transient impulses. The most dangerous, therefore interesting, sane young prisoner I have ever known, abnormally cunning, well illustrates this ungeared characteristic. He said, "I know, sometimes, I am what you call good and then again bad. In my good moods I am ashamed that I was ever bad; and equally in the bad mood I am ashamed of ever being good." His alternate self-disapprobation had no content of intellectual stability or moral responsibility. Although he was only eighteen years old, he was by heredity and habit a confirmed and desperate criminal. Fortunately he died while imprisoned.

Morbidity of body, mind, or the moral sense diminishes individual industrial efficiency and in turn narrows opportunity; leading on to indolence, privations, dissipation, and crimes. The source is held to be in physiological defects; the declaration of Ribot and other eminent psychologists is credited as true, that "The character is but the psychological expression of a certain organized body drawing from it its peculiar coloring, its special tone, its relative permanence." The nature and habit of living matter must exert such powerful influence upon volition that the conception of the individual will, dominating and unaffected by constituents and conditions of the total personality, is deemed no longer tenable. On the contrary it is confidently believed that, quite independent of the immediate conscious choice and will of the prisoner, agencies foreign to himself may be made effective to change his character; that the material living substance of being is malleable under the simultaneous reciprocal play of scientifically directed bodily and mental exercises; and that the agencies are irresistible.

The doctrine of the interaction of body and mind is so well established and altogether reasonable that there is no need here to guard against a fancied materialistic tendency. Rather there is occasion to guard against too fanciful idealism. There may be a grain of truth in the remark of George Eliot: "In proportion as the thoughts of men are removed from the earth in which they live to an invisible world they are led to neglect their duty to each other." Dr. E. H. Hartwell says: "Bodily actions demand our first consideration since without them mental power, artistic feeling, and spiritual insight cannot be made to answer any earthly purpose." To this extent the principle of determinism is espoused; and unhesitatingly alleged free will is invaded. By rational procedure the social in place of antisocial tendencies are trained and made dominant. Thus the man is redeemed.

The original and preferable principle for organizing our reformatories is that of local-centralism. The state legislative control should be limited to a broadly outlined enabling act in harmony, of course, with the general state penological policy, but leaving much freedom of initiative to the local institutional authority—the board of managers. This local authority, in turn, had best limit its functions to fixing, changing, and supervising the administrative polity, leaving the immediate executive management to the resident chief officer—the prison governor. The governing principle of a reformatory must needs be, within certain constituted rights, of monarchical type, but exercised with much discretionary flexibility; approximately as a community under martial law, where both civic and military functions obtain. Such a blend is practicable and useful; indeed it is requisite.

. It is important that the subordinate staff shall remain subordinate; that each officer and employe shall confine his reformative activity to his own assigned specific duties. The chiefs of the several departments may properly constitute a coterie for the study of prison science, for consultations and advising, but they should each act entirely within his own particular sphere and under authoritative direction. And the rank and file of the staff should remain as the soldier, and never independently assume the rôle of the reformer. No outside training school for prison officers can ever supply a suitable reformatory prison staff. Both the selection and training of assistants is best when controlled by the governing head of each reformatory. The civil service system wards off some improper demands for appointments but at the same time restricts the range of selection and hinders prompt sifting out of the unfit. Its serviceableness, however, preponderates.

So delicate and easily disturbed is the generative reformative process that outsiders—the would-be special philanthropists, professional religious revivalists, advertising salvationists—should generally be excluded; or if at all admitted to any participation, their ministrations should, under the direction of the governor, be made to fit into the established culture course. Even a resident official chaplain may inadvertently interfere with the germination of reformations. I have found the resident chaplain to be less desirable for religious ministrations than an itinerant service. One mind, and that the mind of the resident reformatory governor, must have and hold and wield every operating agency—impel, steady, and direct the whole and every item of the procedure. Such completeness of control requires an exacting and strenuous disciplinary régime which for effectiveness must include the principle and exercise of coercion.

A majority of prisoners instinctively respond to the inherent persuasion of the combined agencies; and of those who do not a majority readily respond to the moral coerciveness of the agencies. Some, only a small ratio, do not respond at first, except to some form of corporal coercion—some bodily inconvenience and discomfort. These, the irresponsive, who for the good of the prison community and for the public safety most need reformation, should not be neglected nor relegated to incorrigibility until every possible effort has unavailingly been made for their recovery. The advantages proffered are, naturally, not appreciated until availed of and enjoyed. Some cannot adopt and carry into execution measures calculated for their own good without the intervention of coercion. Adjustment to environment, even if it is compulsory, leads from the avoidance of bodily risks to the avoidance of social risks and thus to non-criminal habits, which, when duly formed, no longer need the prop of compulsion. "Compulsion first, then the sense of duty, automatic, the connection expanding into knowledge of ethical habit, then the habit creating conviction, then relations, then the capacity for general ideas." Thus coercion is often 'of initial indispensable educational value. Not infrequently prisoners who were assisted out of a stalled condition by means of an applied physical shock have expressed to the manager their grateful acknowledgments therefor. Many

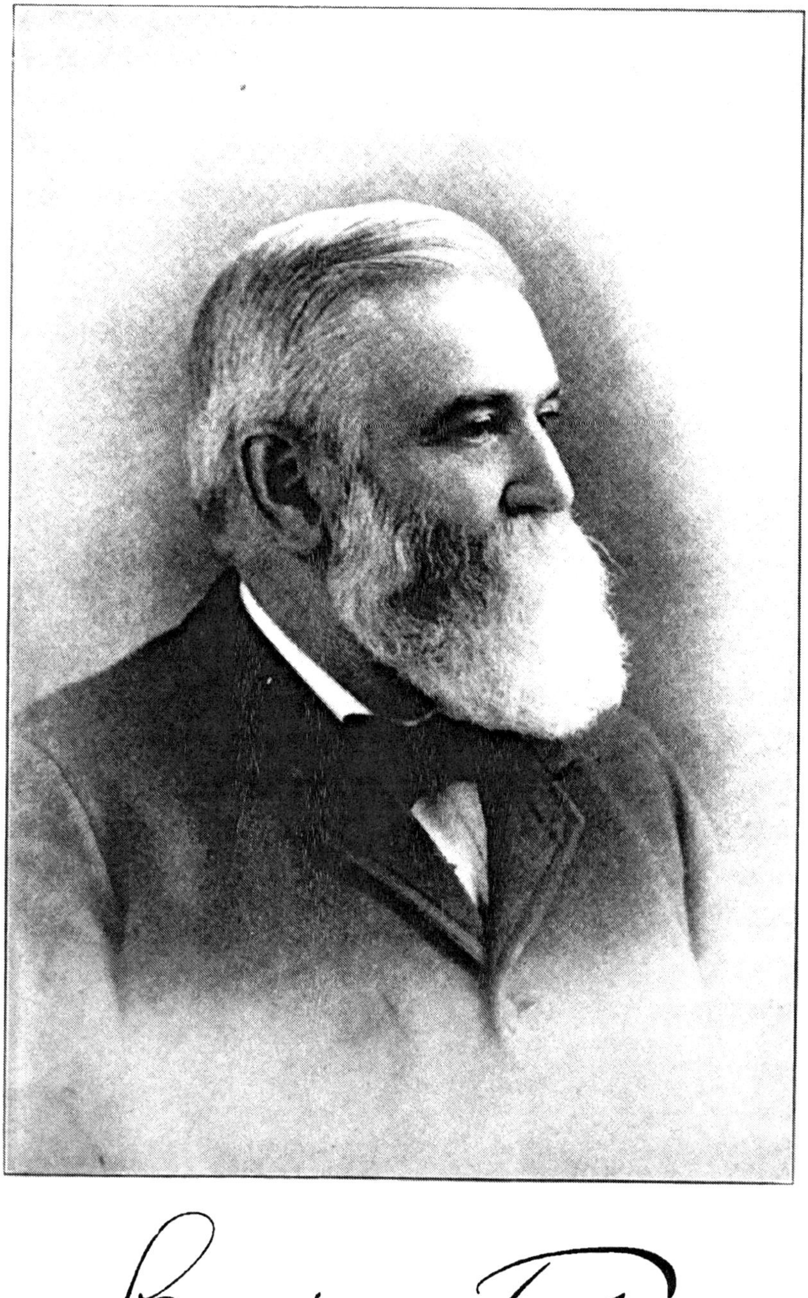
Gardiner Tufts

such prisoners who without the physical treatment would have remained long in the ranks of the incorrigible have, after the simple treatment, developed well and ultimately established themselves in the confidence of their community as reliable, useful inhabitants.

There should be within the reformatory course a reserve of penological surgery similar in beneficent design and in scientific use to the minor surgery of the healing art of medicine.

THE PROCEDURE

Efficiency of the reformatory procedure depends on completeness of its mechanism composed of means and motives; on the force, balance, and skill with which the means and motives are brought to bear upon the mass, the groups, and the individual prisoners; and not a little on the pervading tone of the reformatory establishment. A mere enumeration of means and motives of the mechanism is, briefly, as follows:

1. The material structural establishment itself. This should be salubriously situated and, preferably, in a suburban locality. The general plan and arrangements should be those of the Auburn Prison System plan, but modified and modernized as at the Elmira Reformatory; and ten per cent of the cells might well be constructed like those in the Pennsylvania System structures. The whole should be supplied with suitable modern sanitary appliances and with abundance of natural and artificial light.

2. Clothing for the prisoners, not degradingly distinctive but uniform, yet fitly representing the respective grades or standing of the prisoners. Similarly as to the supply of bedding which, with rare exceptions, should include sheets and pillow slips. For the sake of health, self-respect, and the cultural influence of the general appearance, scrupulous cleanliness should be maintained and the prisoners kept appropriately groomed.

3. A liberal prison dietary designed to promote vigor. Deprivation of food, by a general regulation, for a penal purpose, is deprecated; it is a practice only tolerable in very exceptional instances as a tentative prison disciplinary measure. On the other hand, the giving of food privileges for favor or in return for some special serviceableness rendered to the prison authorities is inadvisable and usually becomes a troublesome precedent. More variety, better quality and service of foods for the higher grades of prisoners is serviceably allowable even to the extent of the à la carte method, whenever the prisoners, under the wage system, have the requisite

credit balance for such expenditure. Also, for some of the very lowest intractable prisoners, a special, scientifically adjusted dietary, with reference to the constituent nutritive quality, and as to quantities and manner of serving, may be used to lay a foundation for their improvement, otherwise unattainable.

4. All the modern appliances for scientific physical culture: a gymnasium completely equipped with baths and apparatus; and facilities for field athletics. On their first admission to the reformatory all are assigned to the gymnasium to be examined, renovated, and quickened; the more defective of them are longer detained, and the decadents are held under this physical treatment until the intended effect is accomplished. When the population of the Elmira Reformatory was 1,400, the daily attendance at the gymnasium averaged 429.

5. Facilities for special manual training sufficient for about one-third of the resident population. The aim is to aid educational advancement in the trades and school of letters. This special manual training, which at Elmira Reformatory included, at one time, 500 of the prisoners, covered in addition to other exercises in other departments mechanical and freehand drawing; sloyd in wood and metals; cardboard constructive form work; clay modeling; cabinet making; chipping and filing; and iron molding.

6. Trades instruction based on the needs and capacities of individual prisoners, conducted to a standard of perfect work and speed performance that insures the usual wage value to their services. When there are a thousand or more prisoners confined, thirty-six trades and branches of trades may be usefully taught.

7. A regimental military organization of the prisoners with a band of music, swords for officers, and dummy guns for the rank and file of prisoners. The military membership should include all the able bodied prisoners and all available citizens of the employes. The regular army tactics, drill, and daily dress parade should be observed.

8. School of letters with a curriculum that reaches from an adaptation of the kindergarten, and an elementary class in the English language for foreigners unacquainted with it, through various school grades up to the usual high-school course; and, in addition, special classes in college subjects and, limitedly, a popular lecture course touching biography, history, literature, ethics, with somewhat of science and philosophy.

9. A well-selected library for circulation, consultation, and

under proper supervision, for occasional semi-social use. The reading room may be made available for worthy and appreciative prisoners.

10. The weekly institutional newspaper, in lieu of all outside newspapers, edited and printed by the prisoners under due censorship.

11. Recreating and diverting entertainments for the mass of the population, provided in the great auditorium; not any vaudeville nor minstrel shows, but entertainments of such a class as the middle cultured people of a community would enjoy; stereopticon instructive exhibitions and explanations, vocal and instrumental music, and elocution, recitation, and oratory for inspiration and uplift.

12. Religious opportunities, optional, adapted to the hereditary, habitual and preferable denominational predilection of the individual prisoners.

13. Definitely planned, carefully directed, emotional occasions; not summoned, primarily, for either instruction, diversion, nor, specifically, for a common religious impression, but, figuratively, for a kind of irrigation. As a descending mountain torrent may irrigate and fertilize an arid plain, scour out the new channels, and change even the physical aspect, so emotional excitation may inundate the human personality with dangerous and deforming effect if misdirected; but when skilfully handled it may work salutary changes in consciousness, in character, and in that which is commonly thought to be the will. Esthetic delight verges on and enkindles the ethical sense, and ethical admiration tends to worthy adoration. The arts, which in essence are the external expression of the idea— the revelation of the reality—have too exclusively remained the heritage of the wealthy and wise; they must ultimately fulfil their God-given design—ennoblement of the common people. "We shall come upon the great canon 'art for man's sake' instead of the little canon 'art for art's sake.'" I have sufficiently experimented with music, pictures, and the drama, in aid of our rational reformatory endeavors, to affirm confidently that art may become an effective means in the scheme for reformation.

In addition to the foregoing items the prisoners are constantly under pressure of intense motives that bear directly upon the mind. The indeterminateness of the sentence breeds discontent, breeds purposefulness, and prompts to new exertion. Captivity, always irksome, is now unceasingly so because of the uncertainty of its duration; because the duty and responsibility of shortening it and of modifying any undesirable present condition of it devolve upon the prisoner himself, and, again, because of the active exactions of the standard and criterion to which he must attain.

Naturally, these circumstances serve to arouse and rivet the attention upon the many matters of the daily conduct which so affect the rate of progress toward the coveted release. Such vigilance, so devoted, supplies a motive equivalent to that of the fixed idea. Then the vicissitudes of the daily experience incite to prudence; and the practice of prudence educates the understanding. Enlightenment thus acquired opens to view the attractive vista where truth and fairness dwell. Habitual careful attention with accompanying expectancy and appropriate exertion and resultant clarified vision constitute a habitus not consistent with criminal tendencies.

At present, owing to absence of exact knowledge of the modes of the mutual dependence of mind and body, it is not possible to wield, with perfect balance, the contingent means and motives, nor accurately adjust the operation of the scheduled elements of the joint composition—the total mechanism. But the fact of interdependence is so well established and so much of the method has been learned from experiment that the principles of mental physiology or physiological psychology should be applied in the reformatory procedure. It is uniformly conceded that the nervous system, centering in the brain, is the organ or instrument of the mind; that the mind is a real being which can be acted upon by the brain and which can act in the body through the brain. For the sake of the authority and simplicity of statement of this elementary biological truth I quote from Professor Ladd as follows:

"The mind behaves as it does because of the constitution and behavior of the molecules of the brain; and the brains behave as they do behave because of the nature and activities of the mind. Each acts in view of the other. The action of each accounts for the other. . . . The physical process consists in the action of the appropriate modes of physical energy upon the nervous and end-apparatus of sense, . . . brought to bear through mechanical contrivances carrying impulses to the mind. And psychical energies are transmuted into physiological processes—a nerve commotion within the nervous system thence propagated along the tracks and diffusing over the various areas of the nervous system."

This brief statement of the dual human constitution, the

102

condition of whose changeable and changing elements at any time so determines conduct, points to the possibility and so to the duty of effecting salutary alterations in the personality of prisoners by means of skilfully directed exercises of mind and body in harmonious mutual conjunction. If there exists a spiritual reality, neither brain nor mind, which manifests itself in both, it is beyond our ken, and the fact need not divert from or hinder rational efforts. For surely the best expression of such a force must be had when the mind and body are best conditioned. Doubtless changes of personality are more easily accomplished in the period of childhood and youth, but throughout the entire conscious life of a man there is no period when the citadel of the personality may not be taken by suitable siege.

A skilful, successful siege, while it encompasses the mass, must also reach to the groups and individual prisoners ministering with much particularity. This is practicable, even with the largest prison population. It is observed that the police of a municipality may know and influence the conduct of every inhabitant; that the "organization" of a political party knows the distinctive character of each elector and the agency effective to influence his political action; that at our National Military Academy the marking system reveals the idiosyncrasy of each cadet and gives reliable data for forecasting his career. In like manner the governing authority of a reformatory may and should have knowledge of each prisoner and, definitely, the use and effect of agencies directed for his advancement.

Such particularity is facilitated by group formations, great and small, composed of prisoners whose similar characteristics permit their treatment in group connection. In order to meet the several similarities the groups will form and reform and change kaleidoscopically, but always with prescribed order and precision of selections, so that in the round of groupings the special needs of each are duly treated. Fully a hundred such groups existed at the Elmira Reformatory within a general prison population of fifteen hundred, and the individualism helped to solidify and at the same time steady the mass to stand the necessary strain of the effective disciplinary régime then in vogue.

The words "necessary strain" are used advisedly. Stringency and strenuosity are indispensable principles of administration. Lax, superficial, or perfunctory administration easily transmutes the intended reformatory into a damaging instrument producing deformities instead. Strictness and strenuousness serve also to counteract any possible injurious attractiveness of the unusual cultural opportunities and privileges the reformatory system involves. Not only a solidifying and steadying effect is wrought, but at the same time the irresponsive prisoners are sifted out and settled to their appropriate place.

Every separate reformatory institution has its own particular tone, derived originally from the central controlling individual, fed, fanned, and reflexively disseminated. This institutional tone is an impalpable something which, like the consensus of public opinion, is always a powerful determining factor. As the hundred instrumentalists of a great orchestra reach their highest excellence by inspiration of their leader, so the most effective reformatory work must have its tone of inspiration. It is the product of a quality rather than of external influences. Important as it is that the governing head should do and say the wisest things, it is of vastly more importance that he possess within himself the manly qualities and glowing interest which, when generally communicated, insure the best success. Such inwardness is self-propagative.

With the utmost confidence in the category of principles arrayed, and supplied with the completest reformatory mechanism, yet, when confronted with the duty to effect reformations, so lofty and complex is the problem, so delicate are the processes, and so much is the skill required, that it is not surprising if incredulity should arise. But when the problem is resolved into two essential elements it seems more simple. These elements are the formation of desirable habitudes, and development of individual economic efficiency.

The only useful knowledge we can have of the springs of character is to be derived from intelligent observation and true interpretation of the customary behavior. That every individual has characteristics fixed in his innate constitution or nature—a certain temperament and natural tendencies—cannot be denied. But external circumstances have already somewhat modified the original characteristics; and none can name the limit of further possible modifications to be effected by different circumstances and very different customary conduct. While the force of the original nature should not be utterly disregarded, and some regard must be had to the influence of exceptional flowering reason, new dominating tendencies like an acquired or second nature may be created.

Nature—custom—reason; the greatest of these is custom. Criminal behavior may but express a want of regulated channels for the flow of vital force or lack of force. As the stagnant pools of a barren rivulet exhale malaria, and as the freshet serves to spread pollution, so a low rate of vitality may account for vagrant impulses, and, when under even normal pressure, insufficiency or irregularity of ducts of habit may produce pernicious conduct. Habit is formed by practice. By practice new nervous paths are made and connected. Movements of body and mind become more and more under conscious direction of the subject—from mere automatism through various stages until permanent change is wrought. Repeated efforts and movements which tend to produce right habits and, at the same time, disuse of every unsuitable activity, may become so fixed in the constitution that when any spring of action is touched, desirable action will follow and with reasonable certainty of result as a consequence of collaborated forces of mind and body. The degree of perfection of habit may be fairly estimated by the promptness and uniformity of the action responsive to the stimulus.

A signally distinguishing characteristic of the American Reformatory Prison System is the importance attached and the attention given to methodical treatment of the material organism for renovation—mayhap a little of refining effect and adjustment of sense to mind. Such physical training is believed to be a rational basal principle of reformatory procedure.

Another distinguishing feature, still more important because it is the germinal, all-embracing principle from which every progress proceeds, is the use of the economic motive and training to thriftiness. This principle, which is inherent in human nature and in the nature of things, plainly written in history, manifest in current affairs, present in every normal consciousness, the ground principle so long obscured from our educational systems and religious observances by reason of mediævalism and institutionalism, so blurred in our common life by excess and artifice, so misused in prison labor systems, is now rallied for its appropriate use in the scheme for reforming prisoners.

Successful legitimate industrial performance involves native or acquired capacity and disposition for useful work. This in turn demands such development of physical energy that exertion is pleasurable or not painful; it requires a degree of mechanical and mental integrity which verges on morality and, indeed, is of the same essential quality; there must be sufficient dexterity for competitions, and stability equivalent to reliability that insures a commercial value to the services. It is the observation of experience that such an effect can be produced by industrial training; and, moreover, the possession of means, produced by exercise of the honest qualities made necessary to successful labor, conveys to the workmen a stimulus as of achievement, the ennoblement of proprietorship, and suggests some sense of solidarity of interests which prompts to prudence, thence to proper fraternity of feeling and conduct. After such a course of training and actual achievement, when the prisoner is sent out, on conditional release, to the situation arranged for him, possessed of his self-earned outfit of clothing, tools, and money, having left behind a margin of his savings to be added to from time to time or drawn upon to meet exigencies; after his sustained test on parole under the common circumstances of free inhabitancy; is he not, ordinarily, entitled to reasonable confidence that he will live and remain within the requirements of the laws?

The formation of such a new social habitude is an educational, therefore a gradual, process which requires time as well as practice. Whatever of real value may attend the preaching of disinterested benevolence to the outside general inhabitants, it is, as an independent agency, of little use for a community of common convicts. Such of them as might be moved by such an appeal are, usually, scarcely normal, and their responsive benevolent acts are likely to be injurious. Fellow-feeling for comrades may prompt to crimes, collusions, and public disorder.

The same may, properly, be said of prescriptive moral maxims, generally, and of the possible effects of personal entreaty. Also effort such as is commonly made to induce a habit of moral introspection, is believed to be a mistaken policy. The state standard of practical reformations is not the product of inward moral contrition; more naturally contrition is consequent on reformation. When reformation is accomplished contrition is useless and often harmful. It was deemed not an encouraging indication when, as occasionally happened, a prisoner on his admission to the reformatory, answering interrogatories, flippantly said, "I am going to reform"; not encouraging, because it showed no real purpose or some vague diverting notion of reformation quite aside from the real thing. The most hopeful response was felt to be when a desire was expressed and felt to learn some trade or income-giving occupation.

Moral suasion and religion are recognized as reformative agencies in our prison system, but no particular niche is prescribed for them such as is assigned to other agencies. Moral tone and the religious consciousness are flavoring qualities immediately penetrative.

They are attributes inherent in and emanative from the humblest as the noblest effort and exercise intended for any betterment.

Neither punishment nor precept nor both combined constitute the main reliance; but, instead, education by practice—education of the whole man, his capacity, his habits and tastes, by a rational procedure whose central motive and law of development are found in the industrial economies. This is a reversal of the usual contemplated order of effort for reformations—the building of character from the top down; the modern method builds from the bottom upward, and the substratum of the structure rests on work.

This better order of procedure is in accord with the method of human development foreshadowed by the allegorical scriptural Eden episode; and it does not preclude the highest aim and attainment. The far-reaching reformatory possibilities of work are admirably pointed out by Professor Drummond. I quote:

"Work is an incarnation of the unseen. In this loom man's soul is made. There is a subtle machinery behind it all, working while he is working, making or unmaking the unseen in him. Integrity, thoroughness, honesty, accuracy, conscientiousness, faithfulness, patience—these unseen things which complete a soul are woven into the work. Apart from work these things are not. As the conductor leads into our nerves the invisible force, so work conducts into our spirit all high forces of character, all essential qualities of life, truth in the inward parts. Ledgers and lexicons, business letters, domestic duties, striking of bargains, writing of examinations, handling of tools—these are the conductors of the Eternal! So much so that without them there is no Eternal. No man *dreams* integrity, accuracy, and so on. These things require their wire as much as electricity. The spiritual fluids and the electric fluids are under the same law; and messages of grace come along the lines of honest work to the soul, like the invisible message along the telegraph wires."

The principles of the American Reformatory Prison System as here set forth are as yet incompletely practiced; but, more and more, men are learning that the eternal verities are within the acts and incidents of the daily life; that the public safety turns upon a proper adjustment of individual and collective relativeness; and that the fulcrum of leverage is economic efficiency. This better view is fraught with promise for better public protection by means of rational reformation of offenders.

IV

POSSIBLE AND ACTUAL PENALTIES FOR CRIME*

By FREDERICK HOWARD WINES

T O give an account of the criminal codes of the United States, which should be at once intelligible, succinct, and exhaustive, would be an undertaking impossible to accomplish. Crime to a great extent is treated as a matter of purely local interest and importance. Each state and territory has its own code. Each code has been borrowed in part from some one or more of the codes already in force in other states, but modified to suit the views of the compilers. No two codes agree throughout, either in their definitions of crime or in the penalties prescribed for particular offenses. They contain internal evidence of their eclectic origin; and the successive stages in the evolution of criminal statutes might be historically traced, as comparative philologists trace the derivation of words from a limited number of primitive roots. Our statutes, founded upon the common law of England, contain many definitions and distinctions whose resemblance to their English originals is very remote.

Burglary, at the common law, is breaking and entering the dwelling of another by night with intent to commit a felony. This definition does not include (1) breaking without entering, (2) entering without breaking, (3) breaking, or entering, or breaking and entering a dwelling by day, (4) breaking or entering a building other than a dwelling, (5) breaking or entering a structure or inclosure

* In this paper the text of an article appended to the report, by Dr. Frederick Howard Wines, on crime, prepared for publication in the Eleventh U. S. Census (1890), has been reproduced. The volumes containing this report are not readily accessible to the general reader, but the bearing of the facts stated upon the question of definite versus indefinite sentences is so obvious and so important, that no apology is required for reprinting it here. It was meant to be illustrative and explanatory of the statistical tables showing the variations in sentences imposed by the courts and in the prescribed and average duration of imprisonment by states and territories, by sex, color, nativity and race, and by groups of crimes, separately and in combination with each other. These tables, of which there are twenty-seven, fill 90 quarto pages. Mr. Wines also furnished a separate tabular statement of the possible sentences for certain selected crimes, according to the codes in force in 1890, with an elaborate and extensive set of notes attached. The student who desires to go more deeply into this subject is referred to the original census volumes.

not a building, such as a car or boat. All of these acts are included in the popular conception of the word burglary, and that conception has passed into the technical phraseology of the statutes. The Oregon code, for instance, mentions "burglary in the night," "burglary by day," and "burglary not in a dwelling house." In Wyoming, burglary is "breaking and entering, or entering, any building or inclosure with intent to commit a felony;" if the intent is to commit a misdemeanor, the offense is characterized as simple housebreaking. The intent, in the common law, is an essential element of the crime, and it must be intent to commit a felony. But certain codes, like that of New Hampshire, confine it to certain felonious acts, such as murder, rape and robbery, while the majority add to the word felony the words "or larceny," which is perhaps the most common intention of all; and some, like that of New York, substitute the word "crime" for felony, thus including misdemeanors. In many states the fact that a burglar is armed, or makes an assault, or has a confederate present, is an aggravation of the offense, and subjects him to a higher penalty; in others this distinction is ignored.

Arson, at the common law, is the malicious burning of the house of another, meaning by "house" a building, with its outbuildings, finished for habitation. This definition takes no notice of the intentional burning of one's own house, with intent to defraud the insurer or to hide a crime; nor of the burning of other property, as vessels, rolling stock, lumber, grain, fences, bridges, woods and prairies. Nor does it include the burning of buildings not designed for habitation, as mills, warehouses, shops, schools, churches, public buildings, and many others that might be mentioned. The statutes accordingly give very enlarged definitions of the word, which only partially agree with each other. In California, arson is said to be the wilful and malicious burning of any building with intent to destroy it; setting fire to other kinds of property is malicious mischief. Arson of an inhabited building in which there is at the time some human being, in that state, is arson in the first degree; all other kinds of arson are of the second degree. A specimen of another style of definition, in which a long list appears of different sorts of buildings and other property liable to conflagration, is given in the Indiana code. Much is made in some codes of the distinction between buildings within and buildings without the curtilage of a dwelling, but the majority do not refer to it.

Robbery, at the common law, is larceny committed by violence from the person of one put in fear. But the statutes of Missouri and

Kansas make the taking of the personal property of another from his person, or in his presence, by threatening future injury to his person or property or to the person of any relative or member of his family, robbery in the second degree, while robbery in the third degree is nothing more nor less than the offense commonly known as blackmail. The Delaware code makes a separate offense of robbery in a dwelling or on a public highway, with a special penalty. The distinction between robbery armed and unarmed, though not universal, is quite general.

These instances and others which might be given illustrate the difficulties which surround and encumber the correct interpretation of criminal statistics. Many of the crimes and misdemeanors enumerated in the census returns are unknown to the common law. The list of crimes in no two states is precisely the same. None of the codes are complete. There are laches and oversights in all of them. Offenses punishable in one state are not punishable in another, and the same word is not employed in all cases in the same sense. There are codes, for instance, in which the common distinction between grand and petit larceny is ignored or formally disavowed; and the codes in which it is recognized differ so widely in their characterization of the limit which separates the two that it is placed in Georgia at $1.00 and in Maine, Massachusetts, Florida, and New Mexico at $100.

This is the reason why statistics of crime need to be accompanied by a brief statement in outline of the requirements of the law which prisoners are charged with breaking, and of the extent of their resulting liabilities. Tables 123–131 of the Census of 1890 show the average duration of sentences of prisoners in the several states and territories. That average must measurably depend upon the power to punish confided to the courts. It is easy to compare the percentages of the total population in prison in the different states, but such comparisons prove nothing as to the social and moral condition of the people without examination of the lists of punishable offenses in each of them; and these again prove nothing until the average duration of sentence for each group of crimes is also known. The penalties authorized by legislatures and those pronounced by judges must bear some relation to each other, to give value to a criminal code as a general directory to criminal courts. The law and the figures must be read in conjunction, or the meaning of the figures will not be clear, and erroneous deductions from them are likely to be made.

Frederick H. Wines

Some comparisons have been made, in tabular form, between possible penalties under different codes. No exhaustive attempt has been made in this direction, but a few typical offenses have been selected, representing 60,000 prisoners, or three-fourths of the whole number. In the columns of the tables are the minimum and maximum terms of imprisonment prescribed by law—the limits of discretion allowed to the courts in the matter of sentence. The alternative penalties and additional penalties, other than imprisonment, are shown in the notes, which are necessarily numerous.

VARIATIONS IN FORM OF PENALTIES PRESCRIBED

The penalty for any offense may assume either of five typical forms: (1) imprisonment only; (2) fine only; (3) fine or imprisonment; (4) both imprisonment and fine; (5) fine or imprisonment, or both such fine and imprisonment. Each of these varieties of sentence is divisible into three subvarieties: those with a maximum but no minimum penalty, those with a minimum but no maximum, and those with both a minimum and a maximum limit. When there is no maximum limit to imprisonment stated, the natural limit is life. Some states exhibit a partiality for one or the other of these forms, but there are states in which all of them are in use at once.

IMPRISONMENT

In order to furnish a vivid idea of the great facility with which changes can be rung upon so few and such simple elements, attention is called to the following list of terms of imprisonment in the tables:

(1) Maximum terms with no minimum: 10 days, 20 days, 30 days, 1 month, 60 days, 2 months, 90 days, 3 months, 6 months, 1 year, 2 years, 3 years, 5 years, 6 years, 7 years, 10 years, 12 years, 14 years, 15 years, 20 years, 21 years, 25 years, 30 years, life.

(2) Minimum terms with no maximum: 20 days, 30 days, 6 months. (The maximum in these cases cannot be assumed to be life.)

(3) Minimum and maximum terms: 5 days to 20 days; 10 days to 30 or 50 or 60 or 90 days, or to 6 months; 24 days to 1 year; 1 month to 3 or 6 months, or to 1 year; 60 days to 6 months, or to 1 year; 2 months to 1 year; 3 months to 6 months, or to 1 or 2 or 10 years; 4 months to 10 years; 6 months to 1 or 2 or 3 or 5 or 7 years; 1 year to 2 or 3 or 4 or 5 or 7 or 10 or 14 or 15 years, or life; 18 months to 9 or 21 years; 2 years to 4 or 5 or 10 or 15 or 20 or 21 or 25 years, or life; 3 years to 9 or 10 or 15 or 18 or 20 years, or life; 4

111

years to 7 or 8 or 10 years, or life; 5 years to 10 or 15 or 20 or 21 or 30 or 60 years, or life; 7 years to 20 years; 10 years to 20 or 21 years, or life.

FINES

Attention is further called to the following list of fines in the notes to the tables:

(1) Maximum fines with no minimum: $10, $20, $25, $30, $50, $100, $200, $250, $300, $500, $600, $800, $1,000, $2,000, $2,500, $4,000, $5,000, $10,000, $20,000.

(2) Minimum fines with no maximum: $10, $20, $100, $200, $300, $500, $1,000, $10,000.

(3) Minimum and maximum fines: $1 to $20 or $100; $3 to $100; $5 to $20 or $25 or $50 or $100 or $500; $10 to $25 or $50 or $100 or $300 or $500 or $1,000; $20 to $50 or $100; $25 to $100 or $1,000; $30 to $500; $50 to $150 or $200 or $250 or $300 or $500 or $1,000; $100 to $300 or $500 or $1,000; $200 to $500 or $1,000; $250 to $1,000; $300 to $500 or $1,000; $400 to $1,000 or $2,000; $500 to $1,000 or $2,000 or $5,000 or $10,000; $1,000 to $5,000 or $10,000.

A MATHEMATICAL PROBLEM

The subject thus presented offers for the consideration of mathematicians a somewhat formidable problem in permutation. Given, 24 maximum and 3 minimum terms of imprisonment, with 64 variable terms with definite maximum and minimum limits; also 19 maximum and 8 minimum fines, with 42 variable fines with definite maximum and minimum limits. Required, answers to the two following questions: first, In how many ways might these be combined by the framers of criminal codes in the five typical forms mentioned above? and second, How many different individual sentences might be pronounced upon convicted prisoners under the thousands of possible paragraphs or sections which might be devised by the literary ingenuity of the aforesaid legal authors?

FINE AND IMPRISONMENT

The modifications of sentence to simple imprisonment by the introduction of the element of fine, as has been intimated, assume two forms; namely, fine as a substitute for imprisonment and fine as an addition to imprisonment. In either form the law may be, and sometimes is, so framed as to admit of the commutation of fine into imprisonment at a fixed rate, commonly, perhaps, on the basis of the equivalence of one day in custody and $1.00 in cash. Where this is the case, the fine imposed is in effect a prolongation of sentence, and would to that extent increase the averages stated in the table. If some other mode of discharging an impecunious convict is devised, instead of requiring him to work out his fine, the fact remains that a light sentence to prison and a heavy fine might be for many men a more severe punishment than a longer term without this addition. In estimating the comparative severity of different codes, this fact must be borne in mind. It will not answer, from any point of view, to concentrate one's whole attention upon the question of imprisonment alone.

In Europe there has been much discussion of the "scale of penalties," a phrase unfamiliar to American ears. We have a scale, as may be inferred, but it can hardly be said to be graduated with mathematical precision.

Codes with fixed penalties, like the Code Napoleon, accept, on behalf of the legislative branch of the government, the responsibility of apportioning punishment to supposed guilt. The majority of our codes throw this responsibility upon the judicial department, but in varying measure.

SUPPLEMENTARY PENALTIES

But the latitude left to judges and juries has not yet been fully stated. In a number of states, notably in Massachusetts, Michigan and Mississippi, the courts are offered their choice, for certain crimes, between sentences to imprisonment in the state prison or penitentiary and sentences to imprisonment in the county jail. In Alabama and some other southern states, prisoners may even be sentenced to hard labor outside of prison walls, upon plantations or roads or public works. There are additions to imprisonment in other forms, such as disfranchisement and disqualification for office as a witness; and, in Delaware, the pillory and the whipping post. In Rhode Island, every person convicted of murder or arson is thereupon deemed in law to be dead, with respect to all rights of property, to the bond of matrimony, and to all civil rights and relations of whatever nature, as if his natural death had taken place at the time of such conviction. In that state, if any person is sentenced to imprisonment in the state prison for life or for any term of years not less than seven, any creditor may apply to the probate court for settlement of his estate, and letters of administration issue upon such request. In Maryland, parties who marry within the prohibited degrees of consanguinity may be banished from the state. The principle of restitution in cases of crimes against property has been engrafted upon several codes, including those of Delaware, Maryland, and Louisiana.

Sentences are further modified, and their average duration is prolonged, by various provisions as to second and subsequent convictions. Such provisions may be general, or they may be limited in their application to specified offenses. On the other hand, the total amount of imprisonment is not quite so great as it would appear from Tables 114–122 to be, since commutation of sentence, on a fixed scale, as a reward for good conduct in prison, is nearly everywhere the prisoner's right, under what are familiarly known as "good time" laws. Where the indeterminate sentence has found its way into any criminal code, the term of sentence stated in the census returns is the maximum term which might have been imposed for the crimes specified, and this also increases the apparent average duration of sentence in the states which have such codes. This is especially true of New York, with its immense reformatory prison at Elmira.

The whole or a part of a sentence may be to solitary confinement, or the prisoner may be sentenced to be fed on bread and water.

These are further illustrations of the difficulties which surround and encumber the interpretation of criminal statistics. To reduce this mass of confused and conflicting provisions to anything like order or system is a vexatious and wearisome task, in which a moderate degree of success is all that can be reasonably hoped for.

But one of the most striking results of the comparative study of possible sentences for crime is the conviction which it inevitably produces, that criminal law is unequally applied. This may be seen in the tables; first, by an examination of the different penalties in the different states for the same offenses, and second, by a comparison of the penalties for different offenses.

VARIATIONS IN SEVERITY OF PENALTIES PRESCRIBED

It is commonly said that the end sought in the punishment, so-called, of criminals is the protection of society. But injustice to prisoners in the name of the law would be an assault upon the basis of all righteous government. It must therefore be assumed that the criminal law is designed to be just. In other words, it consciously inflicts upon no man a greater amount of suffering than the crime which he has committed merits. The penalties contained in any code are the expression of the moral sense of the turpitude of crime in the minds of those by whom it was adopted and is continued in force. They constitute the only legal measure of possible guilt, leaving the question of actual guilt in each particular instance to the determination of the proper judicial tribunals. It follows that the important point to be considered in any examination of them is the maximum penalties. The minimum penalties are not to be over-looked or disregarded. But the statement of any minimum is comparatively rare.

The maximum penalty for counterfeiting in Delaware is three years; in Maine, Massachusetts, New York, Florida and Michigan it is imprisonment for life. The minimum penalty in Missouri is five years, which is the maximum in Connecticut.

The maximum penalty for perjury in New Hampshire, Connecticut, and Kentucky is five years; in Maine, Mississippi, and Iowa it is imprisonment for life; in Missouri it is death, if the witness designs thereby to effect the execution of an innocent person. In Delaware, on the other hand, perjury is punishable by fine, without imprisonment, not less than $500 nor more than $2,000.

The maximum penalty for incest in Virginia is six months; in Louisiana the minimum penalty is imprisonment for life; in Delaware the penalty is a simple fine of $100.

The maximum penalty for bigamy ranges all the way from one year in Delaware to twenty-one years in Tennessee.

The maximum penalty for rape in New Jersey and Pennsylvania is fifteen years; in Delaware, North Carolina and Louisiana the penalty is absolute and is death.

The maximum penalty for mayhem in Colorado is three years; in Vermont it is imprisonment for life. In Georgia, putting out one eye or slitting or biting off the nose or lip is a misdemeanor, for which the punishment cannot exceed six months in jail, a year in the county chain gang, and a fine of $1,000. On the other hand, the penalty in Georgia for castration is death, but may be commuted by the jury to imprisonment for life.

The maximum penalty for assault with intent to commit rape in Pennsylvania and Kansas is five years; in Massachusetts it is imprisonment for life.

The maximum penalty for arson of an occupied dwelling by night in Connecticut, Arkansas, Wyoming, Colorado and Washington is ten years; in Delaware, Virginia, North Carolina, and Louisiana the penalty is absolute and is death.

The maximum penalty for arson, in the daytime, of a building not a dwelling and without the curtilage of any dwelling, in Kansas is four years; in Maryland, South Carolina, and Georgia, it is death.

The maximum penalty for arson with intent to defraud insurer in Alabama is one year; in Maine the minimum penalty for the same offense is imprisonment for life.

The maximum penalty for breaking and entering a dwelling by night in Arkansas is seven years; in North Carolina the penalty is absolute and is death; in Louisiana it is death, if the burglar is armed or makes an assault; also in Delaware, if the intent is to commit murder, rape, or arson.

The maximum penalty for grand larceny varies from two years in Louisiana and New Mexico to twenty years in Connecticut.

The maximum penalty for forgery varies from three years in Delaware to imprisonment for life in New York and Missouri.

If guilt is measured by penalty, the absence of any accepted standard of measurement is thus a matter of mathematical demonstration.

Still more diverse are the relative estimates of different crimes in the different codes. In the statements which follow, guilt is measured by the maximum penalty for each offense prescribed in the statutes:

The guilt of counterfeiting in Ohio and Minnesota is twice that of perjury, but in Rhode Island and Alabama the guilt of perjury is twice that of counterfeiting.

The guilt of perjury in Indiana is to that of incest as 21 to 5, but in Kentucky the guilt of incest is to that of perjury as 21 to 5.

The guilt of rape in New York is twice that of incest, but three times in Wisconsin, Minnesota, and Kansas, four times in Vermont, five times in Pennsylvania, ten times in New Hampshire, and thirty times in New Mexico.

Delaware, Virginia, Georgia, New Mexico, and Oregon are the only states in which bigamy is regarded as a higher crime than incest. In Virginia the maximum penalty for bigamy is eight years, but for incest only six months, while in Wyoming and Colorado the maximum penalty for incest is twenty years, but for bigamy two years.

The guilt of assault to kill in Mississippi is five times that of assault to rape, but in Delaware and Georgia the guilt of assault to rape is twice that of assault to kill. Assault to kill is punishable in Vermont, Connecticut, Michigan and Arizona by imprisonment for life, and assault to rape by different terms of years, but in Massachusetts assault to rape is punishable by imprisonment for life and assault to kill by imprisonment for one year.

The guilt of mayhem in Ohio is twice that of burglary, but in Michigan the guilt of burglary is twice that of mayhem.

The guilt of arson in Pennsylvania, Ohio, Nebraska, and Kentucky is twice that of burglary, but in Connecticut the guilt of burglary is twice that of arson.

The guilt of burglary in Kentucky and Alabama is twice that of larceny, but three times in Wisconsin and Mississippi, four times in Georgia and Michigan, five times in New Hampshire, and six times in New Mexico.

The guilt of robbery in Vermont, New York, Delaware, Wisconsin, Minnesota, Kentucky, Mississippi and Oregon is twice that of larceny, but three times in Arkansas, four times in Georgia, Florida and Iowa, five times in New Mexico, six times in New Hampshire, and seven times in Louisiana.

The guilt of burglary in Texas is to that of forgery as 12 to 7, but in Arkansas the guilt of forgery is to that of burglary as 15 to 7.

The guilt of forgery in Kansas is four times that of larceny, but in Connecticut the guilt of larceny is four times that of forgery.

With the exception of murder, the highest three crimes in New Hampshire and Alabama are rape, arson, and robbery; in Delaware and West Virginia, rape, arson, and burglary; in Indiana, rape, arson, and the embezzlement of public funds; in Mississippi, rape, arson and administering poison.

The highest two crimes in Virginia, with the exception of murder, are rape and arson; in Minnesota, arson and burglary; in Nebraska, Wyoming, and Colorado, crime against nature and rape; in Utah, rape and administering poison.

The highest crime in New Jersey, except murder, is the crime against nature; in Pennsylvania and Maryland, arson; in Ohio, Illinois, Wisconsin, Kentucky, Texas, Tennessee, Arkansas, Washington, and Oregon, rape.

IMPRISONMENT FOR LIFE

Still omitting all reference to homicide, the maximum penalty for crimes named is imprisonment for life in the following states:

In Massachusetts, for counterfeiting, rape, assault with intent to rape, poisoning a well or spring, arson, burglary, robbery, and embezzlement of public funds.

In Maine, for counterfeiting, perjury, rape, arson, burglary, and robbery.

In Rhode Island, for rape, administering poison, poisoning a well or spring, arson, burglary, and robbery.

In Michigan, for counterfeiting, rape, assault with intent to kill, administering poison, poisoning a well or spring, and robbery.

In Missouri, for the crime against nature, arson, burglary, robbery, and forgery.

In Nevada, Idaho, and Colorado, for the crime against nature, rape, administering poison, arson, and burglary.

In Arizona, for rape, assault with intent to kill, administering poison, arson and burglary.

In Vermont, for mayhem, assault with intent to kill, arson, and burglary.

In New York, for counterfeiting, arson, burglary, and forgery.

In Florida, for counterfeiting, poisoning a well or spring, arson and burglary.

In Iowa, for perjury, rape, arson, and burglary.

In Connecticut, for the crime against nature, rape, assault with intent to kill, and administering poison.

In New Mexico, for the crime against nature, administering poison, poisoning a well or spring, and dueling.

In Montana, for the crime against nature, rape, and administering poison.

In Mississippi, for perjury and administering poison.

In Louisiana, for incest and the crime against nature.

In Nebraska, Wyoming, and Colorado, for the crime against nature and rape.

In Utah, for rape and administering poison.

In Minnesota, for arson and burglary.

In Georgia, for the crime against nature.

In Ohio, Illinois, Washington, and Oregon, for rape.

In Arkansas, for dueling.

In South Carolina, for burglary.

In West Virginia and Texas, for robbery.

In North Carolina, for the embezzlement of public funds.

In the remaining states, namely, New Hampshire, New Jersey, Pennsylvania, Indiana, Wisconsin, and Kansas, life sentences are not authorized by law, except for murder and manslaughter.

DEATH

The death penalty is in force in the following states for the crimes named.

For murder in all the states except Rhode Island, Michigan, and Wisconsin.

In Louisiana, for rape, assault with intent to kill, administering poison, arson, and burglary.

In Delaware and North Carolina, for rape, arson, and burglary.

In Alabama, for rape, arson, and robbery.

In Georgia, for rape, mayhem, and arson.

In Missouri, for perjury and rape.

In Virginia, West Virginia, South Carolina, and Mississippi, for rape and arson.

In Florida, Kentucky, Tennessee, Texas, and Arkansas, for rape.

In Montana, for arson of dwelling by night.

In Maryland, for any variety of arson.

POSSIBLE AND ACTUAL PENALTIES

In order to obtain a complete view of the relations of crime and punishment, the possible sentence authorized by the codes must be compared with the actual sentences imposed by the courts. For this purpose the average sentences for different crimes in the different states are given in Table 123.* A table is also submitted which shows in addition, for certain offenses, in parallel columns, the maximum penalty authorized by law, the highest and the lowest sentence pronounced by the courts, and the average for all prisoners in confinement in each state on that particular charge, June 1, 1890.

Generally speaking, the approximations to equality in the apportionment of actual sentences are greater than in the case of possible sentences. For instance, while the possible (maximum) sentence for perjury ranges from five years to life, the actual average sentences imposed (omitting sentences for life) range from one year in Maine to ten years in Florida. The possible sentences for incest range from six months to life, but the actual average sentences from one year in Pennsylvania to fifteen years in Louisiana. The possible sentences for the crime against nature range from five years to life, but the actual average sentences from one year in West Virginia and Utah to eleven years and nine months in California.

* See Census Report, 1900.

The possible sentences for bigamy range from one year in Delaware to twenty-one years in Tennessee, but the actual average sentences from four months in Montana to four years and three months in Minnesota. The possible sentences for rape range from fifteen years to death, but the actual average sentences from two years in Louisiana (where the maximum penalty is death) to thirty-three years and six months in New Mexico.

The possible sentences for arson range from ten years to death, but the actual average sentences from two years in Arkansas to seventeen years and six months in Rhode Island.

The possible sentences for burglary range from seven years to death, but the actual average sentences from one year and six months in New Mexico to eight years and four months in Georgia.

The possible sentences for robbery range from six years to life, but the actual average sentences from one year and nine months in Delaware to twenty-two years in Alabama.

The possible sentences for larceny range from two to twenty years, but the actual average sentences from 1.136 years in Delaware to 5.556 in Texas.*

The possible sentences for forgery range from three years to life, but the actual average sentences from one year and six months in Arizona to seven years in New York.

In the foregoing statement it will be understood that the averages stated in Table 123 † can only be computed from term sentences, and that the sentences to imprisonment for life or to suffer execution are not included. If an arbitrary figure, based on the ages of prisoners at the time of conviction and their expectation of life, could be substituted for life sentences, the averages would be much greater than they appear from that table to be.

AVERAGE SENTENCES

It will be seen that in almost all cases the average term sentence imposed by the courts is far below the maximum penalty authorized by the statutes. There are some exceptions, as may be seen by consulting the columns for the crime of incest, where the maximum penalty and the average sentence are identical for Arizona, Nevada, Oregon, and California. The contrast between the maximum pen-

---

* The District of Columbia is omitted from this statement, because prisoners sentenced for grand larceny in the District are sent elsewhere to undergo their sentence of imprisonment, and the average stated in the table is for petit larceny only.

† In Census Report, 1900.

alty and the actual average sentence in other cases is very striking, of which the following instances may be mentioned; in Maine, the maximum penalty for perjury is imprisonment for life, but the actual average sentence is one year. It would be fairer, however, to take cases in which the maximum penalty is a sentence for a definite term of years rather than for life, and attention may be called to the maximum penalty for the crime against nature in Mississippi, which is ten years, and the actual average sentence, which is one year; to the maximum penalty for burglary in New Mexico, which is twelve years, and the actual average sentence, which is one year and six months, and to the maximum penalty for forgery in Arizona, which is fourteen years, while the actual average sentence is one year and six months.

The inequality of average sentences for the same offense in different states is also noticeable. The average sentence for perjury in New York is more than double that in New Jersey, and in Florida it is double that in Georgia. The average sentence for incest in Massachusetts is twice that in New Hampshire and ten times that in Pennsylvania. The average sentence for the crime against nature in North Carolina is nine times that in West Virginia, in Alabama five times that in Mississippi, and in Washington twice that in Oregon. The average sentence for bigamy in New York is more than double that in Pennsylvania or Connecticut. The average sentence for rape in Mississippi is six times, and in Texas twelve times, that in Louisiana; in New Mexico it is more than three times that in Arizona, and in California more than five times that in Washington.

The average sentence for arson in New Hampshire is nearly double that in Vermont, in Texas more than three times that in Arkansas, and in Rhode Island about four times that in Pennsylvania.

The average sentence for burglary in California is more than double that in Arizona, and in Vermont more than four times that in Rhode Island.

The average sentence for robbery is less than one year in California, but more than nineteen years in Arizona; and in Alabama four times that in Mississippi.

The average sentence for larceny in Maryland is double that in Delaware, and in Texas three times that in Louisiana.

The average sentence for forgery in Minnesota is more than double that in Wisconsin, and in New York more than double that in New Hampshire or Pennsylvania. Similar instances might be greatly multiplied.

Evidently part of this apparent inequality in the distribution of punishment is due to differences in the circumstances which attended and characterized the commission of the offenses, which were duly taken into account by the courts before which the offenders were tried. Part of it is also explicable on the theory that in some states the number of offenders is so small that the averages stated are of little value.

The value of the table of possible sentences lies in the fact that it gives to students the variations in the codes of the states, in concrete form, and the table is not meant for practical use by lawyers. Any minor errors which may be discovered will not invalidate the value of the table for the purpose for which it was made.

V

SAMUEL JUNE BARROWS

By PAUL U. KELLOGG

IN his verses on Life and Song, Sidney Lanier, the poet of our South-land, lamented that the singer had not yet come who should wholly live his minstrelsy,—live it as if life were caught by a clarionet and its heart were utterly bodied forth in the throbbing of the reed. Last year, one evening in May, the Oratorio Society and the Prison Association of New York united in a service at Mendelssohn Hall commemorative of Samuel June Barrows. The splendid choruses in which for years he had lifted up his voice were interspersed by addresses telling of him as the helper of prisoners, the lover of letters, the lover of justice, the man of peace, the shepherd of souls. These were so many aspects of a life, long and full, which had loosened many of those fetters that bind men to misery (such as crime, bigotry, war and race hatred), and which, in turn, had forged strong, radiant links with music and the other joys of creation. For it was more nearly true of him than of most men, that "his song was only living aloud; his work, a singing with his hand."

Mr. Barrows died of pneumonia on April 21, 1909, at the Presbyterian Hospital, New York. The illness came suddenly in the flood-tide of the year's work; and his very loyalty to the public duties thick upon him, made him loath to be reconciled in laying them down. "I think it is hard to die like a saint," he said. "I am content to die without a crown, just as a decent man." In that way, also, had he lived, simply, unpretendingly, just as a decent man. Yet the International Prison Congress, in assembling in Washington in 1910, meets without its elected president—the first American to be called to the chair of this world's conference. Delegates speaking various tongues and standing high in the councils of the great governments, will mourn not only a fellow member but a friend well nigh as intimate and personal to them as, fifty years before, he had been to the working boys of an East Side night school, who without leave or precedent gave "nine cheers for Barrows" when he left their class. And convicts in the great Federal prisons, shuffling Negroes in the chain gangs of the South, parolemen granted a new chance in life by Australian law he had influenced, children before the new juvenile courts of France, sick men in the disease-beset cell-blocks of our older penitentiaries, young offenders locked in with the hardened rounders of obscure county jails, fair men and women caught in the ignoble meshes of old laws and tyrannies,—all these lost a friend, as surely as their lot, and that of their kind for generations to come, is bound to be influenced by the causes he substantially advanced.

Mr. Barrows's last piece of self-sacrifice was for such a one,—in prison, to be visited though it were at the ends of the world. In March, Mrs. Barrows had set out for St. Petersburg in behalf of Madame Breshkovsky, one of the heroic noblewomen of the Russian revolutionary movement, who in her seventieth year lay sick in the fortress of St. Peter and St. Paul. "I should be glad to give my life for Babushka," he had said, as his wife started alone on this emergent mission to Russia, "and would count it well spent. I cannot go; I think you should go." The cables carried word of his sickness to Mrs. Barrows, but the fastest steamers were unable to bring her back to the United States before his death. We may have faith, however, that husband and wife were not at the last denied such communion as finds expression in Mr. Barrows's stanzas, "The Wireless Message." In boyhood he had operated the key of one of the first telegraph instruments in use, and fifty years later, when they were last on the ocean together, he had written these verses in eager recognition of the second great conquest of space through electricity. He was quick to catch the glint of the universal and spiritual in its meaning; but in a very personal way, also, his words seem to have been half-prophetic of the hours of separation, of yearning and of diminishing strength, when his heart was to reach out over the seas they were then traversing toward the answering chords of her spirit.

> Electric pulses through the viewless air
>   Pitched to some distant tone,
> With ardent zeal their voiceless message bear
>   Through the ethereal zone,
> And at some tuned, receptive point remote,
>   They find their kindred note.

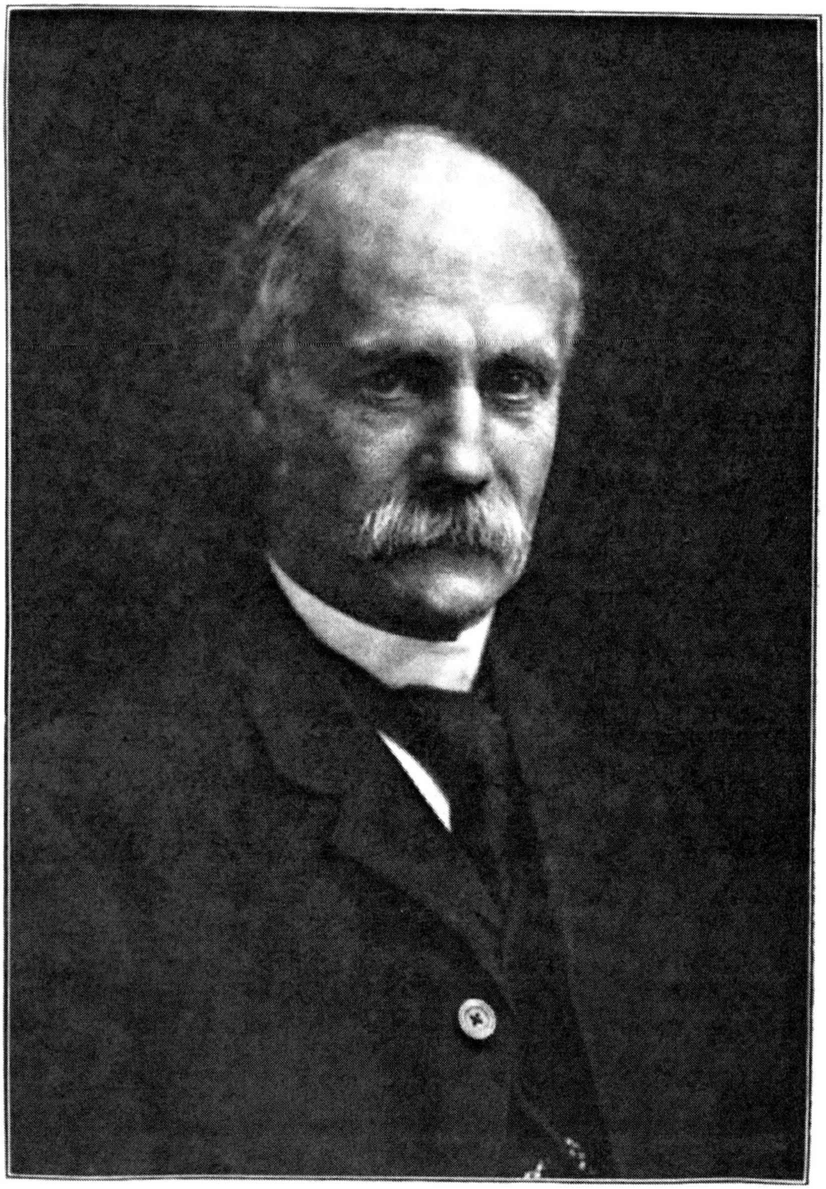

S. J. Barrows.

Self-poised on high the towers of the soul
    Some distant message wait.
Magnetic pulses speed from pole to pole,
    Swift to affiliate; .
But thou, my soul, to gain this wished-for boon,
    Must keep thyself in tune.

Love flashes in the open, shoreless sky,
    Pathway of God and man,
The burning question and the swift reply.
    Shall I the message scan?
And shall I find as these swift pulses dart
    Some message for my heart?

Mrs. Barrows recrossed the ocean less than three months after her husband's death and took up once more the mission to which they had jointly pledged her best efforts. She pleaded before the highest officials of the Czar the cause of the unflinching, white-haired prisoner, whose burning message of a people oppressed had stirred the swift pulses of America. "Sir," said the petitioner, "by a strange coincidence it was my husband who presented to the Russian Ambassador the petition in behalf of Mr. Tchaikovsky, which you were good enough to grant.* As my husband, the man, pleaded for the man, so I, the woman, come to plead for the woman."

Madame Breshkovsky was transferred to one of the better cells in the fortress, and later, was exiled to the penal settlements of Siberia instead of to hard labor in prison,—concessions which the activity of friends in other countries may have influenced, and not the least among them, this "little old lady who had traveled 10,000 miles" once, and again a second time, and who in her undaunted widowhood had ventured into the Island Palace on the Neva. In Babushka's age and exile may the devotion of these two, the simpler tragedy of whose lives was thus bound up in hers, abide with her! May it be to her surety of those "love flashes in the open shoreless sky" which go with her from the bruised hearts of the common people of all the Russias. As a part in Mr. Barrows's life, these were more than the chance incidents of a closing chapter. Love and brotherhood no less than justice were the mainsprings of his being.

* In 1909 the editors of *The Outlook* and Samuel J. Barrows carried a petition to the Russian Ambassador in Washington in behalf of Nicholas Tchaikovsky, known as the Father of the Russian revolutionary movement, who had been eleven months in prison awaiting trial. Mr. Tchaikovsky had spent some years in America and endeared himself to men and women in the United States. The petition was granted; Mr. Tchaikovsky was released on bail, and at his later public trial in March, 1910, was acquitted.

They made his work in prison reform a rebellion against the fixed ideas of punishment and custody; they lent the weight of his own death to the humanitarian protest against the fettering of liberty in the North. In the Russian bureaucracy he saw piled up and solidified the spirit of revenge and repression which his life work it was to fight wherever he found it, whether in old and ruthless laws, in blind court practices, or in those medieval modes of imprisonment which persist among us and which wreak an ultimate vengeance upon keeper and prisoner and society alike.

Separated at his death, in life Mr. and Mrs. Barrows were so truly at one, that a review, however brief, of the work of either must have much of the character of a joint biography. Their collaboration on a volume of reminiscences was one of the plans whose fulfillment his death came to prevent. This sharing of life work was the more remarkable because of the great variety of individual experience which came to both. Here was a man who campaigned in the Indian country, and was a peace advocate; who dug up Greek temples and pulled down old jails; who as a linguist mastered the harshest consonants of the nations, and as a sweet singer sang oratorios, and wrote ballads; here was a newspaper correspondent, preacher, editor, stenographer, penologist, parliamentary leader, polyglot poet and philanthropist. In the early days of our westward expansion, there developed a type of frontier minister who traveled great distances to preach in turn to the scattered settlements—an evangelism of the saddle which brought spiritual courage and vision into the material struggle against the wilderness. In much the same way Mr. Barrows served a later generation facing new issues; his circuit was the humanities.

Mr. Barrows was born May 26, 1845, on the lower East Side, New York. He was a child when his father died after a protracted sickness. His mother earned a living for herself and her four children by making shoe-blacking after an old English recipe. At eight years he went as an office boy to the works of his father's cousin, Richard Hoe, the inventor of the first of the modern American printing presses. The boy worked ten hours a day; his wages were a dollar a week; Sundays he listened through three heavy sermons; evenings he went to night classes; and one school year his employer let his wages go on while the boy attended day school. Colonel Hoe was a friend of Morse, the inventor of the telegraph, and the first private wire in the world was strung to his factory. Twelve-year-old Samuel Barrows operated it. The boy also studied shorthand, and throughout his life was an expert stenographer.* During the war he attempted to enlist in the navy but was thrown out on account of his health; and to retrieve the drains in strength which overwork since childhood had made upon him, he took a position as secretary with Dr. Jackson of the Sanitarium in Dansville, New York. It was there that he met Isabel Hayes Chapin, who was equipping herself as a medical missionary to India, whither she had gone as a bride of eighteen and whence she had returned, a widow, after two short years. Mr. and Mrs. Barrows were married June 28, 1867. They were twenty-two; they had no money; but they were rich in purpose, and with rare courage and mutual helpfulness set about a larger preparation for the work of life.

While Mrs. Barrows completed her medical studies,—those were the days when women students were pelted and ridiculed,—Mr. Barrows served as a reporter on the New York *Tribune*, and for a summer as city editor on the New York *World*, then a religious daily. In 1868 he was appointed stenographic secretary to William H. Seward, who had been Secretary of State in Lincoln's great war cabinet, and he remained in the Department of State until 1874. At one time he' fell ill with typhoid and Mrs. Barrows took his post, the first woman employed in the department. During this period, she completed her medical studies by a year at Vienna, specializing in the eye. "You must go," the young husband had said to her, "if I have to live on pea soup and sleep in a loft." As a matter of fact he lodged in a small room and prepared his own food. Returning to America, Mrs. Barrows was the first oculist to practice at the national capital. She taught also in Howard Medical School and took students as boarders. Earnings from these various quarters now enabled the young wife to make it possible for her husband to complete his own professional education. In this way they took turn about, helping each other.

Mr. Barrows had studied out of hours at Columbian University, Washington (exchanging shorthand for Latin and Greek). He now entered Harvard Divinity School and graduated in 1874 (B. D.). Those were the years when Louis Agassiz was delivering

* Mr. and Mrs. Barrows accomplished jointly what had never been done before— the first verbatim report of one of Phillips Brooks's rapid sermons. Mrs. Barrows has listened to addresses in German by Carl Schurz, translated them mentally, and taken them down in English while in process of delivery. For twenty years she was official reporter and editor of the proceedings of the National Conference of Charities and Correction, and has served various international conventions in a similar capacity, inscribing her notes in whatever language was spoken. Post cards marked with pot hooks by husband or wife carried more intelligence to the other than long letters between less gifted correspondents.

his famous lectures in natural science at Cambridge, and every Sunday the New York *Tribune* reported them at a page in length. The work was done by Mr. and Mrs. Barrows, and their reports were made up by Agassiz into a book.

During the summers of 1873 and 1874, the divinity student was with General Custer (perhaps the most famous of our Western Indian fighters), accompanying expeditions to the Yellowstone and to the Black Hills as correspondent for the *Tribune*. These summers were full of adventure. Correspondent Barrows was the first to report the discovery of gold in the Black Hills; on one occasion a bullet struck a tree just above his head, and on another he narrowly escaped an ambush in which his companion was killed. By good fortune he did not set out the next season (that of the Indian massacre when Custer's whole force was ambushed and killed), but with his family spent the year in postgraduate studies at Leipzig. Returning to this country, Mr. Barrows was made minister of the First Parish, Dorchester, Mass. His first sermon bore these words at the head of the first page, in the shorthand characters from which he always preached—"God is love"; and it has been said of him that he never altogether got away from this text. Four years later he became editor of the *Christian Register*, making that Unitarian journal a national force during the decades of the great church weeklies. In 1897, Rev. Mr. Barrows was elected to the Fifty-fifth Congress, a Republican from a heavily Democratic district, which chose him, while he was in Europe, to lead the revolt against a corrupt representative. Congressman Barrows's first success was in securing permission to send ships to India loaded with grain for the famine sufferers; his chief speech perhaps was one in favor of admitting foreign books and works of art free of duty;—again that balance which has been pointed out as characteristic of the compelling interests in his life. His legislative career was short—one term—but during that time he was instrumental in associating the United States Congress with the parliaments of the world. He was the first American to join the Interparliamentary Union, and ten years later was the active member of the committee in charge of the St. Louis meeting which brought here representatives of the legislatures of civilization.

Mr. Barrows's retirement from Washington was followed by the maturing of his larger work for prison reform. He had been one of the founders of the Massachusetts Prison Association and had helped develop the probation system in that state. In 1896 he was appointed by President Cleveland, Commissioner for the United States on the International Prison Commission. He was a representative of the United States at the quinquennial congresses in Paris and Brussels, and at Budapest was elected president. It was through his efforts that the congress is this year held in Washington. Mr. Barrows was instrumental in securing a federal appropriation of $20,000 for the gathering, and the early work of preparation was done by him. With Mrs. Barrows he had planned a tour of the South American republics to enlist their interest in the Washington gathering. As an outgrowth of the work he was able to carry on through the legations in Washington, Mexico, Venezuela, Colombia, Guatemala, and Panama adhered to the International Congress in the twelve months following his death.

In 1899 Mr. Barrows was appointed corresponding secretary of the Prison Association of New York, and for ten years his influence for progress and breadth of view in penal legislation was cumulative in both state and nation. It was marked by his repeated assaults on the stupid blunder of capital punishment, by his ready recognition of the juvenile court idea, his energetic attacks upon systems of prison idleness, and his unswerving support of the reformatory movement, probation and parole. Mr. Barrows drafted the first probation law of New York state in 1901 and, to quote a recent review by Homer Folks, president of the State Probation Commission, "to his initiative and perseverance we owe its passage." In securing its enactment, Mr. Barrows was obliged to make a number of concessions. "The wisdom of his original position," says Mr. Folks, "has been demonstrated by the actual operations of the statute." Mr. Barrows was a member of the Temporary Probation Commission of 1905–06, which urged further legislation toward a comprehensive state system, and which paved the way for the permanent State Probation Commission, with power of inquiry and suggestion, now serving the commonwealth. These espousals of reform have been linked with a grasp of the technical side of institutional construction and management. Mr. Barrows was a member of the New York State Commission on New Prisons which is charged with the task of replacing old, disease-ridden Sing Sing with a modern plant. To this end he visited Great Britain, Sweden, Finland, Russia, Germany, France, Spain and Portugal. Some of the best energies of the last years of his life were devoted, against domineering political opposition, toward securing the embodiment in the new prison of some of the standards set by modern structures in Europe. At the 1909 session of the New York Legislature, in co-operation with the State Prison Commission, his association strongly urged the establishment of three state work-houses and a reformatory for youthful misdemeanants. When taken sick, he was in Albany in support of bills to make the office of sheriff of Queens county, New York, a salaried one, to establish a board of trustees of labor colonies for the detention, reformation and instruction of persons convicted of vagrancy, drunkenness, etc., and to establish the "John Howard Industrial School" for the educational, industrial, and moral instruction of juvenile delinquents. In behalf of the latter measure, in a report drafted for the Prison Association of New York, and released for publication one week before his death, he made this appeal:

"The poor boy in New York is pretty well taken care of and so is the youthful felon. But the youthful misdemeanant has been overlooked.

"It is appalling to think that by a process of legal indifference and neglect a boy may be sent for six months or a year to a jail where he comes into the most degraded society, where he is without work and without schooling, except the deplorable schooling in crime furnished by older and hardened offenders. A few figures from the official reports of the State Commission of Prisons show how imperative is the need. The number of boys from sixteen to twenty-one sentenced to jails and penitentiaries for the past year outside of Greater New York was 4428 and the number of the same age sentenced in New York City was 14,044, a total of 18,472. In addition, more than 10,000 between the ages of twenty-one and thirty are likewise sentenced to the jails and penitentiaries."

The passage is cited because of its timely bearing, although it is not representative of the lofty utterances which found place in many of Mr. Barrows's speeches and writings, nor of those less frequent instances in which indignation mounted over his persistent kindliness. Then he spoke the wrath that was in him at the continuation of conditions which sicken and besot humanity. His public arraignment was of methods and institutions rather than of men. He was a staunch fighter of the iniquitous system by which sheriffs derive their income from fees for the custody and keep of prisoners in the county jails. He succeeded in helping abolish it in many counties in New York state, and those who love him best feel that he fell a victim to his unending warfare to this end. For the shrievalty has been one of the prizes in local politics in America and in some states the fee system has had to be rooted out one county at a time. The weeks preceding his illness he was engaged in a determined effort to free Queens county, one of the strongholds of the system in New York. Hundreds of impressionable first offenders who should have been placed on probation or in the reformatories, had been held in this old Long Island jail because of the profit in their keep. Mr. Barrows's last letter, written from Albany the day he was taken ill, told how men of both parties were leagued against him with an obdurateness which the graft investigations in the New York legislature the past winter have served to throw light upon. For along with that flexibility in American political life which enables us to adopt new forms of penological activities, we suffer the disadvantage even in our older commonwealths that state work is subjected repeatedly to the whims and perversions of the corrupt elements in the legislatures. The movements to build up the state institutional systems and to free them from political interference, involve, therefore, some of the vital working problems in American democracy; and while at an international gathering we may deplore those obstructionists, our fellow-countrymen, who for petty political ends harassed and half-thwarted this man, we can rightly feel that these legislative campaigns in which he sought the public good with singleness of purpose were in no sense petty, but part of the fundamental strivings of popular government toward the nobler social fabric of the morrow. Nor in the immediate issue were his efforts fruitless. Seven days after Mr. Barrows's death, the bill he had worked for passed both houses of the legislature, so that Governor Hughes, who had recommended it, could put his signature upon it and make it law. There was, nevertheless, a solemn indictment in the circumstances of his death, which those who were responsible for blocking the reforms for which he was straining every nerve, must settle with their consciences as best they may,—those who discounted the disease and criminality bred in jail conditions, and saw only an office for the fall elections, and such fees as have made men rich. And there is a challenge in the circumstances of his death to younger men to carry forward the causes that laid such compelling hold upon his last strength.

In his federal capacity, Mr. Barrows did much work with the Department of Justice toward a revision of the penal law of the United States. He was identified with bills before the last Congress, providing for the parole of United States prisoners, for the appointment of probation officers and the suspension of sentence in United States courts, and for a revision of the statutes relating to the commitment of United States prisoners to state reformatories. He was interested in the work of the local commission which reported in

1909 on the jail and workhouse, in the District of Columbia, and which recommended the establishment of a model system for the national capital.

Mr. Barrows's services were not restricted to New York state and the federal government. They were at the call of prison reform in every commonwealth. This was illustrated in his long volunteer work as departmental editor on the treatment of the delinquent for *Charities Review, Charities and The Commons* and *The Survey*, involving, as it did, a large investment of time and interest. He was repeatedly chairman of committees of the National Prison Association, and the National Conference of Charities and Correction. Among recent undertakings, mention should be made of his work on the committee which stirred up local interest throughout the country in the sanitary conditions of the county jails. He drafted reformatory and probation laws for the new state of Oklahoma, addressing the legislature in their behalf. His visit and good counsel are among the cherished memories of the leaders in the new state. In 1908 he addressed three state conferences on the Pacific Coast and visited penal institutions from San Diego, California, to Seattle, Washington. In January, 1909, he made three addresses to help arouse public sentiment in Milwaukee, Wisconsin, against conditions in the municipal house of correction.

Through reports which he prepared or edited for the International Prison Commission his work as circuit rider in the humanities found widespread application. There were fifteen of these titles,* and they have been circulated in many countries. In some of these reports he had the assistance of many experts; some were drafted by individual authors, himself among others, and Dr. Charles R.

---

* *Reports Prepared for the International Prison Commission by Samuel J. Barrows, Commissioner.*

Report of the delegates of the United States to the Fifth International Prison Congress, held at Paris, France, in July, 1895; by Roeliff Brinkerhoff, R. W. McClaughry, Charlton T. Lewis, Paul R. Brown and S. J. Barrows. Washington, 1896.

The criminal insane in the United States and in foreign countries; by S. J. Barrows. Washington, 1898.

The indeterminate sentence and parole law; by Warren F. Spalding, Martin D. Follett, R. W. McClaughry, a committee of the American Bar Association and S. J. Barrows. Washington, 1899.

Penological questions; by S. E. Baldwin, C. E. Felton, J. B. Chapin, M. J. Cassidy, E. C. Putnam, E. G. Evans, James Allison, Michael Heymann, Mrs. L. M. B. Mitchell and Mrs. L. L. Brackett. Washington, 1899.

New legislation concerning crimes, misdemeanors and penalties; compiled by S. J. Barrows. Washington, 1900.

The reformatory system in the United States; by S. J. Barrows, Z. R. Brockway, F. B. Sanborn, C. D. Warner, C. T. Lewis, J. F. Scott, I. J. Wistar, Bishop S. Fallows, Gen. R. Brinkerhoff, Mrs. I. C. Barrows, Mrs. E. C. Johnson, T. E. Ellison, Henry Wolfer, and T. J. Charlton. Washington, 1900.

Henderson, his successor as president of the International Prison Congress.

Mr. Barrows made these reports, together with his biennial trips to Europe, as American prison commissioner responsible to the United States Department of State, a basis for what was in truth a rare diplomatic service—an informal ambassadorship to all nations in the cause of enlightened justice. Witness, for instance, two letters received shortly after his death, in the same day's mail. One, from Tasmania, told how primitive was the prison system there, and what great changes would have to be made before it could truly be reformative. The writer said that the system set forth in the New York Association's report sent by Mr. Barrows would largely form the key to the improvements advocated: "You have given me fresh courage in this, my life work, and strength to carry it on. You little know how far into the future your kindness will reach." The second letter was from an official of the Transvaal Prison Department, who had received counsel from Mr. Barrows, and who had lent his reports in many quarters, "where they would be more eloquent than I," and made them available for the press. The writer added:

"It is clear that American methods find greatest favor here and we trust in the future that we shall be able to keep in touch with the United States and learn what is taking place. When I tell you that since my first letter to you, we have a reformatory in full working order and classification in all the large prisons, and that this session

Prison systems of the United States; by S. J. Barrows, Frank Strong, B. F Smith, C. L. Stonaker, T. D. Wells, H. S. Landis, C. A. Plummer, G. S. Griffith, F. G. Pettigrove, O. M. Barnes, Frank Conley, A. E. Harvey, C. B. Denson, J. D. Lee, I. J. Wistar, Nelson Viall, G. N. Dow, S. A. Hawk, N. D. McDonald, and P. W. Ayres. Washington, 1900.

The cost of crime; by Eugene Smith. Washington, 1901.

Growth of the criminal law of the United States; by D. K. Watson. Washington, 1902.

The Sixth International Prison Congress, held at Brussels, Belgium, in August, 1900. Washington, 1903.

Penal Codes of France, Germany, Belgium, and Japan; by R. Bérenger, E. Jarno, Alfred Le Poittevin, Wolfgang Mittermaier, Hermann Adami, Adolph Prins, and Keigo Kiyoura. Washington, 1901.

Modern prison systems; by C. R. Henderson. Washington, 1903.

Programme of questions for the Seventh International Prison Congress. Washington, 1904.

Tuberculosis in Penal Institutions; by Julius B. Ransom, M.D. Washington, 1904.

Children's courts in the United States; by S. J. Barrows, R. S. Tuthill, T. D. Hurley, Thomas Murphy, J. M. Mayer, R. J. Wilkin, B. B. Lindsey, Mrs. H. K. Schoff, Bert Hall, A. F. Skinner, G. W. Stubbs, Mrs. H. W. Rogers, and C. C. Eliot. Washington, 1904.

Report of proceedings of the Seventh International Prison Congress, held at Budapest, Hungary, in September, 1905. Washington, 1907.

of Parliament will see introduced the principles of indeterminate sentence, parole and probation and other improvements in the treatment of juvenile delinquents, you will see that your action in sending me your books was not entirely in vain."

The meeting of the International Prison Commission in Paris in the July following Mr. Barrows's death, was made the occasion of expressions of regard on the part of fellow members. Doctor Guillaume of Switzerland, the secretary, reviewed Mr. Barrows's work from the time of his attendance at the Paris Congress in 1895. The Congress was founded through the efforts of an American, Dr. E. C. Wines, but the United States had never taken the steps necessary to formally become a party to the international body. This followed in 1896, and Mr. Barrows was appointed American Commissioner. From that date forward, he sought in the reports, in the regular sessions of the international commission, and in the quinquennial congresses to act as interpreter of the vital advances in penology which were being carried forward in America. Through his efforts, more than through any other agency, have European students and commissions become acquainted with the work of the American reformatories, the juvenile courts, the junior republics, the indeterminate sentence, probation and parole as practiced in the more progressive states. It is perhaps difficult for Americans to appreciate the eager welcome accorded these discriminating official reports on the contributions which the new world has been making to the practice of social control and regeneration. In Mr. Barrows, they found a spokesman who was afire with the fresh inspiration which comes of a new continent where civilization is less trammeled with precedent, but who, nevertheless, was in no sense a provincial; whose alert interest and foreign tours of inspection made it possible for him to relate what he put forth to the laws and institutions of the mother countries. From them, in this humanitarian balance of trade, he drew as well as gave. At the Brussels Congress of 1900, Mr. Barrows presented reports on the indeterminate sentence and conditional release. "There it was," said Dr. Guillaume, "that he won all our hearts." M. Maus, chief of the Bureau of Justice for Belgium, in reporting the section on penal legislation, quoted especially his saying that it would be no more absurd to let a patient, whether well or not, leave a hospital on a fixed day, than to let the release of a prisoner be entirely a matter of the calendar. "We do not ask you to abandon what you have already created in Europe," said the American Commissioner, "but to adopt what you find true in our experience." He showed how

Americans have taken the good wherever we have found it—such inspiration as has come to us, for instance, from the Irish prison system, or the reform schools of continental Europe. The report on American reformatories which he transmitted to another section of this Congress, led to a request for still further documents "so as to build on this sure foundation," and his report on children's courts to the following Congress at Budapest was characterized as "popularizing this new institution in all civilized countries." At Budapest also he gave a public lecture on child-welfare work in the United States and was charged with the presidency of one of the sections in which the discussion ranged in three languages. He communicated the official letter of invitation from President Roosevelt for the Congress to come to America and his election to the presidency was by acclamation. Two years later at Lausanne, he reported to the International Commission on the progress of the work, and again to quote Dr. Guillaume "we saw for ourselves with what devotion he fulfilled his duties."

Space forbids excursions into the other fields of interest which Mr. Barrows explored with such keen zest throughout his life. His religious experience began with folded arms beneath the teacher's quick rattan in the old Cannon Street Church, New York, as related in his book, A Baptist Meeting-House. As a stripling, he was known as the "Boy Preacher," frequenting the docks and climbing on barrels or the first keg at hand, to beg the sailors to enter the good road. He picked up words of greeting from strange tongues, and kept track of the cruisings of the ships making port. Soon after his majority he became a Unitarian, and what a friend has called his "incessant helpfulness" was but a practical living out of the catholicity of his faith. Margaret Deland drew not a little of the material for her novel, John Ward, Preacher, from his early book, The Doom of the Majority of Mankind, and one of his recent articles, The Church I Am Looking For, published anonymously in *The Independent*, provoked much discussion. The writer had looked for a vineyard in which to work; instead they had set him to building fences. He was a strong advocate in the peace movement, a leader in the Mohonk conferences on the Negroes, Indians, and international arbitration, and in each of these fields took a lifelong and active interest. It was Howard University (colored) which granted him the degree of doctor of divinity in 1897. Owing to his interest in legal questions he became an active member of the American Society of International Law.

Mr. Barrows was a frequent editorial contributor to magazines, notably *The Atlantic, The North American Review, The Outlook* and *The Independent,* his writings showing both a constructive earnestness and an inimitable humor. In 1908 he prepared a series of articles for *The Outlook* on the temperance movement and became a formidable figure in the new discussion of the liquor question. His readiness to assume emergent tasks in addition to his serene mastery of routine responsibilities was illustrated in the spring of 1906, when he acted as executive secretary of the Russian Famine Relief Committee, which collected over $50,000 in this country. He was one of the first to listen and act when Nicalos Shishkoff came single-handed to this country and made his urgent appeal for the Volga provinces; and the following summer (1907) Mr. and Mrs. Barrows travelled seven days and nights, going and coming, from Moscow, to spend one day with him at Samara. No trouble was too great for him to take for a friend.

The following paragraphs are from a resolution adopted May 1, 1909, by the Ministerial Union of Boston, Massachusetts, where for twenty-five years Mr. Barrows was a resident; four years as we have seen as minister of the First Parish, Dorchester; sixteen as editor of the Christian Register and afterward as member of Congress from the Tenth District:

"Many of us knew him personally, and to the respect and admiration which all felt, added our warm friendship and love. . . . We knew him as one of the best of men, large-hearted, unselfish, loving and lovable. . . . He served with untiring zeal every cause involving the welfare of humanity,—political emancipation at home or abroad, equal suffrage for men and women, the temperance movement, the industrial emancipation of women and children, a wiser and more liberal philanthropy, the humane treatment and reformation of prisoners, and care for them when discharged,—in every way manifesting his belief in a brotherhood of universal goodwill and peace. A master of languages, acquainted with many lands by frequent visits, an international messenger of mercy and peace, he was a true 'citizen of the world.'

"Nor can we forget his delight in music, poetry, and art, his love of nature, his keen sense of humor, his happy, youthful spirit, his courtesy, sympathy, and loyalty, which made him dear to young and old. Shall we not believe that he has left us but to continue his progress, 'onward and upward forever?'"

A hundred stories could be told of the approachableness and

ineffable sympathy of the man. "You need not be afraid to disturb me by writing upon this subject," was his answer to a letter from an unknown questioner,—"I am always deeply interested in having something done." He often told how he taught a new play at jackstones to the newsboys at the corner where he took the car. Passing by, some days later, he saw one of them nudge a playfellow: "There he goes," he overheard, "there's the feller that interduced 'skunks' inter Dorchester." But neither his ever-present sympathy, nor his patient reluctance to retort in the face of opposition or attack, nor the glamour of philosophy which shone in his face, was cloak for inaction. He was the fastest horseman in the Massachusetts regiment of which for fifteen years he was chaplain. As a youth, in the days of the draft riots, he stamped out the firebrands which a mob had thrown into a store they were about to loot. As a reporter, he made some of the famous "beats" of his day—one, a great wreck on the Atlantic Coast, and another, a New Jersey execution. The hanging was delayed until a late hour and, when the correspondents posted to the telegraph office, they found it closed. Barrows connected the wire which had been cut off and sent his message in with his own hands—the only one to reach New York in time for press.

A member of the Handel and Haydn Society in Boston, Mr. Barrows became a member and director of the Oratorio Society in New York. He learned the piano at fifty, and at the time of his death was practicing two hours a day on the organ at St. George's. He composed the words and music of many hymns, the harmony of an organ prelude, the lively music of such fancies as The Echo Queen, and The Beacon Street Tramp, a "Panethnicphilanthropometric Play" which he wrote and took part in with much gaiety.

Mr. Barrows spoke French, German and Modern Greek, read Dutch and Italian and was learning Spanish for his South American trip. The address of the American Commissioner in Hungarian was a feature of the great Budapest Prison Congress. This last incident illustrates the painstaking thoroughness with which Mr. Barrows put himself into an undertaking which would make for common understanding among men. In the months preceding the Congress he studied the Hungarian grammar and vocabulary, in order to enable him to take some part in informal conversation. He wrote out his speech in English, and not wishing to trust it to an ordinary translator, unfamiliar with penology, he translated it into German for a German friend, who in turn translated it into Hungarian. He then practically committed it to memory, and after reaching Austria-Hungary, was drilled in it by a Hungarian professor, much as you would practice a song. When he delivered it, all this exacting work of preparation was forgotten. He began in French, then changed to Hungarian and voiced his admiration for the Magyar people. What he told them was not the customary platitudes, but how, as a child in New York, he had been lifted to the shoulder in a crowd that he might see Kossuth. Not a man in that room of Hungarians had ever seen the great exile. At Mr. Barrows's words they jumped to the tables and applauded vociferously. The national feeling in 1905 in Budapest was so intense that at this banquet the musicians did not dare play the national hymn; and in introducing the story, Mr. Barrows explained that he gave it only as an historical incident. The next morning, every newspaper in Hungary had his address in full; and the words of fraternal liking of the American Commissioner, unknown the day before, were repeated throughout the empire.

Mr. Barrows was not only a polyglot, but a distinguished student of the dead languages of the East. In the *Unitarian Review* of Boston, of which from 1877 to 1888 he was associate editor, he published many essays on Assyriology and the Bible, the Comparative Mythology of Ancient Peoples, and the like.

It was the life and culture of the Greeks which laid closest hold upon his hours of leisure and which had artistic sequence in the work of his daughter, Mabel Hay Barrows Mussey, in reviving the Greek drama in America. Mr. Barrows spent a year in Greece with Dörpfeld, the famous German archæologist, and was with him when he dug up the Homeric city of Troy. He was the author of The Isles and Shrines of Greece. Dr. Henderson, his successor as president of the International Prison Commission, said of him at the Paris meeting in 1909: "By the side of the old songs of Homer, which he loved, he sought to place the sweet melodies of hope for the convicted." Homer was, in truth, his heart's companion, and at his summer home on Lake Memphremagog in lower Quebec, the first two hours after sunrise were given over to reading the new meaning of a student of peoples into the ancient lines. It was in this camp started by the Shaybacks,—as the Barrows had called themselves when they first explored the region thirty-three years before,—at Cedar Lodge, and Cabin June, and Birchbay, that the marvellous family life of this American household found its amplest expression. Hoe, Seward, Agassiz, Phillips Brooks, Brockway, Dörpfeld, Custer,—those were various men to mark a man's life intimately, and they but stand for a hundred other men whom he counted as friends, whose names would be equally familiar to an international congress. But here—and this is of greater meaning—about their open fires and under the log rafters, "Uncle June" and "Aunt Isabel" have been in a very real sense foster parents to a company of children of the world, knowing no race, or creed, or color as not of kin. Here was an everyday embodiment of that universal sympathy, gentle, resistless, which marked Mr. Barrows's play, and work, and preaching—which made fraternalism the great tenet of his democracy and made the uncrowned decent living of this man at once a harmony and a social force. Here was a man who held fellowship with the ancient Greeks, with the famine-lean peasants of the Volga provinces, with the prisoner of the meanest jail, with the masters of music and art and government, with the God of the mountain peaks of his northern lake,—"Nor time nor space nor deep nor high" could keep his own away from him.

VI

GEN. RUTHERFORD B. HAYES*

By W. M. F. ROUND

EX-PRESIDENT Rutherford B. Hayes, twice a congressman, thrice governor of Ohio, once a military officer of high position and renown, once President of the United States, had also another side to his character than that indicated by these honorable titles. He was eminently and before all things a philanthropist, a lover of his fellow men and a worker for their interests.

A careful study of his life from early manhood until his too early death shows him to have been identified with many of the great reforms of his time. Quietly, unostentatiously, valuing his great honors for what they were worth, but never parading them, Mr. Hayes was easily a leader in the movement for the uplifting of the colored race in the South and for the improvement of the penal system of the country.

There was no subject touching the elevation of humanity in America, no matter how deep the problem involved, but that General Hayes brought the most untiring efforts to help in its solution and gave both his time and his name to the organization of practical charities. Beginning in his own city among his own neighbors, he was known as a generous giver, a thoughtful adviser, a sympathetic helper, wherever there was need.

In the larger affairs of the national organization of charities this good man permitted himself to be loaded with onerous duties, never once counted his ease or the leisure which he had the right to enjoy, and did perhaps more than any other man in the country to give stability and character to the Prison Reform movement, to the cause of the education of the colored man, and to a reasonable amelioration of the woes of the Indian. Calm, painstaking, with a singularly clear vision for the main facts and issues, never wavering in the slightest where a question of principle was involved, General Hayes was a tower of strength to any movement to which he lent his name,

*From the Proceedings of the Annual Congress of the National Prison Association of the United States, held at Baltimore, December 3-7, 1892, page 266.

R. B. Hayes.

and knowing the prestige that belonged to an ex-President of the United States, he lent his name only where he was willing to follow with his entire influence and his whole personality. There was no clearer headed or more conscientious public man in this country than he was. His patience in bearing the atrocious calumnies of an opposing party was heroic.

It is as a prison reformer that the writer of this article has best known General Hayes and his work. In 1870, there was called at Cincinnati a National Prison Congress—which perhaps had a wider influence than any that has been held since—and we find General Hayes presiding at the congress. At that time he was governor of Ohio. All the surviving members of that congress bear testimony to the heartiness with which Governor Hayes entered into the deliberations, and from that moment he linked himself with the advanced guard of prison reformers. He has never fallen behind.

At that time the indeterminate sentence was only named to be considered a scheme of visionaries and was regarded as an attack upon established theories of punishment for crime. Governor Hayes at once recognized in it the keynote of the new penology and the solution of many of the most vexed problems of crime treatment. He, however, with singular wisdom refrained from making it the burden of his public utterances, but lost no opportunity to aid the scheme and its gradual introduction into his own and other states. He engaged in every movement of the prison reformers, and was one of the original incorporators of the National Prison Association of the United States.

Upon the death of Dr. Wines the National Prison Association of the United States, having accomplished a large work in the organization of the International Penitentiary Commission and the establishment of international penitentiary congresses, became inactive. The work inaugurated by it in Europe went on most successfully, but the National Prison Association itself held no meetings. In 1883, it was found desirable to reorganize the National Prison Association. A call was issued by the Prison Association of New York for a meeting to be held at Saratoga at the same time as the meeting of the National Social Science Association. Four men of the original members of the association responded to the call. To make a quorum required five, and the writer of these lines went out to search for the fifth, finding the late Irenæus Prime in a Saratoga boarding house just recovering from a severe illness, who at a great risk to his health left his room to complete the quorum. Then and there General

Hayes was elected president of the National Prison Association. There was great uncertainty as to the success of its reorganization, but in the minds of those who had the matter in hand there was no doubt as to its need. A full statement of the cause was written to General Hayes, who at once accepted the position of president of the association, and from that moment he has held a laboring oar in the organization and upbuilding of this great body, which is perhaps to-day as influential as any similar organization in the country or in the world. The journey from Fremont to New York was never too long for him to take to attend the meetings.

A man full of cares and occupations, he always found time for a careful and thoughtful consideration of every question that came before the association. He has never missed a meeting of the National Prison Congress, and his speeches from the first have had the truest ring of the reformer. In his Toronto address we find him denouncing the jail system of the country and proposing measures for its reformation. We find him demanding the entire separation of young and old offenders. We find him advocating the permanent confinement of habitual criminals in his Boston address. We find him pleading for a recognition of the common humanity in criminals alike with honest men. In Nashville we find him making an earnest plea for the indeterminate sentence. In Cincinnati we find him pleading for a better education of criminals in prison industry and in letters; always in the front rank and always following up his words by his utmost personal influence in his own state and in the nation.

Under the presidency of General Hayes the National Prison Association in its organization and re-organization has grown from its five members in Saratoga in 1883 to more than two hundred, and numbers all the leading prison men of the country. There is not one of them but has felt a warm feeling of fellowship and love for President Hayes; that they could freely approach him for advice, and fully depend upon him for support in any measure of reform that they wished to introduce.

It is not alone in the field of prison reform that General Hayes has won distinction as a philanthropist. His presidency of the board of managers of the Slater fund has led him to a most thorough study of the social condition of the Negro at the South, and of methods for his uplifting. The writer of this article can remember a conversation with General Gordon, of Georgia, in which he said that he had never seen in his life a man who had so thoroughly mastered the difficulties that beset the problem of the colored race in the South as General

Hayes. In the war he had taken his life in his hand to fight for this race, had thrown all the weight of his character against slavery; as a President he had undertaken the problem of reconciliation between North and South, fully recognizing the rights of both the vanquished and the victorious; and later on, as a citizen, had studied the whole problem of the Southern social condition without prejudice or sectional bias. His faith in the future of the colored man of the South was very great, but his uplifting was to depend upon his education, and his education to be effected and controlled by the race that had been his master. It must be a process of generations. In the administration of the Peabody and Slater funds he was a tower of strength and of wise counsel.

In all matters of education General Hayes was deeply interested. As a trustee of the Ohio University he advocated the most advanced methods, the most liberal scheme of education. As a private citizen in Fremont, there was not a detail of public school management that he was not familiar with, and there was not an educational movement in the whole country based upon novel or advanced ideas that he did not find it worth while to study, and if possible, to approve.

When the scheme for the Burnham Industrial Farm was laid out, sitting face to face with General Hayes in an hour's conversation the organizer unfolded to him the principles that were to underlie that institution. The need had already been apparent to both. Intelligent questions as to the smallest details of the plan, wise criticisms of some features, warnings as to some dangers, all fell from the lips of this great-hearted public man, and at the conclusion of the conversation he put forth his hand and said, "You are on the right track; never be discouraged. You will certainly succeed." He was from that hour a warm friend of the movement. Among the most cherished traditions of the Burnham Farm is the memory of a visit of several days' duration, and hanging on the wall of the Brothers' Room is a cordial letter expressing approbation of the system. During that visit there was not a boy there with whom Mr. Hayes did not have a personal talk as to his future nor a brother with whom he did not leave a new impulse of zeal by his inspiring words. He followed the growth of the movement step by step and had planned another visit during the coming summer.

In his charities, in his works of public philanthropy, in his efforts for education, he was most generously unsparing of himself and most conscientious. He never permitted his name to be used in connection with any enterprise until he had sifted it to the utmost. He never permitted his name to be used in connection with any enterprise to which he did not give his own personality. If he accepted a title, he accepted the duties that went with it, and performed them in the most careful and methodical manner. His opportunities for enriching himself by the use of the prestige that naturally attached to him were very great. He put them by with admirable firmness, and the dignity that belonged to a man who had held the first office in the gift of the nation was never lowered by any act of his daily life. Those who knew him best, most closely, the citizens of his own town, bear testimony to the simplicity of his character, to the tenderness of his heart, to the generosity of his nature, to the wisdom of his counsel.

He will be remembered in the pages of our national history as a brave soldier, a noble man, a good President and one of the foremost of American philanthropists, who carried the duties of the first citizen of the country with entire integrity. Because he lived and labored he has left a higher standard of American manhood.

[The revival of the American Prison Association after the death of Dr. E. C. Wines was chiefly due to the initiative of Mr. Round. He, more than any other individual, was responsible for the enlistment of President Hayes in the movement, and his unpaid and valuable service as Secretary of the Association deserves the grateful praise of all who are interested in its work and success.—EDITOR.]

VII

BIOGRAPHICAL SKETCHES

FRANCIS LIEBER

D R. FRANCIS LIEBER, to whom reference has been repeatedly made in the preceding pages, is entitled to more than the bare mention of his name. He deserves, indeed, an article to himself.

He was born in Berlin, in 1800; saw the French troops enter the Prussian capital, after the battle of Jena; swore upon his knees, in 1813, to assassinate Napoleon; enlisted in the Prussian army at the age of fifteen, under Blücher; and fought in the battle of Waterloo, receiving two wounds at Namur, one of which was through the neck and came near proving fatal. He was an early member of the German Turn-Verein, and in 1819, for little or no apparent reason, was for four months a political prisoner. He was again imprisoned in 1824 at Kopenick, a suburb of Berlin, and was released (but upon conditions) at the expiration of more than seven months, only at the personal intercession of Niebuhr, the historian, in whose family he had been a tutor when Niebuhr was Prussian Minister at Rome. Young Lieber had, in 1821, while a student at Dresden, been deeply smitten with philhellenism, and in 1822 he sailed, with a company of juvenile enthusiasts in the cause of human freedom, for Greece. He returned from this expedition penniless and disillusioned, having lost all and achieved nothing. As Col. Napier said of those who shared his aspirations, "All came expecting to find the Peloponnesus filled with Plutarch's men, and all returned thinking the inhabitants of Newgate more moral." It was then that Niebuhr took him to his own home, and healed his more than half-broken heart. He was finally pardoned by Frederick William IV, in 1824.

In 1826 he became a voluntary exile from his native land, spent nearly a year in England, and finally landed in New York in June, 1827. He proceeded directly to Boston, where he established a gymnasium and swimming school. He became the editor of the Encyclopedia Americana, published by Carey, Lee and Carey in Philadelphia, of which the first two volumes were printed in 1829. In September and October, 1833, he drew up the plan adopted for the organization and government of Girard College.   In 1835, he was elected professor of history and political economy in the university of South Carolina, a position which he held for twenty years, and then resigned.   In 1857, he was chosen professor of history and political science in Columbia College, New York.   Dr. Lieber's favorite aphorism was *"Nullum jus sine officio, nullum officium sine jure."*   In his inaugural at Columbia College, in 1859, he said that right and duty are like Castor and Pollux or St. Elmo's fire, an electrical phenomenon sometimes witnessed at sea, in which a blue flame appears at one or both ends of a yard-arm.   The appearance of two flames presages a fine sailing; if only one is seen, it is a sign of foul weather.   In his house he gave a conspicuous place to the inscription, "Patria cara: carior libertas: veritas carissima."   His biographer, Mr. Thomas S. Perry, declares that his life was moulded by that thought.

There are in his Life and Letters many indications of his interest in the prison question.   He visited the Eastern Penitentiary of Pennsylvania in October, 1831, of which he writes in his diary: "The best prison in existence, according to de Tocqueville and de Beaumont.   I shall make myself well acquainted with this subject, for I feel sure it will be one of the greatest interest to me, inasmuch as right and wrong have always occupied my mind."   In May, 1832, we find him at Sing Sing, where he met Mr. Crawford, the English Commissioner to inspect and report upon American prisons.   In 1834, he mentions in his diary, among the subjects continually in his head, that of "penology."   He coined this word from his brain; later he defined it in a letter to de Tocqueville, as "that branch of criminal science which occupies itself (or ought to do so) with the punishment and the criminal; not with the definition of crime, the subject of accountability and the proving of the crime, which belong to criminal law and the penal process."   In a letter to Privy Councillor Mittermaier, in 1836, he wrote: "Do not feel that I shall give up writing my 'Penology.'   It is one of the thoughts which have taken possession of my mind, and it will occupy me until I have mastered it. I hope to show that it is the duty of the state to reform the criminal; at all events it must be her aim not to make him any worse."

This thought was in his mind, evidently, when in 1844, in conversation with Frederick William IV, King of Prussia, praising and defending the Pennsylvania system of prison discipline, he said: "When you bring together six criminals who have each six degrees of evil in them, you will increase this to twelve by bringing them in communication with each other."   Under the seal of the strictest

Francis Lieber

secrecy, he wrote de Tocqueville: "The king is unconditionally for the Pennsylvania system, but most of his Ministers are not." Humboldt, among others, opposed it. At this interview, Lieber implored the king to "put an end to the scandalous public executions." These he called "extramural;" the words extramural and intramural, which are now a part of the English vocabulary, were both his invention. He was nevertheless a firm believer in the necessity for capital punishment, and ridiculed the arguments adduced in opposition to it. The king desired to appoint him Inspector General of Prussian Prisons, and lecturer on penology to the universities, but Lieber declined this offer.

In 1848, he was appointed by the meeting of the "Friends of Prison Discipline" chairman of a committee on the pardoning power and its abuses. He wrote a paper dealing with this question, which was read at their meeting in Philadelphia the following year, and incorporated in the annual report of the New York Prison Association.

How far he was from accepting the basis of the new criminology, or at least from adopting its conclusions, may be inferred from his definition of punishment as "the intentional infliction of some sufferance as deserved sufferance, in which it differs from the infliction of pain by the surgeon." (Civil Liberty, p. 462.) Also, from the following observations on the subject of pardon: "The reported reformation of the criminal must in no case form the sole ground for pardoning. This is acknowledged, I believe, by almost all penologists of note and practical knowledge; and, where it has been tried to hold out an abridgment of the punishment as a reward for good behavior, the consequences have been bad. The hope of pardon for good behavior, which of course can never be absolutely known, leads to hypocrisy, and prevents the very reformation sought for, because it does not allow the prisoner to enter into that state of calm resignation which, according to all experience in criminal psychology, is an indispensable requisite for reformation."

Admitting the correctness of his understanding of the word punishment, reformatory treatment of a criminal undergoing the penalty of his crime is surely something quite different. We must also sharply discriminate between pardon, or executive clemency, and an abridgment of his term of incarceration promised to the convict in the criminal code, in case he complies with certain prescribed conditions. He earns his release under the commutation laws, by "good behavior," or by good conduct coupled with industry; but under the indeterminate sentence, this is not true. He must prove that imprisonment and the training given him while in prison have effected such a change in his attitude to society that he may now be safely set at large; and the evidence is threefold. It includes diligence in the culture of his native intelligence, as well as in labor, and obedience to the rules under which he lives. More than that; his release must not so shock the moral sense of society as to negative whatever deterrent influence may attach to the spectacle of his merited suffering by reason of deprivation of his personal liberty.

Dr. Lieber's view of the relations between criminal justice and a person accused of crime is expressed in a paragraph on the characteristics of "a fair and sound penal trial," in Civil Liberty and Self-Government (Chapter VII), as follows: "The person to be tried must be present (and of course living). No intimidation before the trial, or attempts by artifice to induce the prisoner to confess; a contrivance which protects the citizen even against being placed too easily in a state of accusation. The fullest possible realization of the principle that every man is held innocent until proved otherwise, and bail. A total discarding of the principle that the more heinous the imputed crime is, the less ought to be the protection of the prisoner; but, on the contrary, the adoption of the reverse. A distinct indictment, and the acquaintance of the prisoner with it sufficiently long before the trial to give him time for preparing the defence. That no one be held to incriminate himself. The accusatory process, with jury and publicity; therefore an oral trial, and not a process in writing. Counsel or defenders for the prisoner. A distinct theory or law of evidence, and no hearsay testimony. A verdict upon evidence alone and pronouncing guilty or not guilty. A punishment in proportion to the offence and in accord with common sense and justice; especially no punitory imprisonment of a sort that necessarily must make the prisoner worse than when he fell into the hands of the government, nor cautionary imprisonment before trial, which by contamination must advance the prisoner in his criminality. That the punishment must adapt itself to the crime and criminality of the offender; that nothing but what the law demands or allows be inflicted; and that all that the law demands be inflicted. No arbitrary, injudicious pardoning, which is a direct interference with the true government of law." Although, in this passage, he advocates "a punishment in proportion to the offence," nevertheless, in his Manual of Political Ethics (Book IV, Chapter III) he denies that punishments are equivalent to offences, "as the fines for most crimes were called in the early penal tariffs so peculiar to the Teutonic tribes. Punishment is by no means intended as a moral or social atonement for the offence;" and he remarks, "All who are acquainted with the moral treatment of criminals know well that this supposition, that the moral account is balanced by the suffering of penalty, as debt and credit are in money matters, is one of the most common obstacles to finding entrance into an obdurate heart."

He was clear in his rejection of inquisitorial, as opposed to accusatorial, criminal procedure. "Perhaps there are no points so important in the penal trial in a free country, as the principle that no one shall be held to incriminate himself, that the indictment as well as the verdict must be definite and clear, and that no hearsay evidence be admitted. . . . In the inquisitorial process, the process depends upon the questioning of the prisoner. An accused man cannot feel that perfect equanimity of mind which alone might secure his answers against suspicion. . . . The government prosecutes; then let it prove what it charges. So soon as this principle is discarded, we fall into the dire error of throwing the burden of proving innocence wholly or partially on the prisoner. . . . A fair trial for freemen requires that the preparatory steps for the trial be as little vexatious as possible. They must also acknowledge the principle of non-incrimination. This is disregarded on the whole of the European continent. The free range of police power, the mean tricks resorted to by the 'instructing' judge or other officer, before the trial, in order to bring the prisoner to confession, are almost inconceivable, and they are the worse because applied before the trial, when the prisoner is not surrounded by those protections which the trial itself grants."

These observations have a distinct bearing upon the unwarranted and illegal use made by police officials in the United States, of "the question," as practiced under medieval canon law by the Roman Inquisition in order to extort from the accused a confession of his personal guilt and also the denunciation of his accomplices or other suspected persons. Torture was associated with the question. In what is called "the sweat-box," where the police apply to the arrested suspect what is known as "the third degree," there is too much reason to believe that torture in various forms, mental and physical, is still practiced, though all civilized nations have agreed to abolish it.

A voluminous author, two of Dr. Lieber's books may here be especially mentioned: He was the American translator of de Beaumont and de Tocqueville's great work on The Penitentiary System in the United States (Philadelphia, 1833), to which he prefixed an introduction and appended valuable notes. The Pennsylvania Prison Discipline Society published (1838) his Essay on Penal Law and Solitary Confinement at Labor. The same society also printed his Letter on the Relation between Education and Crime. The legislature of New York published an article from his pen on The Abuse of the Pardoning Power. The legislature of South Carolina published a letter of his on The Penitentiary System.

Among his friends he numbered some of the most illustrious men of the old and the new worlds. In Europe: Niebuhr, Ranke, Bunsen, de Tocqueville, von Holtzendorff, Mittermaier, Bluntschli, Alexander von Humboldt, and others. In America: Kent, Story, and Greenleaf; Calhoun, Clay, Webster, Choate, and Sumner; Audubon, Agassiz, Henry, Bancroft, Longfellow, Hilliard, Everett, Howe, and many more of like social, political, scientific, and literary standing.

DR. THEODORE W. DWIGHT

Concerning Dr. Theodore W. Dwight, not so much of general interest can be written. He was not, like Lieber, a great writer of books; and he did not lead so adventurous and varied a life. Born at Catskill, New York, in 1822, he was a grandson of the first Timothy Dwight, and first cousin to the second Timothy Dwight, both presidents of Yale College. He was graduated, at the early age of eighteen years, from Hamilton College, in which he was first a tutor and afterward professor of law, history, civil polity and political economy. In 1858, he left Hamilton, to become professor of municipal law in Columbia College, in the city of New York. Later, he was made dean of the new Columbia Law School. He retired from the latter position in 1891, one year before his death. In the thirty-three years during which he followed the vocation of a teacher, ten thousand students passed under his instruction.

Besides holding the presidency of the New York Prison Association, he was, at different periods of his life, a member of the constitutional convention of 1867, of the state commission of appeals (1874–75), of the commission to establish the Elmira state reformatory, of the board of state charities, and of the State Charities Aid Association. He represented the state of New York at the International Prison Congress of Stockholm, in 1878. He was the first president of the Dante Society of New York, first president of the University Club, etc.

Dr. Dwight was for a time associate editor of the *American Law*

Register. He was also editor of Johnson's Cyclopedia, and of the American edition of Maine's Ancient Law.

EDWARD LIVINGSTON

Edward Livingston, whom Sir H. S. Maine, the author of Ancient Law, characterizes as "the first legal genius of modern times," was an American citizen of unquestionably eminent Scottish lineage, having been a direct descendant in the male line, from Sir Alexander Livingstone, one of the two joint regents of the kingdom during the minority of James the Second, who was Keeper of the King's Person. The New York branch of the Livingston family is derived from a younger son of Alexander, the fifth Lord Livingstone, who was one of the guardians of Mary Queen of Scots, and whose daughter Mary Livingstone, was one of the four Maries, maids of honor to the queen. Robert Livingston, the second of the name to emigrate to the New World (the first, who was a brother of the first Earl of Linlithgow, having been Baron of Nova Scotia), settled at Albany, where he obtained, by purchase from the Indians, an estate of 160,000 acres, with a frontage of twelve miles upon the Hudson River. This estate was erected into the Lordship and Manor of Livingston, and the patent confirmed, in 1715, by George the First. Edward Livingston was a great-grandson of Robert, the first Lord of the Manor, and first cousin once removed to Robert, its third and last proprietor, who divided it fairly among his surviving children.

Edward Livingston was the youngest of eleven children of Robert R. Livingston, one of the judges of the Supreme Court in the colony of New York. Ten of the eleven lived to old age, ranging from sixty-six to ninety-eight years. Edward was born at Clermont, May, 1764, and was therefore twelve years old at the date of signature of the American Declaration of Independence which was framed by a committee of five, of whom Chancellor Livingston, Edward's older brother, was a member, and among the signers will be found the name of Philip Livingston, cousin to the supreme judge who was Edward's father.

Graduated from Princeton College in 1781, at the early age of seventeen years, he at once entered upon the study of the law, first at Albany, and later in the city of New York, where he was admitted to the bar in 1785. Among his fellow-students he numbered James Kent, Alexander Hamilton, and Aaron Burr. In 1794, he was elected as a Representative in Congress from New York, and remained a member of the House for six years, where he opposed the passage of the alien and sedition laws, and cast his vote for Jefferson as President of the United States. To show the strong bent of his mind and heart, it may be mentioned that during his first term at Washington he moved the appointment of a committee " to inquire and report whether any and what alterations should be made in the penal laws of the United States, by substituting milder punishments for certain crimes, for which infamous and capital punishments are now inflicted;" and again, a year later, of a committee "to inquire whether any and what alterations are necessary in the penal laws of the United States, and that they report by bill or otherwise." Of both these committees he was made chairman, but it is believed that neither filed any report.

The President, Mr. Jefferson, appointed him in 1801 attorney of the United States for the district of New York. The same year, the Council of Appointment at Albany selected him for the mayoralty of New York City. As mayor, he urged the establishment of a public institution, to be jointly maintained by the city government and the Mechanics' Society, for the employment of (1) strangers, during the first month of their arrival; (2) citizens who from the effects of sickness or casualty have lost their usual employment; (3) widows and orphans, incapable of labor, and (4) discharged or pardoned convicts from the state prison. In his communication to the society, setting forth this scheme, which was not carried into effect, he says of the penitentiary system, then in its infancy, "It is a great, I had almost said a godlike experiment, worthy of the free country in which it is made, honorable to the men who planned and highly creditable to those who conduct it." But he pointed out that the unreformed, discharged convict is the chief obstacle to the hopes of its friends, and remarks: "Thus the institution, instead of diminishing, may increase the number of offences. This partial defect, so easily remedied, may ruin the system, and put a stop to the fairest experiment ever made in favor of humanity."

In 1803, a serious epidemic of yellow fever devastated the city, causing a general exodus of the inhabitants. The mayor remained at his post, visiting the sick at their homes in person, and doing all in his power to alleviate their calamity and distress, even to the point of exhausting the supply of wine in his private cellar, so that when at last, he himself succumbed to the disease, and his physicians called for a bottle of Madeira to be administered to him, there was not a bottle of that or any other kind of wine to be found in his house. During this period of absorbing labor and anxiety, a great misfortune

Edw Livingston

befell him. Customs collections were at that time paid to the District Attorney. Not through any act of his own, but in consequence of the rascality of one of his subordinates, it was discovered that he was indebted to the government in the sum of nearly fifty thousand dollars. "Without waiting even for an adjustment of his accounts, he voluntarily confessed judgment in favor of the United States for $100,000 in order to cover the amount which the adjustment should show to be the real balance against him. At the same time he conveyed all his property to a trustee for sale, and an application of the proceeds to the payment of his debt. The property conveyed consisted of real estate, which, though not very marketable, he valued at a sum sufficient for the security of the government. And he immediately resigned both offices." In December, within two months after retiring from the mayoralty, he embarked for New Orleans, the metropolis of the Louisiana Territory, which had been ceded that year by Napoleon to the United States.

His reputation, and the letters he carried with him, insured him from the beginning a commanding position at the bar. He could speak French, Spanish and German; and he had much more than the ordinary practitioner's acquaintance with Roman law. "He had been in Louisiana but little above a year, when the legislature adopted an entire system of practice proposed and framed by him. It is embodied in an act, passed on the 10th of April, 1805, consisting of twenty-two sections, and extending only to twenty-five printed pages."

During that period of stirring events of which the culmination was the battle of New Orleans, Livingston, who had served in Congress with Andrew Jackson, having been duly commissioned as a captain of engineers, served as a volunteer aid to the General, and was in fact his principal and most trusted adviser.

In 1820, he was elected a member of the lower house of the Louisiana legislature, which named him as a member of a commission of three to prepare a code of civil rights and remedies. In 1821, he was elected by joint ballot to revise the entire system of criminal law of the state.

The province of Orleans, even under French rules was governed by the penal laws of Spain, which were continued in force by different acts of Congress, until 1812, when Louisiana ceased to be a territory; but a like provision was inserted in the constitution of the new state. There were a few offenses which were defined and tried according to the common law of England; but Livingston, quoting Lord Bacon, said of the medieval code which it was his aim to replace: "Our laws endure the torment of Mezentius, the living die in the arms of the dead."

The Livingston Code, which is styled "A System of Penal Law," was divided into four parts: A code of crimes and punishments, a code of procedure, a code of evidence, and a code of reform and prison discipline, besides a book of definitions. The machinery proposed for the working of the system comprehended a house of detention, a penitentiary, a house of refuge and industry, and a school of reform. He proposed and urged the abolition of the death penalty. "He offered a substitute which, whatever might prove its effect as a public example, would certainly not have held out to the ordinary transgressor an alternative much less terrible than death. It was imprisonment for life in a solitary cell, to be painted black without and within, and bearing a conspicuous outer inscription, in distinct white letters, setting forth the culprit's name and his offense, and proceeding with a fearfully graphic description of his doom: 'His food is bread of the coarsest kind; his drink is water mingled with his tears; he is dead to the world; this cell is his grave; his existence is prolonged, that he may remember his crime and repent it, and that the continuance of his punishment may deter others from the indulgence of hatred, avarice, sensuality, and the passions which lead to the crime he has committed. When the Almighty, in his due time, shall exercise toward him that dispensation which he himself arrogantly and wickedly usurped towards another, his body is to be dissected, and his soul will abide that judgment which Divine Justice shall decree.'"

Livingston was a believer in the strictly solitary form of imprisonment of convicts. His biographer says that "he obtained information and statistics from the other twenty-three states, as well as from Europe, and minutely examined and reviewed the whole history of the systems of Massachusetts, New York, and Pennsylvania. His conclusion was that under the best scheme of penal jurisprudence to be devised, the inflexible sentence of the law upon every convict of a penitentiary sentence should be confinement in a solitary cell, with sufficient wholesome but coarse food, but without occupation or any human attention, except needful ministration to physical wants and private religious instruction." While he sought to unite the punishment of crime with the reformation of the offender, it is evident that he laid undue relative stress upon retribution and deterrence as ends in prison discipline; also, that his conception of a truly reformatory discipline was vague. He favored the gradual relaxation of the severity of solitary confinement; and among the privileges to be won by good conduct and general tractability, he laid emphasis on education, recommending the appointment of a teacher in prison, the granting of permission to read books of general instruction, and admission into a class for instruction. After a sufficiently prolonged period of solitude, too, the prisoner might even enjoy the privilege of laboring in association with other prisoners. And he proposed giving to every prisoner a share of the profits of his labor, on his discharge.

Like Dr. Wines, Livingston insisted that criminals are susceptible of reformation. In his own words: "Convicts are men. The most degraded and depraved are men; their minds are moved by the same springs that give activity to others; they avoid pain with the same care and pursue pleasure with the same activity that actuate their fellow mortals. It is the false direction only of these great motives that produces the criminal actions which they prompt. To turn them into a course that will promote the true happiness of the individual, by making them cease to injure that of society, should be the great object of criminal jurisprudence. The error, it appears to me, lies in considering them as beings of a nature so inferior as to be incapable of elevation, and so bad as to make any amelioration impossible; but crime is the effect principally of intemperance, idleness, ignorance, vicious associations, irreligion, and poverty,—not of any defective natural organization; and the laws which permit the unrestrained and continual exercise of these causes are themselves the sources of the excesses which legislators, to cover their own inattention or indolence or ignorance, impiously and falsely ascribe to the Supreme Being, as if he had created man incapable of receiving the impressions of good. Let us try the experiment, before we pronounce that even the degraded convict cannot be reclaimed. It has never yet been tried. . . . But to think that the best plan which human sagacity could devise will produce reformation in every case, that there will not be numerous exceptions to its general effect, would be to indulge the visionary belief of a moral panacea, applicable to all vices and all crimes; and although this would be quackery in legislation, as absurd as any that has appeared in medicine, yet to say that there are no general rules by which reformation of the mind may be produced is as great and fatal an error as to assert that there are in the healing art no useful rules for preserving the general health and bodily vigor of the patient."

155

He clearly apprehended the desirability of separating juvenile offenders from mature and experienced criminals, and aimed to provide for them in a separate establishment—a school of reform, for which the state of Louisiana, so many years after his death, has made tardy provision; but it is not even yet completed and occupied. The only hint of his acquaintance with the underlying principle of the indeterminate sentence is the provision that, irrespective of the length of the sentence pronounced upon a juvenile delinquent, no boy should be discharged during his minority, except by apprenticeship; but for girls, the age limit was fixed at nineteen years. His penal code was based on the principle of definite, inflexible, time sentences throughout.

Another feature of his system was the recognition of the intimate relation between crime and voluntary pauperism in the form of idleness or vagrancy. He regarded remunerative employment as the surest antidote to crime, and dreaded the influence of lack of employment on the discharged convict, since it could only tend to insure his relapse and possibly final downfall. He thought, too, that governments are morally obligated to support such members of society as are incapable of maintaining themselves, and have the "corresponding right to test the genuineness of that of incapacity; a right which cannot be exercised without at the same time exercising a strict tutelage and thorough control over all who either are incapable of self-support or pretend to be so." Hence he made a house of refuge and of industry an integral part of his completed scheme; and he proposed placing the entire group of institutions under a single governing head.

Much in this account of his views and his aims reminds one of the very similar opinions of Vilain XIV, who was in a very real sense the father of modern penitentiary reform.

Before finishing the task to which he had been assigned, he was again in 1822, elected a member,—but from the New Orleans district,—of the national House of Representatives. He continued to give his spare time to its prosecution, and the four codes were in large part ready for the press—indeed, some fifty pages were already in type—when, in November, 1824, at his residence in New York, a conflagration in the middle of the night destroyed the manuscript copy and nearly all the notes used in its preparation. Nothing remained for him to do, but to rewrite the whole.

After six years in Congress, he failed, in 1828, of re-election, but was, at the next session of the Louisiana legislature, elected to the United States Senate, taking his seat in that august body on the day of the inauguration of his friend, General Jackson, as President. He obtained leave to introduce a bill, accompanied by a memorial for the incorporation, into the federal statutes, of the code which he had prepared for his adopted state. It was printed, for further consideration, but at the ensuing session its author had ceased to be a senator, and the subject has not again been taken up by Congress.

President Van Buren tendered him, in 1831, the position of Secretary of State, which he accepted. During his first year of service as a member of the cabinet, occurred the official visit of M. de Tocqueville to the United States, for the purpose of examining our penitentiary system. It needs scarcely be said that Mr. Livingston did everything in his power to facilitate his studies.

On the 29th of May, 1833, he resigned the office of Secretary and was appointed Envoy Extraordinary and Minister Plenipotentiary to France. He returned to America in 1835, and died in 1836.

No American book has ever attracted such attention from the civilized world or been so universally and so highly praised, as Livingston's Code. Victor Hugo said of it: "Un beau livre, un livre utile, un livre modèle." It was reprinted in England and in France. The great German jurist, Mittermaier, who had never met Livingston, before he could present his letters of introduction, rushed into his arms at his hotel and hugged and kissed him. M. Villemain, the French publicist, wrote him: "Such a reform in penal jurisprudence reflects more credit upon our modern times than the greatest discoveries in the arts, in literature, and in science; in fact, it is the perfecting of the first of sciences—social science!"

Those who may wish to know more about this remarkable man in detail are referred to the delightful memoir of him by Charles Havens Hunt,* of which the foregoing sketch is mainly a mere abridgment, much of it in the very words of his biographer.

It is only just to the memory of Jeremy Bentham, to add that Livingston acknowledged in a personal letter to him, that the perusal of his writings first gave method to his ideas, and taught him to "consider legislation as a science governed by certain principles applicable to all its different branches, instead of an occasional exercise of its powers, called forth only on particular occasions, without relation to or connection with each other."

* Published by Appleton, N. Y., 1864.

DOROTHEA LYNDE DIX

Miss Dix was of New England birth and parentage, Maine claiming her as a native, where she was born April 4, 1802, though her early life was spent in Massachusetts. It was there that she began her work for jails and prisons, by securing certain reforms in the East Cambridge jail. That was in 1841. By the year 1845 she had traveled more than ten thousand miles in the United States and had studied the conditions of eighteen state penitentiaries, three hundred jails and houses of correction and more than five hundred almshouses, as we know from the notes she made. Her Remarks on Prisons and Prison Discipline in the United States was published in 1845.

Yet all this was but the day of small things, compared with what she accomplished later, for she not only visited every part of the United States, from Maine to California, but Canada and Nova Scotia. She spent two years in England and on the Continent studying the conditions of prisons and the care of the insane, in nearly every country, everywhere influencing legislation in behalf of reform. More than twenty legislatures in this country, the federal government and the British Parliament recognized her services by formal resolutions. Wherever she went she found something that called out her service, as, for instance, securing proper life-boats for the storm-lashed shores of Sable Island, with the result that the very next day after her boats arrived there, one hundred and eighty persons were saved from a wreck, who must have perished but for this timely provision.

During the Civil War Miss Dix served as a nurse, and later had charge of a great part of the nursing force; and when the war was over she raised money to build a soldiers' monument, and more than twelve thousand sleep under its protection in one of the national cemeteries, where it stands "the first object visible over the low level of the peninsula to vessels coming in from sea to the Roads, the reverential tribute of a heroic woman to the heroic men she honored with all her soul." In recognition of her work the United States government gave the following order: "In token and acknowledgment of the inestimable services rendered by Miss Dorothea L. Dix for the Care, Succor and Relief of the Sick and Wounded Soldiers of the United States on the Battle-field, in Camps and Hospitals during the recent War, and of her benevolent and diligent labors and devoted efforts to whatever might contribute to their comfort and welfare, it is ordered that a Stand of Arms of the United States National Colors be presented to Miss Dix."

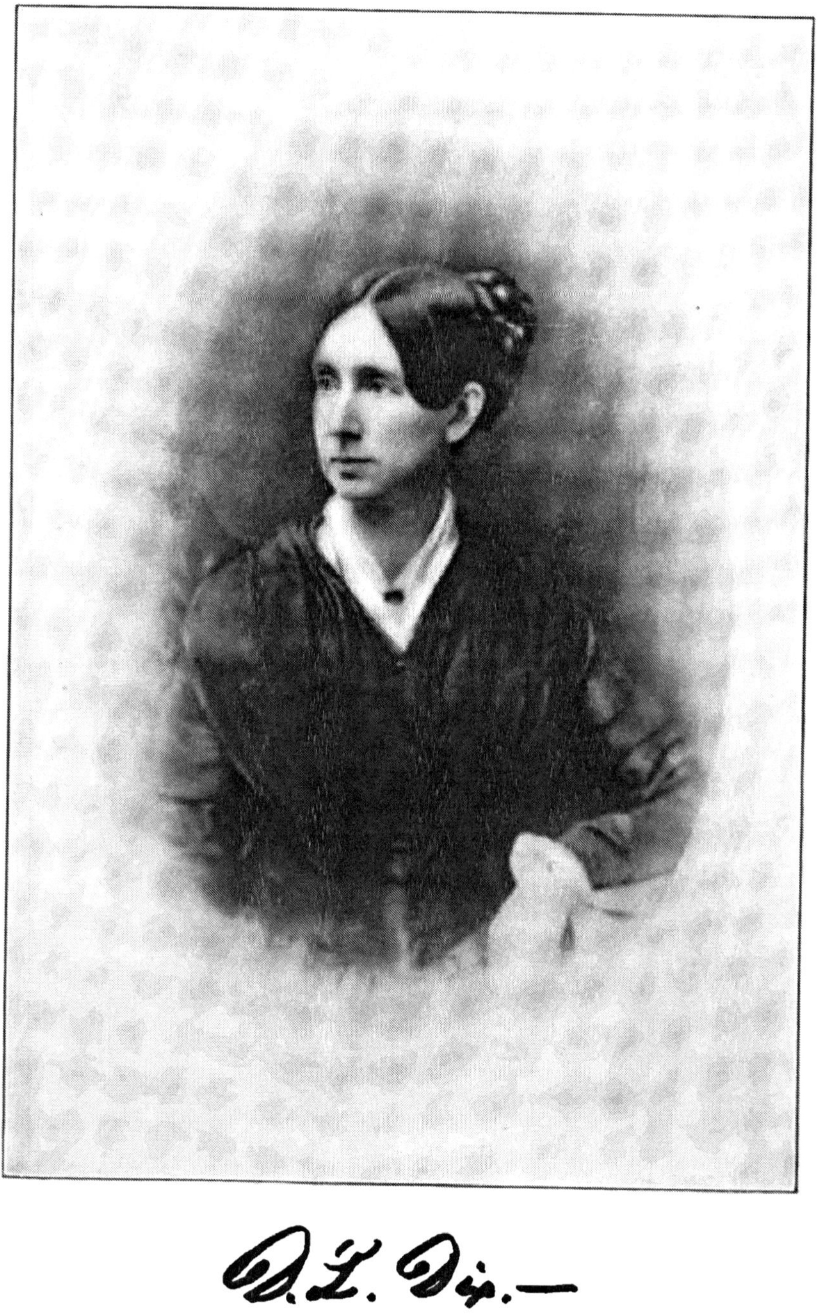

D. L. Dix.—

These beautiful flags were bequeathed by Miss Dix to Harvard College, where they hang over the main portal of the stately building erected in memory of the sons of Harvard who fell during the war.

Miss Dix died July 17, 1887, and it was said of her at that time that she was "the most useful and distinguished woman America has produced." Her biographer, Francis Tiffany, gives her a still higher place: "Here is a woman who, as the founder of vast and enduring institutions of mercy in America and Europe, has simply no peer in the annals of Protestantism. To find her parallel in this respect, it is necessary to go back to the lives of such memorable Roman Catholic women as St. Theresa of Spain or Santa Chiara of Assisi."

ELLEN CHENEY JOHNSON

Ellen Cheney Johnson was born at Athol, Massachusetts, December 20, 1829. She received her education in the public schools and at the Francestown Academy in New Hampshire. She married Jesse C. Johnson, a merchant of Boston. Both she and her husband were interested in philanthropic work, and for many years their home near the State House, was a gathering place for public spirited citizens. She was active in the work of the Sanitary Commission during the Civil War, and afterwards continued her work in behalf of the widows and orphans of soldiers. She was an early advocate of a separate prison for women and was one of those whose efforts led to the creation of the Reformatory Prison for Women that was opened in 1877. She was appointed a member of the Board of Commissioners of Prisons when it was reorganized in 1879, and in January, 1884, was appointed superintendent of the Reformatory Prison for Women at Sherborn, Massachusetts. Her work at that place made it a world-famous model of prison administration. She died in London while in attendance upon the Women's Congress, where she went to speak on prisons for women, on June 28, 1899.

GARDINER TUFTS

Gardiner Tufts was born in the city of Lynn, Massachusetts, July 3d, 1828. He was said to be a lineal descendant of Edmund Ingalls, the first settler of Lynn. He was the son of Deacon Richard and Rebecca Tufts. In 1854 he married Miss Margaret A. Harris of Ipswich, who, with three daughters, survived him.

At the age of thirty-two Colonel Tufts was elected a member of the state legislature. In 1862 he was appointed by Governor Andrews as Military Agent of Massachusetts, with office at Washington, D. C., the first appointment of its kind, it is said, by any governor. This position he held all through the Civil War. Remaining in the state employ, he was afterward appointed treasurer and steward of the Reformatory Prison for Women at Sherborn, and after a few months' service in this position, he was made superintendent of the State Primary School, at Monson. In 1885 he was chosen by Governor Robinson to be superintendent of the new State Reformatory, and on December 20 of that year he formally opened it and served most efficiently till the time of his death.

Colonel Tufts died November 23d, 1891, of pneumonia, after a brief illness. This was brought on by a severe cold contracted during his attendance at the National Prison Congress, held in Pittsburgh a few weeks before. Funeral services were held at his house, and immediately afterward in the guardroom of the Reformatory; and in the afternoon of the same day at Lynn, in the old First Church. He was buried with military honors, the services being in charge of the Loyal Legion. A bust of Colonel Tufts was placed in the State House, Boston, and a fine portrait of him hangs in the chapel of the Reformatory.

INDEX

INDEX

ADLER, FELIX: Extract from address on manual training, 20

ADMINISTRATION. See *Discipline*

ALABAMA: Commutation of sentence law, 24

ALTRUISM IN OUR PRISON SYSTEM, 93

AMERICAN PRISON ASSOCIATION: Financial support, 84; Hayes, R. B., presidency, 84, 142; Organization and first congress, 78; Reorganization in 1883, 141; Wines, E. C., secretaryship, 75. See also *Cincinnati Prison Congress* •

AMERICAN REFORMATORY PRISON SYSTEM (Z. R. Brockway), 88

AMERICAN SOCIAL SCIENCE ASSOCIATION, 76, 78

ARISTOTLE AND PLATO: Conceptions of goodness and virtue, 89

ARSON: Defined, 109

ATTITUDE OF THE STATE TOWARD THE PRISON SYSTEM, 93

AUBURN SYSTEM OF PRISON DISCIPLINE, 4

AVERAGE SENTENCES, 120

BACON, FRANCIS: Quotation from, 89

BARROWS, ISABEL C.: Breshkofsky, Madame, devotion to, 124, 125; Marriage, 127; Medical studies and skill in stenography, 127; Sharing of life work with Mr. Barrows, 126

BARROWS, SAMUEL JUNE: Birth, 126; Camp life in Canada, 138; article on (by P. U. Kellogg), 123-139; "Citizen of the world," 136; Death, 123; Early life and privations, 126; Election to Congress, 128; Family life and wide sympathies, 138; Federal penal reforms, 131; Fee system, fight against, 130; Hungarian speech at Budapest, 137; International Prison Commission;—Reports, 132; Tributes, 134; International Prison Congress, work for, 129, 134; Interparliamentary Union, interest in, 128; "Isles and shrines of Greece," 138; Marriage, 127; Ministry in Dorchester (Mass.), 128; Musical and linguistic talents, 137, 138; Prison Association of New York, secretaryship, 129; Religious opinions, 135; Varied activities in the cause of prison reform, 132; Western experiences, 128; The wireless message, 124

BECCARIA, CESARE, 86

BIOGRAPHICAL SKETCHES, 145-160

BONNEVILLE DE MARSANGY: First argument for conditional liberation, 38

BOSTON PRISON DISCIPLINE SOCIETY, 4

BRESHKOFSKY, MADAME, 124, 125

BRITISH SOCIAL SCIENCE ASSOCIATION, 78

BROCKWAY, Z. R.: American reformatory prison system, 88; Early advocacy of indeterminate sentence, 31, 32; Experience in prison administration, 77; Genius and hero, 87; Superintendence of Elmira Reformatory, 32, 33

BURGLARY: Defined, 108

BURNHAM INDUSTRIAL FARM, 143

CALIFORNIA: Commutation of sentence law, 14

CAPITAL PUNISHMENT: Death penalty in various states, 119; Livingston, Edward, proposed substitute, 154

CAPITALISTS OF CRIME, 42, 56

CENTRALIZATION OF CONTROL OF STATE PRISONS, 5, 63

CINCINNATI PRISON CONGRESS (1870): Account, by F. B. Sanborn, 78, 79; "Declaration of principles," 39; Analytical index, 35; Completeness, 3;

Discussion and condensation, 78; Text as adopted, 39; Text as originally submitted by Dr. Wines, 45; Unanimous adoption, 34; Vote for calling international congress, 34

CLASSIFICATION OF PRISONERS AND PRISONS: Cincinnati Congress declarations, 39, 41, 46, 54; Three general divisions of prisoners, 95

CLOTHING AND BEDDING FOR THE PRISONERS IN REFORMATORIES, 99

COLONIAL CONDITIONS: Intercourse, etc., 1

COMMUNITY OF INTEREST BETWEEN OFFENDERS AND THE STATE, 94

COMMUTATION OF SENTENCE: Federal prisoners in state prisons, rights of, 14; Legislation by various states, 13, 14. See also Sentence, length of

CONDITIONAL LIBERATION. See Indeterminate Sentence

CONNECTICUT: Commutation of sentence law, 14

CONSTRUCTION: Cincinnati Congress declarations, 43, 61–62; Reformatories, best type of buildings, 99

CONTRACT SYSTEM. See Labor-Contract System

CONVICT LABOR. See Labor

CORPORAL PUNISHMENT: Irrational and ineffectual, 12; Physical coercion sometimes requisite, 98

CRIME: Defined, 39, 45; Prevention of, Cincinnati Congress declarations, 41, 55

CRIMINAL CAPITALISTS, 42, 56

CRIMINAL INSANITY: Cincinnati Congress declarations, 42, 56

CRIMINAL LAW IN THE UNITED STATES. See United States Criminal Law

CRIMINAL LUNACY. See Criminal Insanity

CRIMINAL PROCEDURE IN THE UNITED STATES. See United States Criminal Procedure

CRIMINAL STATISTICS: Cincinnati Congress declarations, 43, 60; Value affected by variations in codes, 110

CRIMINALOID CLASS, 94

CROFTON, SIR WALTER, 16, 26, 27, 76

DEATH PENALTY. See Capital Punishment

DEFECTIVES: Prisoners of inferior class, 95; Special treatment at Elmira Reformatory, 96

DEFINITIONS OF CRIMES, 108

DETERRENT PRINCIPLE IN PUNISHMENT 91

DISCHARGED PRISONERS: Cincinnati Congress declarations, 42, 56

DISCIPLINE: Abolition of cruel punishments in New York, 10; Auburn system, 4; Cincinnati Congress declarations, 41, 46–48, 50, 51; Contract system, demoralizing to discipline, 8; Disciplinary punishments, necessity of, 5; Fundamental principles, 18; Irish convict system, 27; Mark system, 26; Moral axioms, 18; Opposing theories of government, 11; Pennsylvania system, 4, 146, 154; Political control, effect of, 6; Rewards and punishments, 12, 39, 46; Social principle, necessity of recognizing, 55

DISGRACE NOT OFTEN FELT BY PRISONERS, 92

DISREGARD OF CONSEQUENCES BY CRIMINALS, 91

DIX, DOROTHEA LYNDE: Biographical sketch, 158

DRUMMOND, PROFESSOR: Remarks on value of work, 107

DWIGHT, THEODORE W.: Biographical sketch, 150; Contract system, characterization of, 7; Investigation (with Dr. Wines) of prisons in the United States and Canada, 17

EDUCATION: Cincinnati Congress declarations, 40, 49; Duty of the state, 20; Moral, mental, and industrial instruction, 19; Schools of letters in a reformatory, 100. See also Industrial Training; Moral and Religious Training

ELIOT, GEORGE: Quotations from, 97

ELMIRA REFORMATORY: Brockway, Z. R., superintendency, 32, 33; Commission on site and plan, appointment, and report, 26, 29; Completion of building, 32; First suggestion of industrial reformatory, 32; Indeterminate sentence in act of incorporation, 32

FEE SYSTEM: Fight against, 130

FINES: Variations in, 112

GOODNESS: Defined by Plato and Aristotle, 89

GREECE: Description of scenery (E. C. Wines), 74

HARTWELL, E. H.: Quotation from, 97

HAYES, RUTHERFORD B.: American Prison Association, presidency, 84, 142; Biographical sketch (W. M. F. Round), 140; United States, presidency, 84, 140, 143

HOWARD, JOHN, 52, 86

HOWE, SAMUEL G.: Conditional liberation, 30; Experiences in Greece, 72

HUBBELL, GAYLORD B.: Irish Convict system, 27; Political control at Sing Sing prison, 6; Proposed reformatory prison in New York, 28

ILLINOIS: Commutation of sentence law, 14

IMPOSSIBILITY OF PERFECT JUSTICE, 90

IMPRISONMENT FOR LIFE IN VARIOUS STATES, 117

IMPRISONMENT, TERMS OF. See Sentence, Length of

INDEMNIFICATION FOR WRONGFUL IMPRISONMENT, 42, 56

INDETERMINATE SENTENCE: Bonneville de Marsangy, first declaration of principle, 30; Brockway, Z. R., early advocacy, 31, 32; Cincinnati Congress declarations, 40, 48; Howe, S. G., early mention of conditional liberation, 30; Protecting society from crime, 95; Recommendation in first report of Elmira Reformatory commission, 29; Time sentences wrong in principle, 18

INDUSTRIAL TRAINING: Cincinnati Congress declarations, 41, 52; Manual training and trades instruction in reformatories, 100; Reformatory possibilities of work, 107; Value of manual training, 20

INTERACTION OF BODY AND MIND, 97

INTERNATIONAL PRISON COMMISSION: Reports edited by S. J. Barrows, 132; Tributes to S. J. Barrows, 134

INTERNATIONAL PRISON CONGRESS: Barrows, S. J., services, 129, 134; London Congress (1872), 37; Refusal of appropriation by Congress in 1876, 83; Sollohub, Count, earliest suggestion, 33; Stockholm Congress (1878), 37; Vote passed by Cincinnati Congress, 34; Wines, E. C., work of, 36, 75, 80

IOWA: Commutation of sentence law, 14

IRISH CONVICT SYSTEM, 27

JOHN HOWARD INDUSTRIAL SCHOOL, 130

JOHNSON, ELLEN CHENEY: Biographical sketch, 159

JURY, 97, 99, 101, 106

JUVENILE COURTS. See Children's Courts

JUVENILE DELINQUENTS: Youthful misdemeanants, 130. See also Children's Courts; Probation

KANSAS: Commutation of sentence law, 14

KELLOGG, PAUL U.: "Samuel June Barrows, a circuit rider in the humanities," 123

LABOR: Competition with free labor, 52. Contract System; Cincinnati Congress declarations, 41, 53; Discipline, demoralization of, 8; Education of prisoners rendered impossible, 20; Improvement on idleness, 5; Objections, 7. New York: Investigating commission's conclusions, 24; Large earnings of state prisons, 22; Proposed law, 24; Overwork system, 9, 12; Productive or profitable labor, 21, 22, 23

LADD, PROFESSOR: Quotation from, 102

LEWIS, CHARLTON T., 86

LIBRARIES IN PRISONS AND REFORMATORIES, 19, 100

LIEBER, FRANCIS: Biographical sketch, 145; Books and translations, 150; Criminal procedure, views on, 148; Opinions, 148; Theory of punishment and pardons, 147

LIVINGSTON, EDWARD: Ancestry and birth, 151; Death, 157; Louisiana criminal code, 153; New York City, mayoralty of, 152; Penal code, 154; Solitary imprisonment, belief in, 154; Substitute for death penalty, 154; United States penal code, 157

MACONOCHIE, ALEXANDER, 26, 46, 77, 86

MAINE: Commutation of sentence law, 14

MARK SYSTEM OF PRISON DISCIPLINE, 26

MASSACHUSETTS: Commutation of sentence law, 14

MICHIGAN: Commutation of sentence law, 14

MILLIGAN, REV. JOHN L., 16

MIND AND BODY: Relation between, 102

MINNESOTA: Commutation of sentence law, 14

MISDEMEANANTS: Lack of provision for, 130

MISSOURI: Commutation of sentence law, 14

MONTESINOS, COLONEL, 52, 86

MORAL AND RELIGIOUS TRAINING: Moral suasion and religion, 106; Optional religious opportunities, 101; Regenerating influence of religion, 19, 40, 48; Religious agencies not always desirable, 98

MORAL STATE OF PRISONERS, 89

NATIONAL PRISON ASSOCIATION. See *American Prison Association*

NATIONALITY IN PENAL SYSTEMS, 3

NEVADA: Commutation of sentence law, 14

NEW HAMPSHIRE: Commutation of sentence law, 14

NEW JERSEY: Commutation of sentence law, 14

NEW YORK: Centralization of control of state prisons, 5; Commutation of sentence law, 13, 14; Constitutional amendment, proposed, 10; Prison Association (see *Prison Association of New York*); Proposed prison labor law, 24; State Reformatory at Elmira. See *Elmira Reformatory*

NEWSPAPERS IN PRISONS AND REFORMATORIES, 60, 101

OFFICERS OF PRISONS AND REFORMATORIES, 48, 49

OHIO: Commutation of sentence law, 14

OREGON: Commutation of sentence laws, 14

ORGANIZATION OF REFORMATORIES, 97

OVERWORK SYSTEM OF PRISON LABOR, 9, 12

PARDONS: Cincinnati Congress declarations, 43, 57; Lieber, Francis, theories, 147

PARENTAL RESPONSIBILITY, 44, 62

PENNSYLVANIA: Commutation of sentence law, 14; Prison Society, 4

PENNSYLVANIA SYSTEM OF PRISON DISCIPLINE: Brief definition, 4; Lieber, Francis, advocacy, 146; Livingston, Edward, belief in solitary imprisonment, 154

PENOLOGICAL SURGERY, 99

PENOLOGY: Word coined by Dr. Lieber, 146

PHILADELPHIA PRISON DISCIPLINE SOCIETY, 4

PHYSICAL CULTURE IN REFORMATORIES, 100

PHYSIOLOGICAL DEFECTS AS SOURCES OF CRIME, 96

PLATO AND ARISTOTLE: Ideas of goodness and virtue, 89

POLITICAL CONTROL OF PRISONS: Hubbell, G. B., testimony, 6; Instability of administration, 39, 47; Political appointments not necessarily bad, 5; Prison Association of New York, efforts at reform, 4, 8; Proposed constitutional amendment in New York, 10

POSSIBLE AND ACTUAL PENALTIES FOR CRIME (F. H. Wines), 108

PREPARATORY LIBERATION (Bonneville de Marsangy), 30

PREVENTION OF CRIME. See *Crime, Prevention of*

PRISON ADMINISTRATION. See *Discipline*

PRISON ARCHITECTURE. See *Construction*

PRISON ASSOCIATION OF NEW YORK: American Prison Association, part in organizing, 76; Barrows, S. J., secretaryship, 129; Commission to investigate prisons in the United States and Canada, 17; Income at different periods, 76; Investigation commission of 1866, 8; Political control, war against, 4, 8;

Reconstruction of New York prison system, committee appointed, 16; Wines, E. C., secretaryship, 4, 15, 75, 76

PRISON CONSTRUCTION. See *Construction*

PRISON DISCIPLINE. See *Discipline*

PRISON LABOR. See *Labor*

PRISON LIBRARIES, 19, 100

PRISON NEWSPAPERS, 60, 101

PRISON OFFICERS, 48, 49

PUNISHMENT: Definitions, 39, 45; Theories, 88

QUEENS COUNTY (N. Y.): Jail, 130, 131

REFORMATION: American reformatory prison system (Z. R. Brockway), 88; Cincinnati Congress declarations, 39–41, 45–52; Contract system opposed to reformation, 7; Economic motives, 105; Essential elements of the problem, 104; Livingston, Edward, opinions, 155; Mental physiology in reformatory procedure, 102; Physical training, 105; Primary object of penal justice, 17, 39, 46; Standard of requirements, 94; Stringency and strenuosity in administration, 103

RELIGIOUS TRAINING. See *Moral and Religious Training*

RESPONSIBILITY: Parental responsibility, 44, 62; Responsibility of society for crime, 42, 57

RETRIBUTIVE THEORY OF PUNISHMENT, 88

REWARDS AND PUNISHMENTS IN PRISON DISCIPLINE, 12, 39, 46

RHODE ISLAND: Commutation of sentence law, 14

RIBOT: Quotation from, 96

ROBBERY: Defined, 109

ROUND, W. M. F.: Biographical sketch of Gen. R. B. Hayes, 140

SANBORN, FRANK B.: "E. C. Wines and prison reform: a memoir," 64

SENTENCE: Length of; Average sentences, 120; Cincinnati Congress declarations, 41, 43, 54, 59; Possible and actual penalties for crime, 108

SEWARD, WILLIAM H.: Gift of prison library, 19

SEYMOUR, HORATIO, 86

SING SING PRISON: Evils of political control, 6

SOLITARY CONFINEMENT. See *Pennsylvania System of Prison Discipline*

SOLLOHUB, COUNT: Characterization of America, 3; Prison industries, 52; Suggestion of an international prison congress, 33, 80

STATE CONTROL OF PRISONS, 5, 63

SUPPLEMENTARY PENALTIES, 113

TAPPAN, A. B.: Proposal for an industrial reformatory in New York, 25

TCHAIKOFSKY, NICHOLAS, 125.

TENNESSEE: Commutation of sentence law, 14

TUFTS, GARDINER: Biographical sketch 159

VARIATIONS IN SEVERITY OF PENALTIES PRESCRIBED, 114

VAUX, RICHARD: Estimate of Dr. Wines, 70

VERMONT: Commutation of sentence law, 14

VIRTUE: Defined by Plato and Aristotle, 89

WHEELER, WILLIAM A., 11

WINES, ENOCH COBB: American Prison Association, secretaryship, 75; Books on travel and education and on China, 67; Character and influence, 71; Dates of birth and death, 65; "Declaration of principles (Cincinnati Congress of 1870), formulation of, 3, 4, 34, 39, 45; Easthampton (N. Y.) pastorate, 70; Education and marriage, 66; Educational work, 67, 68; Fundamental principles of prison discipline, 18; Greece, travels and descriptions, 72–75; Honors and achievements, 37, 82; International Prison Congress, work for, 36, 75, 80; Investigation (with Dr. Dwight) of prisons in the United States and Canada, 17; Labor investigation commission, membership, 24; Memoir (by F. B. Sanborn), 64; Mosaic legislation, book on, 69; Prison Association of New York, secretaryship, 75, 76; Services to prison reform in New York, 25;

Sketch of life and services (by F. H. Wines), 3–38; Slavery, views on, 68, 69; "State of Prisons," publication, 38, 87; Travel, study and correspondence, 15, 16, 77; Union with Messrs. Sanborn and Brockway in prison reform work, 4; Vaux, Richard, warm admiration, 70; Washington College (Pa.), professorship, 70; Zeal and sincerity, 81

WINES, FREDERICK HOWARD: Historical introduction, 3; Possible and actual penalties for crime, 108

"THE WIRELESS MESSAGE" (S. J. Barrows), 124

WISCONSIN: Commutation of sentence law, 14

WOMEN IN PRISON ADMINISTRATION, 45